Jackie

The Price
of the Pedestal

Jackie

The Price of the Pedestal
Lee Guthrie

DRAKE PUBLISHERS INC.
NEW YORK

Published in 1978 by
Drake Publishers, Inc.
New York, New York

Library of Congress Cataloging in Publication Data

Guthrie, Lee.
   Jackie: the price of the pedestal.

   Includes index.
   1. Onassis, Jacqueline Kennedy, 1929-
2. United States--Biography.
CT275.0552G84   973.922'092'4   [B]   78-3212
ISBN 0-8473-1801-X

Printed in the United States of America

CONTENTS

Jackie
The Price
of the Pedestal

For my children:
Donald . . . Cathy . . . Sean
for delight beyond description

ACKNOWLEDGMENTS

I wish to thank David Ragan, author of the voluminous *Who's Who in Hollywood, 1900-1976* (Arlington House) and editorial director of Macfadden Entertainment Magazines, for his pertinent advice and generous aid.

I am grateful to Ted Gottfried for suggesting this project. Because of it, I have realized certain truths about money, power, and sex of which I had previously been only dimly aware.

Finally, I want to thank my editor for helping to make the book better than it would otherwise have been.

Prologue

What an incredible life she's had! The legends of no queen—ancient, medieval, or modern—can quite match the extraordinary existence of Jacqueline Bouvier Kennedy Onassis. With considerable help from the media, Jackie has become a legend in her own lifetime. She has become the world's leading celebrity—a condition that she clearly enjoys and manages with immense panache.

Born a few months before the stock market crash of 1929, the Great Depression never toucher her . . .

There have always been men eager to protect her from life's grimmer realities. Her father set the stage. He adored her. Why shouldn't everyone else? Her stepfather treated her like one of his own children. The rich and handsome young Senator from Massachusetts married her when she was twenty-four—although even he could not protect her from the forces of history.

His brother took her under his wing—although there were many others vying for the role of her official protector. And then, unbelievably, the dark forces of irrationality claimed her brother-in-law, too.

This time, she was rescued by a modern pirate, a Mediterranean womanizer, social climber, and shipping tycoon who also happened to be one of the richest men in the world. His money enabled her to indulge the acquisitive side of her character without restraint. She became the world's most profligate shopper.

It seemed a tawdry sequel to Camelot.

The tycoon eventually tired of his once-valued prize, but by then he was too tired and ill and old to divorce her. Death released him from the marriage.

All these men have enabled her to live in beautiful places:

—Lasata, the Easthampton estate of her grandfather with its rolling lawns and lush orchards, its hidden garden and private riding ring.

—Merrywood in Virginia and Hammersmith Farm in Newport, Rhode Island, the spacious and tranquil estates of her stepfather.

—Hyannis Port, with its cool nights and sunny days in constant harmony with the roar of the surf and the sharp salt smell of the Atlantic.

—And, Skorpios. For seven fabled and endlessly chronicled years, it was her very own island, a fantasy come true in the blue Ionian Sea.

These days, she spends most of her time in Manhattan—she works as an editor there—and drives on the week-ends to a rambling barn of a house in the New Jersey hunt country.

At an age when most women are settling into middle age and becoming grandmothers, Jackie shows up at the theatre, the ballet, museum openings, and parties with a variety of men, many of them younger than she is. The flashbulbs go off and Jackie smiles and opens her eyes very wide. In the photographs that will inevitably appear in the next day's papers, she will look dazzling.

Apparently, age cannot wither nor custom stale her almost infinite capacity to charm . . .

How on earth does she do it?

Chapter One

Daddy's Girl

Chapter One

Daddy's Girl

From the beginning, she did things her way. Expected to arrive in the middle of June, she did not make her appearance until the end of July. Her parents had planned for her to be born in Manhattan. She preferred the country. And so on July 28, 1929—a hot and humid Sunday—Jacqueline Lee Bouvier was born in Southhampton's small community hospital.

She weighed eight pounds and her tiny head was covered with jet black hair just like her father's.

Jack Bouvier's heavy-lipped, dark good looks and constant pursuit of women had earned him an apt nickname as a young man. His envious friends called him "The Sheik." In his forties and fifties, he was frequently mistaken for Clark Gable, a mix-up he relished.

His full name was John Vernou Bouvier III. His father was attorney and stockbroker John Vernou Bouvier, Jr., a man whose intense pride in his family's history and tradition was not shared by the eldest son who bore his name and was reared to someday take over the leadership of a family that had become one of the most illustrious in America. There was a fortune to match.

In addition to Jack, there was his younger brother William Sergeant—always known as "Bud"—and his three sisters: Edith and the twins, Maude and Michelle.

The first Bouvier to arrive on the shores of the New World came to fight for the American cause in the Revolutionary War. Even though Andre Eustache Bouvier went back to France, he never forgot the heady experience of fighting for freedom in the ranks behind Marquis de Lafayette, the French aristocrat who had taken up the American cause of independence from England.

The father's stories of America fascinated his son, Michel, who emigrated to the United States when he was barely out of his teens, married Louise Vernou, and founded a dynasty.

For over a hundred years, the Bouviers, almost as if it were the normal course of events, made immense amounts of money, entered into brilliant marriages, produced huge families, and lived into their eighties. From the time he was a little boy, Jack Bouvier had been told that he was expected to do the same.

Indications are that he tried, but only sporadically. Jack's school years were undistinguished, a fact that greatly troubled his father who had been graduated from Columbia as a Phi Beta Kappa. After Jack's graduation from Yale, he went to work on Wall Street and proceeded to carve out his primary career as a ladies' man.

Unfortunately, World War I intervened. To avoid the draft, Jack enlisted in the Navy, then set about pulling strings in Washington via his Wall Street and Yale connections. Before long, he was transferred to the Aviation and Signal Corps of the Army and spent most of the war at Scott Field in St. Louis, Missouri. Unlike his brother, Bud, he had no desire to see combat.

When the war ended, Jack returned to New York and resumed his career on Wall Street and his status as one of New York's most eligible bachelors. The first thing he acquired was a Park Avenue apartment where he was soon throwing parties that were at least partially responsible for naming the post-war decade the "Roaring Twenties."

Jack Bouvier's nephew, John Davis, the son of his sister Maude, has written a perceptive description, both physical and psychological, of his dashing uncle:

"A man with a great sense of style, an innate flair, he made the most of his good looks by paying inordinate attention to his clothes. Almost everything he wore he had made to order. His tailor gave his suits a Continental cut, emphasizing the chest with wide lapels, indenting the waist and flattening the hips. Tripler made his shirts with high collars and long sleeves, for Jack liked to show plenty of collar and cuff, and Tripler also made his ties, which he preferred paisley, wide and long.

"Jack Bouvier's ancestry was just as British as it was French, yet his Provencal blood prevailed, giving him a dark complexion that he made even darker by exposing himself regularly to a sun lamp. . . .

"Jack's personality, too, was more Mediterranean than Anglo-Saxon. Like most Mediterranean men, he was highly susceptible to the fascination of beautiful women and big money, but soon tired of a woman, and spent money faster than he earned it. Unconventional, and lacking in the middle-class virtues, Jack Bouvier had the narcissistic vanity of a Roman and the theatrical flamboyance of a Neapolitan. Unlike many of his classmates at school and college, he was essentially a loner who was reluctant to share the spotlight with others. In company he was more theatrical than social, preferring to make a dazzling impression on people rather than expend a great deal of effort to get to know them. As a man of distinctly erotic temperament, male company bored him; he much preferred the society of women. Since he was so Mediterranean in appearance and personality, and yet came from a family of wealth and long-standing social position, Jack Bouvier was a rather unique being in New York society: a member of the upper class who was more Latin than Anglo-Saxon. The ranks of the Social Register at the time were almost entirely filled with people of British, Scotch, Dutch, or German ancestry, and if there were French members included, chances were that their ancestors had come from northern France, not the Midi. In a sense, Jack and Bud Bouvier were the closest things to Italians in society."

As the great bull market of the twenties roared toward its catastrophic collapse in the Great Depression, Jack Bouvier's life seemed, at least from the outside, like an almost unattainable golden dream, the sort of life that F. Scott Fitzgerald's Jay Gatsby yearned for.

Jack's career on Wall Street boomed right along with the stock market. He was a specialist on the floor, now, trading in just a few stocks and earning about $75,000 a year. In addition, he had amassed, through his own speculations, a fortune of $750,000. Clearly, by the time he was forty, he would be a millionaire in his own right.

Maybe it was time to get married.

* * * * *

Compared to the Bouviers, Janet Lee's family were *nouveaux riche*. Descended from poor immigrants who'd come to America in the great wave of Irish immigration two generations back, the family fortune had been made by Janet's father, James Thomas Lee. After working his way through City College and Columbia Law School, he practiced law, speculated in real estate, became a vice-president of the Chase National Bank, and eventually ended his career as president and Chairman of the Board of the New York Savings Bank.

In 1903 he married Margaret Merritt, and the couple had three children: Marion, Winifred, and Janet. After Lee had put together his multi-million-dollar fortune, he decided to take on another challenge and climb the social ladder. In the summers, he moved his family to East Hampton, and Lee's three daughters were soon on the best of terms with the Bouvier twins, Maude and Michelle.

Jack Bouvier was fourteen years older than his twin sisters. During their teens, he scarcely noticed them. Almost overnight, it seemed, they had become dazzling young women. And their friends had become dazzling young women, too. One in particular caught Jack's eye, even though she had been in and out of the Bouvier summer place, Lasata, for years.

The romance blossomed quickly. Janet Lee and Jack Bouvier began seeing each other in the summer of 1927. The following winter their engagement was announced, and on July 7, 1928, they were married. Jack was 37, Janet was 21.

Janet Norton Lee was a small, delicate girl with enormous eyes and a determined, inner nature completely at odds with her fragile exterior. She was a fiercely competitive and daring horsewoman who collected ribbons and trophies with astonishing regularity. Even after her two daughters were born, Janet seldom missed competing in the National Horse Show held at Madison Square Garden.

The local gossip mongers naturally considered Janet the *nouveaux riche* making a brilliant marriage to the rich and handsome Jack Bouvier. As their subsequent lives would show, however, it was Janet, and not her husband, who had the spirit and nature of a true aristocrat.

But the future cast no shadows on that beautiful summer day that Janet Lee and Jack Bouvier were married in St. Philomena's Church in East Hampton. Janet was attended by six bridesmaids, and her two sisters were matron and maid of honor. The bridesmaids wore yellow chiffon gowns and green straw hats. Marion and Winifred wore pale green dresses and yellow straw hats.

It was the social event of the season. A society writer for one of the New York dailies seemed carried away by all the elegance: "Have you ever glimpsed the loveliness of a bed of nodding green and gold jonquils in the sunshine? Surely you've all seen a stately bride bedecked in satin, lace and silver? Combine these effects and you'll have a glowing picture of Mrs. John Vernou Bouvier III, stepping into the sunshine from the door of quaint St. Philomena's Church yesterday with her attendants about her."

The reception for five hundred was held at the Lee home on Lily Pond Lane. Society band leader Meyer Davis and his orchestra provided dance music, Jack had a heated argument with his new father-in-law. Late in the day, Jack and Janet drove to New York and spent their wedding night at the Savoy-Plaza. The next day they sailed for Europe on the *Aquitania*.

* * * * *

No one could have been happier over this improbable marriage than Jack's father, John Vernou Bouvier, Jr. (or "Grampy Jack," as his grandchildren called him). There had only been two sons to carry on the Bouvier tradition, and Bud, Jack's younger brother, had been on an increasingly downward spiral since his days of glory as a combat officer in World War I.

After early financial successes in the oil business in Oklahoma, both his fortunes and his personal life had decayed. His drinking reached such proportions that his wife left him, taking their only child, Michel, with her. Emmy Lou said she would go back to him if he would quit drinking and get his life in order. Bud, for whatever reason, wasn't able to do this, although there is much evidence that he tried. Everyone had feared he would show up drunk at Jack's wedding. To the contrary, he performed his duties as best man with both competence and good will.

But a few months later, when it was Maude's turn to be married at Lasata, Bud's condition had worsened. A month after Maude's wedding, the family arranged for Bud to enter a private sanatorium where he stayed for six months. He made some progress, but not nearly enough. Shortly after he was released in April, his condition was soon no better than it had been before his expensive hospital sojourn.

Bud, in a desperate last attempt to throw off the bonds of alcoholism, took his son to California for an idyllic month of outdoor living near Los Olivos. If the boy could have stayed with him, Bud's story might have turned out differently. But in August the child returned East and Bud's decline was rapid.

He began drinking again, more heavily than before. On October 8, 1929, he was found dead in his room.

* * * * *

As this family tragedy was coming to its climax, Jack Bouvier's attention was dominated by his wife's pregnancy. At thirty-eight, Jack Bouvier was about to become a father. If he had known that the baby girl who arrived that Sunday afternoon in Southampton would become one of the world's most celebrated women—First Lady of the United States and wife of one of the world's richest men—he would no doubt have considered her future an appropriate one. After all, she *was* the daughter of Jack Bouvier, wasn't she?

A year after Jacqueline Lee Bouvier was born, her maternal grandfather gave the young family a Park Avenue duplex. By this time, the Great Depression was nearly a year old, but the Bouviers and the Lees and other rich American families continued to live much as they had lived for decades. They suffered substantial financial losses, of course, but few of them were wiped out. The cushions, the reserves, the slush funds, may have been depleted, but the day-to-day comforts continued. The servants remained employed: cooks prepared the food, maids cleaned the houses, nurses brought up the children.

And, in the case of Jack and Janet Bouvier, grooms continued to care for Janet's three horses: Stepaside, Clearanfast, and Danseuse.

When Jackie was barely a year old, Janet had her astride a pony. Janet would hold the lead lines herself and slowly walk the pony so that her daughter, hardly able to walk yet, would get the feel of a horse under her and learn to command an animal with the same natural, unthinking ease with which she commanded her own body.

Janet's patience, and Jack's—she frequently assigned the leading chores to him—paid off. By the time Jackie was five, she was skilled and confident enough to ride a hunter at her mother's side. The two of them, mounted on a pair of chestnut mares, took third prize in the Family Class at the East Hampton Horse Show.

When she was six, she was entered in a jumping class in the Southampton Horse Show. Competing against her were children considerably older than she: ten, eleven and twelve years old.

On one of the rounds, Jackie brought her pony in crooked. It shied the jump, and Jackie was thrown off. Furious, the little girl was back on her feet in seconds, trying to remount the pony from the wrong side. By the time a judge reached her, the audience had burst into applause. What a gutsy little kid!

Puzzled, young Jackie asked her mother on the way home why the people had clapped when she fell off her horse.

Janet felt this was a serious matter. She pulled the car over to the side of the road and gave her oldest daughter her complete attention. "Those were terribly silly people," she said. "They didn't understand what really happened. You should be ashamed of handling your pony so carelessly. He might have been hurt."

Jackie said nothing, but the child's perceptive intelligence had no doubt discovered that, in spite of her mother's displeasure at her carelessness, even mistakes can be turned to your advantage if you show courage and tenacity.

The speculative fancies that hindsight affords are usually seductive but not always accurate. The formation of character is a mysterious process, as the great novelists have always known. And in an age of glib, do-it-yourself psychology which perhaps treats human nature as far more malleable and subject to improvement and change than it really is, one must warily tread the quicksands of long-distance character analysis. Still, it is difficult not to imagine some of the effects on Jackie's personality of her precocious career as an equestrienne. She learned early in life to compete in the full glare of judges and audience. She learned that winning is important and that it seldom occurs by accident. Total self-control and unwavering self-confidence are needed if one is to carry off life's prizes. One must never doubt one's own importance and ability to perform brilliantly.

But these hard lessons were softened by a childhood that could hardly have been more privileged. Jackie garnered her first press notices on the occasion of her second birthday. A society reporter wrote: "Little Jackie Bouvier will not make her bow to society for another sixteen years or more, but she was a charming hostess at her second birthday party given at the home of her parents, 'Rowdy Hall' on Egypt Lane."

In the spring of 1933, Jack and Janet Bouvier had a second daughter, Caroline Lee. Jackie was moved out of the nursery and into her first "grown-up" bedroom. She liked her new independence. Besides, she had a favorite rag doll, Sammy, to keep her company every night now that the nurse was devoting most of her time to the new baby.

One day Janet got a call from the police. They had a pretty, black-haired child at a nearby precinct who had confidently given them her phone number. She had stopped a patrolman in Central

Park and announced, "My nurse is lost."

Jackie's forthrightness was not always quite so appealing. An elevator operator in the Park Avenue apartment house had a crest of blonde hair that stood up from his head as if it were starched. Baby sister, Lee, always the diplomat, told the man one day that he looked "pritty." Older sister Jackie turned to her little sister with a withering look and said scathingly, "How can you say such a thing? You know perfectly well that Ernest looks just like a rooster."

* * * * *

Summers were spent in East Hampton. There life, at least for the Bouviers, revolved around horses and horse shows. Winters were spent in Manhattan. Jackie attended Miss Spence's school and quickly earned a reputation as a prankster and rebel.

Finally, the school's famous headmistress, Ethel Stringfellow, told Jacqueline she needed discipline in order to do her best just like her beloved horses had to be properly schooled and trained if they were to win prizes. Jackie got the message. She settled down to become the good, often brilliant, student that she remained right through her college years.

This idyllic existence was shattered for Jackie when her parents separated late in 1936, several months after her seventh birthday. Jack Bouvier's fortunes had declined so badly as a result of the depression and his own bad judgment that he had been forced to accept largess from Janet's father. James Lee was willing to help his son-in-law, but only if certain conditions were met. He insisted that Jack Bouvier give up several of his clubs and, in general, tone down his flamboyant style of living. Jack had no choice but to comply but, inwardly, he seethed. His resentment did not help his marriage.

Then there were the other women. After spending the first fifteen years of his adult life as a ladies' man, Jack found it impossible to change after his marriage. Janet required fidelity. Jack didn't know the meaning of the word.

They signed a six-month separation agreement that ran from October 1, 1936, to April 1, 1937. Jack agreed to pay Janet $1,050 per month in child support and maintenance. She retained custody of Jackie and Lee, but their father's visitation rights were liberal. He had moved from the spacious Park Avenue duplex to one room in the Westbury Hotel.

When the separation agreement ran out in April, Janet agreed to give the marriage another try. The Bouviers were together again as a family for five months. Then, at the end of August 1937, Jack and Janet separated permanently, although the divorce did not take place until 1940.

The break-up of the Bouvier marriage was not friendly. The Bouviers had nothing good to say about the Lees. The Lees had nothing but harsh words for the Bouviers. Both families tried to win the primary affection of Jacqueline and Lee.

Jack, who wanted his daughters to consider the Bouviers as their "real" family, indulged them to a degree that neither his income nor the times warranted. Jackie and Lee soon understood that their father's generosity depended on how much attention they paid to him. Perhaps more than most growing girls, they learned how to court their father and appease his vanity.

One trump card that Jack held in the battle for his daughters' affection and loyalty, according to Bouvier family historian, John H. Davis, was his flamboyant and theatrical personality:

"Living with their mother was colorless and dull compared to living with Jack. Being with their father was a 'treat.' Staying with their mother was humdrum. Because going to their father's was always such an exciting experience, Jack influenced his daughters profoundly during the most receptive time of their lives, transmitting certain qualities to them that they would one day project to the entire world.

"One of these was a sense of style. Jack Bouvier not only paid very careful attention to his own wardrobe but he insisted that the women in his life be equally well-dressed. . . . To receive a compliment from Jack on the way one dressed was a great tonic to one's morale, and Jacqueline and Lee made sure the compliments would be forthcoming. What their father liked, they wore. . . .

"Another quality Jack transmitted to his daughters was an appreciation of what makes women desirable. . . .One quality he always admired in women was unapproachableness. The more a woman refused his advances, the more he was attracted to her. Then, when she finally gave in, he would lose interest in her and move on to someone else. Thus, he would admonish his daughters time and again never to throw themselves at anybody, to be always reticent with men and play hard-to-get."

* * * * *

Jack had his daughters all day on Sunday, for half of all their school vacations, and six weeks each summer. During the Bouvier half of their summers, life for Jackie and Lee was centered on Lasata, their grandparents' sumptuous country retreat in East Hampton.

Lasata symbolizes a way of life that gradually disappeared after World War II. The ivy-covered stucco house stood on twelve carefully tended acres. The grounds, which required the attentions of a full-time gardener, included a tennis court, an orchard, a corn-field, a formal, sunken garden just behind the main house, a grape arbor, a cutting garden, stables, and a riding ring.

Sunday lunches at Lasata were tumultuous affairs. Jack would extravagantly praise his daughters and berate his nieces and nephews for not showing them the deference they deserved. Jack's fatherly monologues set his sisters' teeth on edge but they said nothing. *Their* children, in turn, would tease Jackie and Lee even more and not always gently. The two girls didn't care. Their father's praise was more than worth it.

After lunch, most of the clan would head for the Maidstone Club for tennis, golf, or swimming. The Bouviers owned a cabana at the Maidstone and on most Saturdays and Sundays in July and August, Jack Bouvier lay in the sun all day, building the tan that he would maintain during the winter with a sun lamp.

If Janet hadn't remarried, it is probable that the delights of Lasata in the summer would have been enough to lure her daughters into the Bouvier camp permanently as they grew older. But Janet remained single for only two years. Her new husband was Hugh D. Auchincloss, a man whose social standing equaled that of the Bouviers and whose fortune was considerably larger. Of Scots descent, "Hughdie" resembled Jack Bouvier neither physically nor temperamentally. Auchincloss, a stockbroker, was a basically conservative man who possessed the Scottish virtues of thrift, stability, and hard work.

Janet and Hugh were married in June 1942. It was the begin-ning of the end for Jack Bouvier's hopes that he could eventually woo his daughters away from their mother. Jackie and Lee not only moved away from New York, but their new life was lived on a grander scale than the Bouviers could provide.

After a few years of working in Washington in the thirties, Auchincloss had decided that he wanted to live there permanently. He bought Merrywood, a magnificent Virginia estate that overlooked Washington from the hills above the Potomac. In addition to being much bigger than Lasata, Merrywood's forty-six acres also boasted a swimming pool.

Merrywood was home to Hugh's three children from two previous marriages in addition to Janet's two daughters. And when Jackie was in her teens, her mother and stepfather had two children of their own. Eventually, Merrywood was home to seven children who apparently got along amazingly well.

When the Virginia summers became too hot and humid to endure, the Auchinclosses would move, en masse, to Hammersmith Farm on the outskirts of Newport, Rhode Island, where Hugh had grown up.

Beginning in 1944, however, Jackie spent most of her time during the academic year at Miss Porter's school in Farmington, Connecticut. One of her roommates there was Nancy Tuckerman. They have remained friends and confidantes ever since. (Nancy became Jackie's White House social secretary in June, 1963, and continues to this day to function as a part-time personal secretary, handling phone calls and much of Jackie's mail.)

Janet and Hugh decided that for Jackie to keep Danseuse in the school's stables would be an unwarranted expense. Jackie, who loved the gentle mare as if she were human, appealed to her Bouvier grandfather for the $25 a month stabling cost.

Grampy Jack came through for her:

Dear Jacqueline: What in one aspect might be viewed as a sumptuary extravagance may, on the other hand, from the mental and physical standpoint, be regarded as a justifiable necessity.

Within this generalization naturally falls Danseuse. Psychologically she aids you. Spiritually she provides a wholesome release from sordid worldly cares. Therefore I will engage to meet her keep of $25 a month until April next.

Are you or am I in these dreadful days justified in such an indulgence? I think not, but with the necessity for maintaining Danseuse both of us are in concurrence.

Affectionately,
Granddad

* * * * *

Jackie loved her years at Miss Porter's (even though she once wrote to a classmate: "I just know no one will ever marry me and I'll end up as a housemother at Farmington.") She earned an A-minus average, she had her beloved horse nearby, and she only had to contend with one roommate and not a houseful of Bouviers, Auchinclosses, or Lees. It was perhaps easier to be herself away from the constantly conflicting claims of her various families.

Jack Bouvier, of course, frequently drove up to Farmington to visit his oldest daughter and watch her perform in school theatricals and local horse shows. They played in father-daughter tennis matches. Grandly, in true Bouvier style, he would take Jackie and several of her friends to lunch at the Elm Tree Inn. "Everybody ordered steaks and two desserts," Jackie has said. "We must have eaten him broke."

When Jack learned that Jackie would be going to Vassar in Poughkeepsie, N.Y., an easy commute from Manhattan, he was delighted. This would be a four-year victory over Janet and the Auchinclosses, who, he knew, were making strenuous efforts to include his daughters in *their* family events. Jackie would naturally gravitate to New York on week-ends rather than Merrywood. His bachelor apartment at 125 East 74 Street would be waiting for her.

As he anticipated, Jackie found it a convenient place to sleep over when she had a date in the city. Almost too convenient. Jackie's cousin John Davis describes her father's feeling on the matter in his history of the Bouviers:

"During the winter of 1948 Jack would repeatedly charge his eldest daughter with coming to his apartment only when it suited her convenience, pointing out that she would arrive breathlessly a half hour before her date or her dance, then depart as soon as she got up the next morning. And he would often complain to his sisters that she took advantage of him, that she would write or phone only when she needed her allowance, which at that time was fifty dollars a month."

In the years of college and young adulthood events often move so fast that it is easy for the young person to appear inconsiderate to a person whose life has begun to slow down. Jackie's behavior then was similar to that of many college girls who happened to have parents living in Manhattan. But her father obviously felt he had been singled out for callous treatment.

After Grampy Jack's death in 1948, Lasata was sold and Jack could no longer use the spacious country house with its gardens, stables and riding ring to lure his daughters to spend most of their summers with him. After Lasata was gone, Jack rented a small cottage for himself—it was not near the ocean—and space in a nearby stable for Danseuse. He would not allow Jackie to keep her horse at Hammersmith Farm, fearing that if he did, he would never see her at all.

When Jackie told him she wanted to go to Europe the summer after her freshman year at Vassar, he at first opposed the idea. Jack was convinced it was another of Janet's schemes for keeping his daughters from him. Eventually, however, Jackie broke down his resistance. Jack agreed to the two month junket and paid her expenses.

Chaperoned by Helen Shearman, her Latin teacher from Holton-Arms, a Washington, D.C., day school that Jackie attended for two years before she entered Miss Porter's, she traveled with three schoolmates: Julia Bissell and Helen and Judy Bowdoin, stepdaughters of Edward F. Foley, Jr., who was then Under Secretary of the Treasury.

Foley pulled a few diplomatic strings and came up with an invitation to a Buckingham Palace garden party for the group. The standard uniform in those days for a royal garden party was a "dressy" dress (preferably a flowered print), a cartwheel straw hat, and elbow-length white gloves.

So when Jackie and her travelling companions boarded the *Queen Mary* for the leisurely ocean crossing, the trunks contained all the finery required for attending the British royal family.

Unfortunately, when the great day arrived, the English weather did not co-operate. It rained. And rained. And rained. The hundreds of people who would have been quite comfortable spread over the palace grounds were jammed together under the refreshment canopy. Still, Jackie and her friends managed to go through the receiving line twice. King George VI and his wife smiled pleasantly both times. Later, they saw Winston Churchill. The irascible English statesman graciously shook hands with all the pretty American college girls.

After sightseeing in London and the English countryside, the group took the boat train to Paris, toured the chateau country, made a brief stop at Juan Les Pins on the French Riviera, then proceeded to Switzerland and Italy: Milan, Venice, Florence, and Rome.

Jackie was mesmerized by Europe, especially France. She

immediately set about finding a way to go back. She persuaded both the Vassar and Smith administrations to let her apply for the Smith College program for junior year abroad. She was admitted to the program conditionally: she had to take extra courses in French. And she passed them all.

It wasn't just the lure of French culture and the opportunity to study at the Sorbonne that appealed to her. If she were on the other side of the Atlantic, all the pressure from her various families would diminish considerably. If she stayed at Vassar, she would constantly have to "choose" between her mother, the Auchinc022closes, and Merrywood and her father, the Bouviers, and her father's apartment on East 74th Street.

But in Paris this painful and often confusing emotional juggling act wasn't necessary. Jackie could spend her time on her studies and her own pursuits without having to consider the effects of her decisions on her parents.

Most of the Smith College group lived in Reid Hall, a Sorbonne dormitory for American students. Jackie, however, wanted to live with a French family. She rented a small room in the home of the Comtesse de Renty, a noblewoman whose husband had died in a German concentration camp. She now made her living by running a boardinghouse for students. Jackie was one of seven paying guests at 78 avenue Mozart.

The vibrance and elegance of the French capital, the intense student life of the Sorbonne, and the sophistication of the American colony suited Jackie perfectly. She couldn't ignore the contrast between her Parisian life and Vassar's staid atmosphere. The American college was like a convent, and if there was anything that didn't suit the determined and outspoken Jackie Bouvier, it was a cloister. Before Christmas had arrived, she resolved not to return to Vassar for her senior year.

She spent the summer after her year at the Sorbonne traveling in Europe, first with Claude de Renty, her landlady's daughter, and later with her stepbrother, Hugh D. Auchincloss, Jr., better known as "Yusha." Early in the summer, while she and Claude were still on their no-frills trip, Jackie wrote to Yusha, "We really saw what it was like with the Russians with Tommy guns in Vienna. . . . We saw Vienna and Salzburg and Berchtesgaden where Hitler lived; Munich and the Dachau concentration camp. . . . It's so much more fun traveling second and third class and sitting up all night in trains, as you really get to know people—and hear their stories.

When I traveled before it was all too luxurious and we didn't see anything."

Later, Yusha met her in Dublin and they toured Ireland—yes, Jacqueline Lee Bouvier kissed the Blarney stone—and then crossed the Irish Sea to Scotland, ancestral home of the Auchinclosses, where they drove north to John o' Groats, in Caithness.

While Jackie traveled in Europe and her sister, Lee, spent the summer on a ranch in Wyoming, their father was recovering from a cataract operation. A further blow was dealt Jack Bouvier when he learned that Jackie did not plan to return to Vassar. She had decided to finish college at George Washington University in Washington, D.C. To Jack, this meant nothing except a stunning victory for Janet and the Auchinclosses.

He was both surprised and delighted, then, when Jackie became engaged, early in 1951, to John G. W. Husted, Jr., son of a well-known New York banker. This meant that after their marriage, she would be living in Manhattan again.

The story is told that John Husted's mother once offered Jackie a boyhood snapshot of her son.

"No, thanks," Jackie said. "If I want any photos, I can take my own."

The engagement was eventually broken off. While it lasted, however, Jackie made frequent trips to New York, spending every other week-end at her father's apartment. Naturally, Jack was thrilled.

But the summer after Jackie finished college, she was off to Europe once again, this time acting as guide and traveling companion to her younger sister. Jackie and Lee rented a car and drove from Paris to Spain and then through Italy. They were in Florence when Jackie turned 22. While in the city of the Medicis, they managed to get themselves invited to Bernard Berenson's elegant villa just outside the old city.

The aging art critic made an enormous impression on Jackie. Ever since that summer day in 1951, she has considered Berenson one of the most impressive persons she has ever met.

Earlier that year, several months before her graduation, Jackie had entered *Vogue's* Prix de Paris contest, open to college women only. Those who entered were required to plan an entire issue of *Vogue,* write four papers on fashion, a personal profile, and a brief essay on "People I Wish I Had Known." Jackie chose three esthetes: Diaghilev, a Russian ballet impresario, English writer

Oscar Wilde, and French poet Charles Baudelaire.

Beating out 1,279 other contestants, Jackie won first prize: a six-month stint on Paris *Vogue* followed by six months in *Vogue's* New York office. Again, Jack Bouvier's hopes were raised. After Paris, where Jackie would again be unavailable to the Auchinclosses, she would be in New York for six uninterrupted months. He had no doubt that his bright and articulate daughter would be offered a permanent job by the *Vogue* editors—which she would undoubtedly accept. After all, she had frequently expressed an interest in journalism.

Again, Jack's plans fell through. Janet and Hugh convinced Jackie to turn down the prize. She had been away from home too much in recent years, they said. Finally, after prolonged discussion, Jackie agreed not to accept the Vogue prize. Later, she would tell friends she feared that if she ever returned to Paris, she would stay there forever.

Jack was crushed. More than anything else, what he wanted was to have Jackie near him. Again and again, those hopes were shattered.

* * * * *

While Jack Bouvier regarded Hugh Auchincloss as his opponent in the years-long battle for his daughters' loyalties and affection, Jackie always saw "Hughdie" as "a wonderful stepfather." When she and Lee were motoring through Italy that summer, Jackie wrote Hugh a sweet and affectionate letter:

"I began to feel terribly homesick as I was driving. . . . I started thinking of things like the path leading to the stable at Merrywood, with the stones slipping as you ran up it . . . and Hammersmith with the foghorns blowing at night. All the places and feelings and happiness that bind you to a family you love . . . something that you take with you no matter how far you go—"

Earlier, when she was still a student in Paris, she had written to Yusha in a similar vein: "I always love it so at Merrywood—so peaceful—with the river and the dogs—and listening to the Victrola. I will never know which I love best—Hammersmith with its green fields and summer winds or Merrywood in the snow, with the river and those great steep hills."

If Jack Bouvier had known about those letters, his heart would have broken for sure.

Ironically, it was through one of Hugh's friends that Jackie got her job in journalism. The friend was Arthur Krock, Washington bureau chief for the New York *Times.* On Jackie's behalf, he called Frank Waldrop, editor of the *Times-Herald,* a now-defunct Washington daily.

"Are you still hiring little girls?"

Waldrop said he was.

"Well, I have a wonder for you," Krock said. "She's round-eyed, clever, and wants to go into journalism. Will you see her?"

Waldrop said he would. They set up an appointment for early December. When she arrived, Waldrop asked bluntly, "Do you want to go into journalism or do you want to hang around here until you get married?"

"No, sir," Jackie said. "I want to make a career."

"Well, if you're serious, I'll be serious," Waldrop said. She would start her new job just after New Year's Day. "Don't you come to me in six months and say you're engaged," Waldrop added.

Jackie was given the Inquiring Photographer column. When she took over the column, in fact, the editors renamed it the Inquiring Camera Girl. For years, the job had been handled by a man. The editors had long wanted a woman to take over the job and give it a lighter touch.

The person running the column had to think up a human interest or topical question every day and then get ten or twelve people to answer the question and allow their photographs to be taken. Thinking up the questions was the hardest part of the job. The pay for Jackie's new assignment was $42.50 a week.

After the election in November, when Dwight Eisenhower defeated Adlai Stevenson, Jackie posed a political question: "Who will be Washington's No. 1 hostess now that the Republicans are back in power?"

Among the persons she queried was the wife of the new GOP vice-president, Richard M. Nixon. Pat Nixon told Jackie: "Why, Mrs. Eisenhower, of course. I think her friendly manner and sparkling personality immediately captivate all who see or meet her. She is equally gracious in small groups or long receiving lines, where she has the knack of getting acquainted with each person, instead of merely shaking hands with the usual phrase, 'How do you do?' The people of America will always be proud of their First Lady."

Pat Nixon had just given Jackie a marvelous lesson in the art of being a political wife. (Mamie Eisenhower? Sparkling personality?) Jackie wrote down Pat Nixon's answer, thanked her, and headed back for the office. She had no idea that she would one day be a political wife herself.

* * * * *

Charles Bartlett was the Washington correspondent for the Chattanooga *Times* at this time. A Yale graduate, he had met John F. Kennedy during the war when both their families had wintered in close Florida proximity: Bartlett's parents had a place in Hobe Sound, Kennedy's were at Palm Beach. Bartlett's path had crossed Jackie's several times since she had started working for the *Times-Herald*. Recently married himself, Charles and his new wife thought Jacqueline Bouvier and the handsome, young, bachelor Congressman from Massachusetts an obvious match.

Charlie and Martha Bartlett decided to play Cupid and invited the pair to a dinner party in June, 1951. At first, nothing happened. But by fall, after Kennedy had returned from his family summer retreat in Hyannis Port on Cape Cod, he and Jackie began seeing each other. Their first date was the grandest they would ever have. Kennedy took her dancing at a Washington hotel. It was a strange excursion: a threesome. Tagging along was one of Kennedy's political cronies from Massachusetts.

After that, Jack Kennedy and Jackie Bouvier were rarely seen in public. They spent many evenings with the Bartletts. Occasionally, they would have dinner with Bobby and Ethel Kennedy and then catch a movie. But they were seen together often enough to generate a steady stream of rumors—Washington produces rumors the way Wisconsin produces cheese—concerning the current status of their alleged romance.

Frank Waldrop, Jackie's boss at the *Times-Herald,* naturally heard the gossip. One day he sent her on assignment to Capitol Hill. One of the people she was to get for the column was Kennedy. Before she left, Waldrop couldn't resist adding, "You behave yourself. Don't get your hopes up. He's too old for you—besides, he doesn't want to get married."

Jackie said nothing, just raised her eyebrows by way of replying to Waldrop and went off to do her column for the day.

Kennedy obviously intrigued her more than the proper young stockbrokers and investment bankers whom she had met. Something in her craved excitement and she instinctively knew she wasn't cut out for the kind of placid, conservative life that her mother had led ever since she'd married Hugh Auchincloss. The life that Janet had created with Hugh had nourished Jackie's childhood immensely, but whether she wanted that same life as an adult was an entirely different matter.

Something in her yearned, perhaps blindly, for the same things that her father craved: life on a grand scale, the large gesture, the wide canvas. And if she took him at his word, Kennedy offered all those things and more. He had told her that he was going to be President. Should she believe him? When they first met, the idea seemed preposterous. But after his stunning upset of Henry Cabot Lodge in 1952 when the rest of the country was going solidly Republican . . . well, maybe he could pull it off.

But at first Jack Kennedy's ambition struck Jackie as not entirely plausible. Bouvier family historian John Davis was a Naval officer in 1952, stationed in Washington. He, too, had heard about Kennedy and his cousin. One day at lunch he asked her about the engagement rumors. Jackie dismissed Kennedy as "quixotic" based on his having confided to her that he "intended to become President."

Still, Davis remembers that "it was obvious both from the tone of her voice and her evasiveness that she liked Kennedy."

She obviously reassessed the situation at some point, and it is not unreasonable to assume that Kennedy's resounding victory over Lodge had something to do with it. Quite possibly, the upset may have convinced Jackie that John F. Kennedy was a real winner who could go the distance and take her with him.

Then there was all that Kennedy money. Jackie had grown up in comparative luxury, but she had no money of her own. She was not an heiress. She would not inherit anything substantial from Hugh D. Auchincloss, and her father's share of Grampy Jack's estate had been devastated by bad management and the Great Depression.

If she did not marry well, she would eventually have to work for a living.

Kennedy escorted her to Eisenhower's Inaugural Ball in January, 1953, and they spent much more time together now that Jack was back in Washington and not spending most of his time campaigning in Massachusetts.

His Senate race wasn't the only hurdle that Jack Kennedy faced in 1952. He also had to meet Jack Bouvier. Jackie had not been looking forward to their first meeting. In addition to being a die-hard Republican whose conservative political philosophy was diametrically opposed to Kennedy's Democratic liberalism, Jackie's father had a long memory, especially where money was concerned.

Two years after Franklin D. Roosevelt was elected President in 1932, he appointed Joseph P. Kennedy head of the newly-created Securities and Exchange Commission. Jack Kennedy's ambitious father had been one of the sharpest, shrewdest operators on Wall Street in his heyday. He had built the Kennedy fortune based on tactics and practices that he then outlawed once he took over as SEC chief.

Several of the new regulations were specifically designed to prevent specialists (such as Jack Bouvier) from participating in an upsurge in one of their stocks. In practical terms, this meant that Jack Bouvier was free to risk his own funds when the market was going down in one of the stocks he specialized in but not when it was going up. The new rule was, of course, meant to eliminate the possibility that by the specialists' buying heavily into an upsurge, it would be given an artificial momentum that would eventually benefit only a few insiders. Most of them, needless to say, the very specialists who had created the inflated price in the first place.

In addition to the potential for political dissension between Jack Bouvier and Jack Kennedy, there were the emotional issues. All during their adolescence, Jack Bouvier had warned his daughters about men. His message seemed to be: *Don't trust any of them. They're all rats.* Perhaps because he saw so little of them, Jack was very possessive of Jackie and Lee. Bad enough that he'd had to hand them over to Hugh Auchincloss in 1942. Now, ten years later, the prospect of having them turn from daughters with at least a part-time loyalty to him into wives with full-time loyalty to their husbands was something Jack Bouvier did not like to think about. He knew their marriages were inevitable, but if only they would marry boys from New York, from Wall Street, so that they could once again become a regular part of his life.

But here was Jackie involved with Joe Kennedy's son. Marriage to him would mean that she would be staying in Washington. And she would undoubtedly be called on to play an important role in Jack's plan to become President. The irony of Jackie helping to implement Joe Kennedy's ambition to put one of his sons in the White House could not have been lost on Jack Bouvier.

(left) Jacqueline Bouvier with her mother, Mrs. John V. Bouvier III, at Easthampton, 1935. (Photo courtesy of Bert and Richard Morgan Studio)

(bottom, left) With her father, John V. Bouvier III, just before her eighteenth birthday. (Photo courtesy of Wide World Photos)

(bottom, right) A stint as a photographer for the Washington *Times-Herald* in the early 1950s. (Photo courtesy of Wide World Photos)

(top) John and Jackie relax at the beach in Hyannis.
(bottom) Senator John F. Kennedy and his bride after their wedding in Newport in 1953. (Photo courtesy of Wide World Photos)

(top) The Kennedys at a 1963 mass in Middleburg, Virginia. (Photo courtesy of United Press International)

(bottom) The aircraft carrier USS John F. Kennedy is commissioned while Jackie, Caroline, and John Jr. watch. (Photo courtesy of United Press International)

Composer Leonard Bernstein at a performance with his sister and Jackie. (Photo courtesy of United Press International)

Caroline Kennedy, Jackie Onassis, and Roosevelt Grier at a 1974 benefit show. (Photo courtesy of Wide World Photos)

Soviet Premier Nikita Khrushchev is charmed by Mrs. John F. Kennedy at a 1961 reception in Vienna. (Photo courtesy of United Press International)

(from left) Rose Kennedy, Mrs. James Gavin, Madame Herve Alphand, Mrs. Jacqueline Kennedy, and Madame Charles de Gaulle in Paris, 1961. (Photo courtesy of United Press International)

With her children, Caroline and John Jr., Jackie visits John F. Kennedy's grave on what would have been his 47th birthday. (Photo courtesy of United Press International)

At Senator Robert F. Kennedy's campaign headquarters. (Photo courtesy of United Press International)

(top) Aristotle and Jackie Onassis. (Photo courtesy of United Press International)
(bottom) With Ari at her fortieth birthday celebration. (Photo courtesy of
United Press International)

(top) Christina Onassis, Ted Kennedy, and Jackie accompany the body of Aristotle Onassis to Skorpios. (Photo courtesy of United Press International)
(bottom) Jackie Onassis concludes her first solo editing assignment at the Viking Press. (Photo courtesy of Wide World Photos)

Still, the thought of his daughter as First Lady was most appealing. By God, then everybody would have to notice that she was a Bouvier, through and through. . .

The meeting went well. The two Jacks were both capable of exuding great charm when they chose; each wanted to make a good impression on the other. And the two men *did* have much in common. "They were very much alike," Jackie has said. "We three had dinner . . . and they talked about politics and sports and girls— what all red-blooded men like to talk about."

Jack Kennedy knew that he could not make his bid for the White House without a wife. But to be a politician's wife requires special talents. His mother, Rose, certainly possessed those talents in large measure, but then she had been a politician's daughter, had grown up in the Irish and Italian wards of Boston. Women like Rose were hard to find. They came along only rarely.

For a woman to be a real asset to a politician took more than beauty and more than intelligence. She had to have a similar kind of hunger for power and recognition and yet be willing to sublimate her ambition into his career. (If she were really good at this game, in fact, she could eventually transform it into *their* career. Whether *he* liked it or not. . .)

Jack Kennedy surely sensed that hunger in Jacqueline Lee Bouvier and meeting her father would have explained the source. In addition, she had impeccable family connections, a fact that the often-snubbed Kennedys of Boston would find gratifying. She had grown up in a milieu in which being a wife was a full-time job—literally. It meant planning parties, dinners, charity balls, and horse shows. It meant knowing how to run two or three houses smoothly, with a minimum of fuss. It meant knowing how to deal with servants and other underlings without needlessly ruffling their feathers. Whatever else these abilities are, they are also political skills, requiring one to use power so deftly and unobtrusively that no one is *quite* aware that power is being wielded. The idea is to make one's use of power seem like the natural order of things.

This is not to imply that Jackie married Jack for his money or that Jack married Jackie because he thought she would further his presidential ambitions. They were both incredibly attractive, intelligent, and vital human beings. Articulate and well-read, both had a sharp wit and an innate sense of style. Their falling in love seems the most natural thing in the world. Only a hardened cynic would imply that their love and affection for each other was not the most important factor in their relationship. On the other hand, only a hopeless romantic could think that either Jack Kennedy or Jacqueline Bouvier was unaware of the power, money, and social status that would be traded if a marriage should take place.

* * * * *

In May, 1953, Jackie went to London for the coronation of Elizabeth II and sent back to the *Times-Herald* feature stories which she illustrated with pen sketches. Her efforts ended up on the front page. Jack cabled her: *Articles excellent but you are missed.*

Jackie spent her spare moments in London poking through the Charing Cross Road bookshops. At every stop, it seems, she found a book she knew Jack Kennedy would enjoy. When she checked in at the airport for the return flight, she had to pay over $100 in excess baggage fees.

Her flight back to the States was scheduled to land first in Boston, before terminating in New York. Waiting for Jackie at the Boston airport was Senator John F. Kennedy.

A month later it was official. A few days before they announced their engagement, Jackie called her Aunt Maude, one of Jack Bouvier's twin sisters. "I just want you to know that I'm engaged to Jack Kennedy," Jackie said. "But you can't tell anyone for a while. It wouldn't be fair to *The Saturday Evening Post.*"

"What has *The Saturday Evening Post* to do with your engagement?" Maude asked, puzzled.

Jackie laughed. "They're coming out with an article tomorrow on 'Jack Kennedy—the Senate's Gay Young Bachelor!' "

Chapter Two

Marriage to Senator Kennedy

Chapter Two

Marriage to Senator Kennedy

The comparison is too obvious not to make it: When Jack Bouvier married Janet Lee in 1928, he was thirty-seven years old, a dashing man about town whose womanizing had been the stuff of legend among his wide circle of family, friends, and Wall Street colleagues. He was fourteen years older than his bride.

When Jack Bouvier's daughter, Jacqueline, went to the alter in 1953, she married a man named Jack who was thirty-six years old, a man who had been named in a national poll earlier that year as the country's most eligible bachelor. His pursuit of women was a frequent topic of conversation in Washington. He was twelve years older than his bride.

There's more: Jack Bouvier's wife was considered *nouveaux riche* Irish by the long-established families who summered in the Hamptons. Jacqueline Bouvier's husband-to-be was considered *nouveaux riche* Irish by the long-established families who lived along the elegant streets of Boston's Beacon Hill.

The wedding couple, their parents and relatives, and the 1200 guests who were due to gather at Hugh Auchincloss' Hammersmith Farm that breezy and sunny Saturday in September were no doubt aware, in varying degrees, of the powerful emotional currents running through what was billed as the wedding of the year.

But no one felt those currents as keenly as Jack Bouvier. He had first visited the Auchincloss turf the previous April when he gave his younger daughter, Lee, in marriage to Michael Canfield. After the wedding in Washington, he had gone to the reception at Merrywood with his twin sisters, Maude and Michelle. Its beauty overwhelmed him. No wonder Jackie and Lee didn't want to visit his cramped and sunless apartment in Manhattan. The gulf between the gracious life that Hugh had provided for his daughters and what he had to offer them seemed immense. Only by an incredible effort of will was Jack able to get through the lavish reception without a breach of etiquette or loss of self-control. Lee's wedding had been one of the most harrowing experiences of his life.

And now, a scant five months later, he was expected to endure this shame and humiliation all over again. Only this time the wedding would be at Hugh's farm in Rhode Island with its magnificent hilltop view of Narragansett Bay.

He was determined that for Jackie's sake and for his own self-pride, he would perform magnificently. This time he would not be taken by surprise. He spent weeks putting his outfit together. He had a new cutaway tailored. He bought new gray suede gloves. His striped trousers had to be just the right width.

Jack arrived in Newport the night before the wedding and checked into the Viking Hotel. The deep bronze tan that he had acquired the previous month in East Hampton had not begun to fade. The hotel management had learned that he was the bride's father, and when Jack ordered ice and drinks from room service, they appeared at his door almost instantly. When he went down for dinner, he was given the best table in the dining room. When he went back upstairs and ordered more ice and more drinks, the management was honored to be of service.

By mid-morning of the next day, it was clear that Jack would be unable to attend the wedding and give his beloved Jackie away. The liquor that he had drunk only to steady his nerves had, instead, cruelly undermined his resolve and destroyed his composure. All the feelings of failure that he had been repressing for years flooded over him in one devastating tidal wave.

The new cutaway was never worn and Jack Bouvier never saw Hammersmith Farm. When the time came for Jacqueline Lee Bouvier to be given in marriage to Senator John F. Kennedy, she walked down the aisle on the arm of her stepfather, Hugh Auchincloss. Whatever hurt and embarrassment she felt over her father's failure to be at her side, she hid behind a dazzling smile and an aura of radiant happiness. The show, after all, had to go on.

The Kennedy-Bouvier wedding was certainly a grand display of youth, beauty, class, style, and influence. Boston Archbishop Richard Cushing celebrated the nuptial High Mass and conferred the special Apostolic Blessing sent from Rome by Pope Pius XII. Matron of honor Lee Bouvier Canfield and the nine bridesmaids wore pink taffeta with claret sashes. Jackie's gown was cream-colored taffeta faille. The veil she wore, all the more elegant for being yellowed with age, had been first worn by her grandmother Lee some fifty years earlier. On Jackie's left wrist was the diamond bracelet the bridegroom had given her. Then there was her engagement ring—a square-cut emerald and diamond.

After the ceremony at St. Mary's Church in Newport, everyone hurried to Hammersmith Farm for the reception. Thousands of wedding gifts were displayed in the main house. Luncheon was served on dozens of small tables set up on the farm's carefully manicured lawns. In one direction, cattle could be seen grazing in a meadow. The opposite view showed Narragansett Bay, studded with white sails.

The guest list was a testament to the equalizing power of money. The roster included Social Register friends of the Bouviers and Auchinclosses as well as the Kennedy contingent of Senators, Congressmen, and Boston ward heelers. After lunch, the Meyer Davis orchestra began playing its repertoire of show tunes and old favorites, just as it had played at Jack and Janet's wedding twenty-five years earlier. The socialites got up and danced; the politicians stood around in small groups and watched.

At the end of the day, Mr. and Mrs. John F. Kennedy flew to Acapulco, where they honeymooned in a pink villa overlooking the Pacific. Just a few days after they arrived, Jackie wrote her father a letter of forgiveness and understanding. When Jack Bouvier showed the letter to John Carrere, his partner, there were tears in his eyes. According to John Davis, "Carrere does not remember the wording of the note but recalls that it was one of the most touching, compassionate letters he has ever read, one that only a rare and noble spirit could have written."

* * * * *

The early years of the marriage were not easy for either husband or wife. Living together made their many differences in taste and personality stand out sharply. Jack thrived on politics. Jackie preferred art and culture. Jack, tending to be restless and unable to relax, was often like a thoroughbred in need of a good race. Jackie enjoyed and needed a large measure of quiet in her life. Jack was a steak and potatoes, corned beef and cabbage person. Jackie preferred French cooking and delicate wines. She told one interviewer: "Since Jack is such a violent, independent person and I, too, am so independent, this marriage will take a lot of working out."

They rented a house in Georgetown and Jackie took several courses in American history at the Georgetown School of Foreign Service. Jack Kennedy had read widely in the American past and Jackie obviously wanted to share his avocation. She mastered the courses easily enough but summed up the experience by saying, "American history is for men."

There were other lessons. One day Jack arrived home at eleven A.M. Jackie was puzzled. Usually, he ate lunch at his desk or in the Senate dining room. It turned out that forty people had been invited to lunch. Through a mix-up in Jack's office, no one had bothered to inform Jackie.

She also had to resign herself to the seemingly endless round of dinners of creamed chicken and canned peas, dinners at which politics was the sole subject of conversation. And when they did spend an occasional evening at home, the phone calls were often incessant until bedtime.

And then there was the formidable Kennedy clan, which believed that a certain amount of family roughhouse, physical and emotional, served as a tonic. Not that the Kennedys were the first contentious family Jackie had had to deal with. The Bouviers, during those summer gatherings at Lasata, could have taught even the Kennedys a lesson or two in sibling rivalry. Gamely, Jackie tried to become a true Kennedy. This effort, of course, meant participation in the ritual Kennedy game of touch football. In one of these games, Jackie broke her ankle. She decided there must be an easier, less painful way of showing she had sufficient courage to be a worthy in-law.

That occasion arose when she was staying at the Kennedy house in Palm Beach. Joe Kennedy had clocks in every room of all his houses. Everyone knew when meals were served, and everyone knew he wanted the family in their places five minutes before the meal was served.

One day Jackie arrived fifteen minutes late for lunch. Joe was furious. He began needling her unmercifully. But for all his financial and political intelligence, Joe Kennedy's speech was riddled with cliches. Finally, smiling sweetly, Jackie said, "You ought to write some grandfather stories for the children. Like *The Duck with Moxie* or *The Donkey Who Couldn't Fight His Way Out of a Telephone Booth."*

Dead silence. One simply did not mock Joe Kennedy at his own table.

The silence was broken by Joe Kennedy's roar of laughter. The girl obviously had guts and spunk.

After this encounter, the stubborn Joe Kennedy and the outspoken Jackie Kennedy seemed to share a special rapport. Jackie painted a cartoon in water colors for him. It showed his children on a beach, looking out to sea. The caption reads: *You can't take it with you. Dad's got it all."*

Jackie's whimsical little painting was immediately hung in the elder Kennedy's house at Hyannis Port.

Years later, in the mid-sixties, British writer Robin Douglas-Home said that "the only one who really knew her worth from the beginning was Joe Kennedy. She got on reasonably well with Bobby, but there was little understanding between the other Kennedy women and Jackie. They underestimated her; particularly they never saw that there was a steel mind and an unbreakable will beneath that sweet surface. They know it now."

But the tragedy that would bring those qualities to the surface for the whole world to see was still far in the future.

The immediate problem was Jack's worsening back ailment. As Joan and Clay Blair, Jr., show in their book, *The Search for JFK,* Jack Kennedy had been born with a weak and unstable spine. They got this forthright and unequivocal statement from Dr. Elmer C. Bartels, one of the Kennedy family physicians at the Lahey Clinic in Boston.

Jack and his image-conscious family went to great lengths to make the public believe that he had first injured his back playing football at Harvard, that this ruptured disc had never healed properly, and that it was severely aggravated during World War II when Jack's PT boat was rammed and cut in two. But Jack would have had considerable trouble with his back even without the trauma of the football injury and PT-109 experience.

The Kennedys also tried to give the impression that Jack had contracted malaria in the South Pacific. The Blairs could find no evidence that he had. The malaria story, in all probability, was concocted in 1947 to explain Jack's yellowish skin coloring, when he was diagnosed as suffering from Addison's disease, a failure of the adrenal glands. Family spokesmen said he was suffering a recurrence of malaria rather than admit that the rising young politician had such a serious condition.

The truth is that Jack had been a frail youngster who constantly struggled to live up to his father's impossibly high standards of toughness and manliness. His war experience had left him physically exhausted. When he finally arrived back in the States, Jack Kennedy weighed 127 pounds and was suffering almost constant pain in his spine. In the spring of 1944, about six months after his war-time ordeal, Jack underwent a lumbar disc operation intended to relieve the pressure on his sciatic nerve. The operation seemed to be a success and Jack gained weight and began shouldering the filial responsibilities that had devolved on him after the death of his older brother, Joe Kennedy, Jr.

But his health was still poor. He collapsed at the end of his first Congressional race in 1946 and again the next year in London when it was discovered he had Addison's disease. The newly discovered cortisone treatment controlled the adrenal condition but the rigors of political life and the constant, driving tension and sheer physical drudgery involved in campaigning soon took their toll on his weak back. By the spring of 1954, a year after the marriage, Jack Kennedy was on crutches again.

The couple stayed at Merrywood that summer. Jackie no doubt thought that a few quiet months on her mother and stepfather's tranquil Virginia estate would be better for her husband than the rigors of the Kennedy compound at Hyannis Port. Jackie gave the first big party of her married life here. It was an elegant dinner celebrating the engagement of Patricia Kennedy to Hollywood actor Peter Lawford. Tables were set all around the lighted pool, and before and after dinner, the guests swam and enjoyed the respite from the Capitol Hill pressures that always seemed to mount in June just as the Congressional session was ending.

The summer at Merrywood didn't help. By fall, Jack's weight had dropped to 140 pounds. His doctors recommended surgery: a lumbar-spine fusion. On October 21, 1954, Jack entered New York's Hospital for Special Surgery. The operation was not a success and Jack developed further complications: a staphylococcus infection, which, for a person suffering from Addison's disease, can be fatal. His condition grew so serious that last rites were given him and his family gathered from various points on the Atlantic seaboard.

But he wouldn't give up. After two months in the hospital, he was taken in December to Joe Kennedy's Palm Beach estate to recuperate. When he was no better by February, it was decided to attempt the operation again. He was flown back to New York.

This time the operation was a success and the incision healed without incident. Even so, Jack was often in pain and sometimes had to go back to his crutches. Finally, he got relief from the pain via novocaine injections, a treatment that had been developed by French neurosurgeon Rene Lerich. He received the injections on an irregular basis for the rest of his life.

Back injury or no, however, Jack Kennedy had not been bred to lie in bed and luxuriate in illness. During the eight months that he was away from his Senate duties, he wrote, with considerable help from Ted Sorenson, *Profiles in Courage,* a series of stories about various political risk-takers in the American past whose bravery had never before been chronicled. Jackie, who stayed at Jean Kennedy Smith's apartment during Jack's hospital confinements, functioned as his chief research assistant and part-time secretary. Jack finished the book in Palm Beach during his recuperation.

Profiles in Courage became a best-seller and won a Pulitzer prize. Jack concluded his acknowledgments with this paragraph: "This book would not have been possible without the encouragement, assistance and criticisms offered from the very beginning by my wife, Jacqueline, whose help during all the days of my convalescence I cannot ever adequately acknowledge."

But Jack's illness took its toll on Jackie, too. In 1955, she suffered a miscarriage. And the next year, when she found herself pregnant again—the baby was due in October—Jack was totally absorbed in the feverish and raucous atmosphere of the 1956 presidential race. It was clear that the Democratic nomination would go to Adlai Stevenson, but the second spot was up for grabs. Jack wanted it. A vice-presidential nomination would give him, overnight, national recognition, and if, as expected, Stevenson lost, Jack could use the campaign to grab the top spot on the ticket in 1960. So Jack had been campaigning hard since early in the year. His days and many of his evenings were spent on Capitol Hill, and on week-ends he frequently left Washington for speaking engagements. Jackie was learning the hard lessons of political wifehood.

The Democratic convention, scheduled for August, would be held in Chicago. Several days before the convention began, Jackie, then seven months pregnant, arrived in Chicago with her husband. They checked into a tenth-floor suite at the Conrad Hilton. Jackie, however, spent most of her time alone or with other Kennedy women watching the convention on television, once it got underway. Jack virtually lived at his campaign headquarters in the Stockyards Inn, a hotel just across the street from the Chicago Amphitheatre, site of the convention.

In the week that followed their arrival, Jackie rarely saw her husband. Jack had brought her to Chicago, not for company, but to quell the rumors that there was serious trouble in the marriage. The Newport and Washington gossips were saying that Jackie was hurt and distressed, even angry, that Jack was more interested in winning the vice-presidential nomination than in making sure that Jackie carried this baby to term.

The Kennedy campaign strategists pressured Adlai Stevenson to back Kennedy for the vice-presidential nomination. Stevenson refused. He wouldn't risk alienating the other candidates: Tennessee Senator Estes Kefauver, New York City Mayor Robert F. Wagner, Minnesota Senator Hubert H. Humphrey, and Tennessee Senator Albert Gore. The race for the ticket's second spot was wide open.

The first ballot for the vice-presidential nominees was begun at 2:30 P.M. on August 17. When the roll call of states was completed a half-hour later, Kefauver had 483½ votes to Kennedy's 304. Both of them were considerably short of the 686½ votes needed.

At 3:17 Jackie called Jack at his Stockyards Inn suite. Several reporters and aides were in the living room when Jack returned after taking the call privately. He looked upset. "She's not feeling too well," he said, "The excitement is too much for her." But when the second round of balloting began at 3:23 P.M, Jack Kennedy was once again glued to the television screen.

It's difficult to interpret this brief scenario. Why did Jackie call? To offer encouragement and best wishes to her husband on the second ballot? Or to complain about her isolation and fears for their baby? Did Jack ask her how she was feeling and elicit a confession of loneliness from her? Or did he resent her intrusion by phone into the charged and tense atmosphere of his campaign headquarters? Unless Jackie was suffering severe anxiety attacks or physical pain, she showed a curious lack of sensitivity in calling at such a crucial moment merely to complain.

Jack Kennedy was not used to women complaining, and certainly not at a tense and crucial political moment. His mother, for example, never complained. Joe Kennedy once said of Rose, "In all the years that we have been married, I have never heard her complain. Never. Not even once. . . . That is a quality that children are quick to see."

On the second ballot, Kennedy picked up votes in the South and in Illinois. He began to run ahead of Kefauver. The corridors outside Kennedy's suite were suddenly jammed with reporters and photographers. They'd begun showing up as soon as Jack had begun to overtake Kefauver. Then Lyndon Johnson threw the Texas delegation into the Kennedy column and Joe Kennedy's boy appeared to have the nomination locked up. At this stage in the balloting, he had 505 votes.

Kennedy put on a tie and jacket and headed for the convention, ready to accept the nomination. Jackie and members of the Kennedy family had already arrived at the Amphitheatre and had made their way through the frenetic crowd to the Kennedy box. Reporters observed that Jackie looked "wan and spiritless."

But when the second ballot was complete, Jack Kennedy's tally stood at 653½. He lacked 33 votes of reaching the needed 686½.

On the third ballot, the Kennedy bandwagon fell apart. Sillivan Evans, Jr., publisher of the influential *Nashville Tennesseean,* told Albert Gore that if he didn't drop out of the race and throw his support to Kefauver his political career in Tennessee was over. Gore realized that at this point he didn't have a chance of winning the nomination. He was up for re-election in two years. He did the sensible thing and gave his votes to Kefauver. Then Oklahoma and Missouri switched . . .

The elegant and urbane Adlai Stevenson's running mate would be the folksy Estes Kefauver, he of the coonskin cap. The Democratic ticket once again would illustrate the truism that politics makes strange bedfellows.

Jack Kennedy made the expected gesture of political civility: he asked the convention to make Kefauver's nomination unanimous.

But losing the battle for second spot was a bitter experience. He had never before lost a race of any kind, and he had no intention of doing it again, no matter what.

Jack and his wife flew into Idlewild Airport the next day. They both appeared exhausted. Jack's eyes were rimmed by dark circles and, contrary to his usual practice, he would not talk to reporters.

"I've been in the news enough," he said wearily.

Jackie said nothing. She appeared to be holding herself together through sheer willpower.

Then Jackie left for Hammersmith Farm where her mother would provide nurture and solace while Jackie waited for the new baby. Jack Kennedy boarded a plane that would take him to southern France where Joe Kennedy was "vacationing."

(It's likely that Kennedy and his strategists, fearful that Joe's string-pulling would alienate rather than garner votes at the convention, had persuaded him to leave the country so it wouldn't appear he was either master-minding the effort or attempting to buy his son the vice-presidential nomination. But Jack and his father spoke frequently during the convention, and rumors flew that Joe was calling from Cannes to lobby delegates for his son.)

Several days later, Jackie was rushed to Newport Hospital where she underwent an emergency Caesarean section. But the longed-for baby, a little girl, was born dead.

When Jack Kennedy got the news, he was on a yachting cruise in the Mediterranean. It took him four days to wend his way to Newport where Jackie was convalescing in Newport Hospital. When she left the hospital, to return to her mother's house, she was physically and emotionally exhausted.

For approximately the next six months, Jack and Jacqueline Kennedy were separated, *de facto* if not *de jure*. Jackie had had enough of the lonely life of a political wife, she was tired of hearing rumors about Jack's women, and she had undergone two disastrous pregnancies. Jack didn't seem to miss her. He was hard at work campaigning for Stevenson and Kefauver, storing up IOU's for 1960.

Enter Joe Kennedy. Reports, never authenticated, but strangely persistent, indicate that Jack Kennedy's father was the person responsible for getting the marriage back on the track again. According to one version of this legend, Joe made Jackie an outright gift of one million dollars not to divorce his son now that he was about to make his push for the White House. "Besides," Joe Kennedy might well have said, "think how much you'd enjoy being First Lady and living in the White House."

Other accounts do not mention money. They say that Joe merely had a heart-to-heart talk with both Jackie and his son. As one reporter put it: "Joe is said to have given her an unexpected lesson in how to seek beneath the outer personality for the deeper, hidden traits in her husband. Without this insight from her father-in-law she might not have discovered so quickly the nature of the man she had married."

To Jack, Joe spoke about "the obligations of a husband to his wife" and told him that "he had to do something about dispelling the rumors that he was a playboy and was carrying on with other women. The Old Man had no tolerance for extracurricular *amours* and he told Jack that the only way to avoid such gossip about himself was to spend more time with Jackie—at home and in public."

The difficulty one has in accepting the story of the million dollar reconciliation is that it is just a bit too pat. All parties seem to be playing the roles assigned them by the tabloid press:

—See the ruthless patriarch stop at nothing as he buys his son the presidency.

—See the spoiled and willful woman agree to smooth things over—for a price.

In other words, bribery and blackmail.

It may be that—assuming the story of the million dollar gift from Papa Joe to Jackie is true—the circumstances were less harsh and more complex than the bare bones of the transaction can show. Joseph Kennedy was a shrewd man. He would know that for all her polish and regal poise as a woman from the upper ranks of American society, Jackie was still virtually penniless. He would know that her lack of an inheritance would make her insecure, and he would know that insecurity does not breed success: not in business, not in politics, not in marriage.

Admiring her gutsiness and knowing that he had raised his sons to be dominating and, therefore, difficult men, Joe may have decided to give Jackie a million dollars to put her on a more equal footing with Jack, trusting that the money would lessen her fears, diminish her sense of vulnerability, and make her more willing to risk a by-no-means-certain future with his hard-driving, ambitious, and, yes, philandering son.

Whether Joe Kennedy intervened and to what extent may never be known, but something brought Jack and Jackie together again. And it may have been something as obvious as Jackie fully recuperating from the ordeal of the 1956 Democratic convention and giving birth to a stillborn child.

In March, 1957, the news leaked out that Jackie was pregnant again. The baby was due in November.

Unfortunately, Jack Bouvier learned about Jackie's new pregnancy when he read about it in his evening newspaper. The fact that she hadn't bothered to call him with the good news before her public announcement hurt him deeply. Jack was sixty-six years old now, and his health had steadily worsened after his terrible humiliation at Jackies wedding. In many ways, Jack Bouvier had not been able to hold his head up since that awful day of Hugh Auchincloss's victory and final triumph.

Jack had sold his seat on the Stock Exchange early in 1955 and retired at the age of sixty-four. But his retiremennt gave him little pleasure. At first he made brief trips to Florida or Cuba. But by the time Jackie announced her third pregnancy in March, 1957, his failing health kept him a virtual prisoner in his 74th Street apartment. Looking after him and comforting him as best she could was Esther, his maid.

The only pleasure in life remaining to Jack Bouvier was a letter, a phone call, a visit from one of his daughters. But these treats were rarely forthcoming. Lee lived in London with her husband, Michael Canfield, and she had a small son, Anthony, to look after. And Jackie's life in recent years as the wife of a politically ambitious Senator was both demanding and hectic.

Jack knew that he had "a liver condition." His doctors had not told him he had cancer. Nor had they told Jackie and Lee. Everyone was surprised when Jack's health plummeted in midsummer. On July 27, the day before Jackie's twenty-eighth birthday, her father was admitted to Lenox Hill Hospital. A week later, on August 3, he was dead.

Jack and Jacqueline flew to New York from Hyannis Port. They stayed at Jack Bouvier's apartment and Jackie immediately took charge of the funeral arrangements. She wrote her father's obituary and, using Jack Kennedy as a messenger, told him to deliver it *personally* to the managing editor of the New York *Times*.

Jacqueline would allow no depressing floral displays—no

crosses made out of lilies—at the funeral at St. Patrick's Cathedral. Instead, she ordered summer flowers spilling out of white wicker baskets. For Jack Bouvier's coffin, there was a drape of daisies and bachelor's buttons. "I want everything to look like a summer garden," Jackie told her aunts Maude and Michelle, "like Lasata in August."

There were not many people in St. Patrick's Cathedral that day to mourn Jack Bouvier: his family, his maid, Esther, and a bare two dozen friends and business associates. He was buried at St. Philomena's in East Hampton.

When his affairs were finally settled, Jack Bouvier's daughters each inherited $80,000 after taxes.

Jackie returned to Hyannis Port immediately after her father's funeral, determined to live quietly until the birth of her child. This time Jack was more attentive—he wasn't running for anything that year—and was with her when she entered New York Hospital just before Thanksgiving. And Jack paced in the waiting room like any other expectant father when Jackie was wheeled into surgery on the morning of November 27. By Caesarean section, she was delivered of a daughter at 8:15 A.M. The infant weighed seven pounds, two ounces.

They named her Caroline.

* * * * *

When it was time for Jack to defend his Senate seat against Christian Herter, Jr., in 1958, Jackie campaigned at his side throughout Massachusetts. If a bargain had been struck, she was obviously living up to her side of it. Jack needed a whopping victory in his home state if he expected his party to name him its standard-bearer in 1960.

Jackie couldn't have enjoyed the grueling schedule but she gamely did what she was supposed to and tried to make the best of it even though her statements to interviewers didn't always ring true: "It's the most exciting life imaginable, always involved with the news of the moment, meeting and working with people who are enormously alive, and every day you're caught up in something you really care about. It makes a lot of other things seem less vital. You get used to the pressure that never lets up, and you learn to live with it as a fish lives with water."

At other times, however, Jackie spoke in a more realistic vein:

"Not many people know how physically wearing such a campaign can be. Some mornings you're up at seven and you visit a dozen towns during the day. You shake hundreds of hands in the afternoon and hundreds more at night.

"But you pace yourself and you get through it. You look at it as something you have to do. You knew it would come and you knew it was worth it."

Jack Kennedy was generous in his praise of his wife as a campaigner: "She is simply invaluable. In French-speaking areas of the state, she is able to converse easily with them, and everyone seems to like her. She never complains about the rugged schedule, but seems to enjoy it."

Jackie may have been doing her very best, but no one ever imagined that political life and the rigors of campaigning were things that she thrived on the way her in-laws did. Jean Smith, Jack's sister, put it this way: "I don't think she's mad about politics. She's been brought up in a different kind of world. She's terribly bright; very cultured and not particularly gregarious. It takes a real effort for her to mix with people she doesn't know."

A family friend described her as "more interested in what Byron was doing than what Napoleon was doing. It requires a more rugged, less feminine girl than Jackie to be vitally involved in politics."

Jackie was annoyed by all the discussions of her interest—or lack of it—in politics. She was enough of a politician to know that an image of her as an unhappy wife, grudgingly helping her husband campaign, would benefit neither her nor Jack. Besides, she had a child now, and that provided an excellent excuse on those occasions when she could not face the campaign trail.

Nor was she accustomed to the kind of public criticism that a politician and his family are routinely subjected to. Her friends and family had, on the contrary, all been handled with the proverbial kid gloves by New York society editors.

Jackie hardly knew what to say when reporters asked about her bouffant hair-do. It seems that Middle America thought it "too extreme."

"My husband likes my hair this way," she said.

Then they started harping on her clothes. Why did she buy so many of them in Paris? Was it true she spent $30,000 a year on clothes?

"I'm so sick of that," Jackie said, an edge of impatience in her

voice. "I've never been inside one Paris house mentioned in a magazine article about me. Let me tell you the facts. I couldn't spend that much unless I wore sable underwear."

The "sable underwear" quote was picked up by the wire services and did much to dispel the notion of Jackie as a pampered rich girl who filled her life with clothes-buying expeditions.

Later in the interview she dismissed the idea that she made frequent trips to Paris couturiers: "Every summer, my husband's parents go to Europe and when they come back Mrs. Kennedy brings each of us girls a dress or a suit or a coat. In addition, I've been over to Paris a few times and have picked up a few things."

In spite of Jackie's protests and denials, however, she *did* spend a lot of time planning and acquiring her wardrobe. (Her personal secretary, Mary Barelli Gallagher, says that during 1961, Jackie spent $40,000 on clothes.)

* * * * *

That Senate race was merely a warm-up for what Jackie had to do in 1960. Even though in March she became pregnant again—the baby was due in December—she was almost constantly at Jack's side during the first half of that year when the presidental primaries were held.

The Wisconsin and West Virginia primaries were so close together she didn't have a chance to go back to Washington for a few days' rest. They arrived in West Virginia in mid-April. The primary election to choose a Democratic presidential candidate was set for May 10.

A television interviewer asked Jackie if she enjoyed hitting the campaign trail.

"It's the only way I can see my husband," she said in her whispery little voice.

In a more candid and thoughtful statement, Jackie told another interviewer: "I wouldn't say that being married to a very busy politician is the easiest life to adjust to. But you think about it and figure out the best way to do things—to keep the house running smoothly, to spend as much time as you can with your husband and child—and eventually you find yourself well-adjusted."

The person who gave Jackie the freedom to campaign on a full-time basis with her husband was Maud Shaw, a genuine, old-fashioned English nanny. She was hired by the Kennedys shortly before Caroline was born, and arrived to begin her duties when Caroline was eleven days old, living in the Kennedy house at 3307 N Street, N.W., in Georgetown.

During the campaign, however, Maud Shaw's very large role in Caroline's care and upbringing was definitely downgraded. American voters were presumed to prefer a candidate's wife who took care of her own children. The October 10, 1960, issue of *Life* magazine carried big spreads on both Jackie Kennedy and Pat Nixon. One photo showed Jackie bending over Caroline's crib. The caption began: "Tucking her daughter in for an afternoon nap, Jackie, who does not have a nurse for Caroline. . . ."

After a fierce battle with Hubert Humphrey, Jack Kennedy won the West Virginia primary. He spent the weeks leading up to the Democratic convention criss-crossing the country, his time divided between public speaking engagements and private meetings with politicians, publishers, and pollsters. He wanted his support all lined up so that he could take the nomination on the first ballot.

Jackie retired to the Kennedy compound in Hyannis Port for the summer. She did not attend the convention that August in Los Angeles. This time around, after her very visible role in the primary campaigns, there were no rumors of separation and estrangement that had to be quashed. Jack called her just before he made his stirring "New Frontier" acceptance speech to the convention. "It's a good thing you didn't come out here," he said. "There's too much pandemonium. You can watch me on TV in a few minutes. I'll call you later to see how you liked it."

It was made clear from the beginning that Jackie wouldn't be doing all that much campaigning. Her doctor, she said, had placed severe restrictions on her schedule. Quiet and rest were to be the most important items on her agenda.

Several weeks after Jack was officially named the Democratic candidate, Jackie spoke with reporters in New York. "I feel I should be with him when he's engaged in such a struggle," she said. "If it weren't for the baby, I'd campaign even more vigorously than Mrs. Nixon. I can't be so presumptuous as to think I could have an effect on the outcome, but it would be so tragic if my husband lost by a few votes merely because I wasn't at his side and because people had met Mrs. Nixon and liked her.

"Politics comes into my life twenty-four hours a day," she continued, "and it's such a strange and exciting profession, with crises all the time. Really, I'm grateful to politics because it makes my husband the kind of exceptional man he is."

She was learning.

As the campaign progressed, the polls showed Kennedy and Nixon running neck and neck. And while Jackie "rested," Pat Nixon was wearing her "Republican cloth coat" all over the country, campaigning just as hard as her husband.

Ladybird Johnson, Jean Smith, and Ethel Kennedy turned up at various teas and rallies to explain that Jackie *wanted* to be with them but was having a baby. That line lost its credibility, however, when she was photographed out sailing one week-end with her husband. If she was in good enough shape to go sailing in the choppy Atlantic waters off Cape Cod, then she certainly ought to be able to meet a few voters without suffering major trauma.

During the last six weeks of the campaign, Jackie suddenly became much more visible. She lent her name to a weekly "Campaign Wife" column that was written by the campaign's publicity staff and distributed by the Democratic National Committee. She also recorded a number of radio spots in French, Italian, and Spanish for use on foreign-language radio stations.

As the election grew closer, Jackie increased her efforts. She appeared at the inevitable teas that the Kennedy women had initiated back when Jack first ran for the Congress. She invited the New England and New York national committeewomen to a party in Hyannis Port.

It was announced that she was forming a "Women's Committee for the New Frontier." Nationally known women, expert in foreign policy, education, economics, and health, were invited to meet with Jackie in Georgetown. She asked the thirty-three who showed up if they would "serve as a source of information for my husband. Since I couldn't campaign with him, I wanted to find some way I could help him."

Jack Kennedy, she said, respected women in politics. "He said a long time ago that one woman was worth ten men in politics. They seem to have idealism and they devote the time." (Of course, Jack Kennedy's avowed high estimate of female political abilities didn't prompt him to name any of them to important jobs in government, but that, as they say, is a whole other story.)

Late in October Jackie was hostess at a meeting of Democratic precinct workers—again, all women—who would be responsible for the door-ringing end of the campaign.

Finally, there were no more rallies, teas, or meetings to attend. Everything that could be done had been done and, in any case, time had run out. It was November 8, 1960. Election Day.

Jackie and all the other Kennedys gathered at Hyannis Port. Now it was up to that fickle and unpredictable creature, the American voter.

It was a long wait. The Kennedys, like people all over the country, sat in front of their television sets throughout the night. Finally, on Wednesday morning, it became clear that Kennedy had won, albeit by the narrowest margin in history.

The Kennedys—all of them—left the compound and proceeded to the National Guard Armory in Hyannis, the only nearby hall big enough to house the hundreds of reporters, photographers, and television technicians who had been waiting all night to wrap up their assignments and go home.

Jackie played her role on this occasion with dazzling perfection. Jack introduced his family and said a few words of thanks to the press corps for their patience and good will throughout the long ordeal. Then he turned and reached out his hand to Jackie. She stepped to his side and gazed adoringly at his profile, her face glowing with wifely and maternal comeliness, her hands demurely clasped behind her back.

She smiled engagingly when Jack Kennedy closed the session by saying, "Now my wife and I prepare for a new administration—and a new baby."

For the first time in the history of the republic, the United States of America had a Royal Family.

Chapter Three

The White House Years

Chapter Three

The White House Years

They were a golden couple: young and rich, stylish and energetic. Like the most durable Hollywood stars, the camera loved them. Jack and Jacqueline Kennedy brought theatrical values to Washington. It was a development that would alter the course of history. Television had been there all during the fifties, but no politician had quite known what to do with it until Jack Kennedy came along. The much-publicized campaign debates may have been the decisive factor in JFK's narrow win. Millions of prime-time viewers sat in their living rooms during the autumn of 1960 and watched as Kennedy came across as dominating, forceful, and sure of himself. Nixon, in almost embarrassing contrast, appeared defensive, furtive, and in need of a shave.

The print media also loved the Kennedys. In addition to their photogenic good looks, they were articulate and witty, elegant and poised. They knew they made good copy. And they used that ability to create an image of a storybook marriage, ideal in every way, and of a political administration that was soon to be called Camelot. Only the ancient legend of King Arthur and the Knights of the Round Table could provide a suitable metaphor for all the wondrous events and instant solutions that were soon to emanate from the activist Kennedy White House.

From the very beginning, Jackie generated almost as much interest among reporters as JFK. She handled it beautifully. Her independence, for example, was balanced by her devotion to her husband: "When somebody cuts Jack, she is unforgiving," said sister-in-law Ethel Kennedy. "She has an elephant's memory." There were stories of the hot lunches she sent to his office to insure proper nutrition and the serene home she provided so that Jack could have a haven from the rigors of politics, a game that she personally did not enjoy but knew was indispensable to her husband.

"As a wife, I'm happy if he's happy," Jackie said, "and he's happy doing that—politics and public life."

Her elegant tastes were balanced by her wholehearted acceptance of the tasks of motherhood: "My major effort must be devoted to my children. I feel very strongly that if they do not grow up as happy and secure individuals ... nothing that I would accomplish in the public eye would give me any satisfaction."

Even in this arena, however, she gracefully deferred to her husband: "As long as the father is the figure of authority, and the mother provides love and guidance, children have a pretty good chance of turning out all right."

Behind this continuing barrage of traditional wifely statements, Jackie, as always, did exactly what she wanted to do.

* * * * *

After the election, the Kennedys returned to Washington. Their house at 3307 N Street, N.W., promptly became a secondary headquarters for the upcoming transfer of political power that would take place in January when Dwight and Mamie Eisenhower vacated the White House and Jack and Jacqueline Kennedy moved in.

It was a hectic period. Crowds stood along the sidewalk opposite the house hoping to catch a glimpse of the President-elect or Jackie. Reporters and photographers had the place staked out, waiting for JFK to come out on the front stoop and announce that yet another Cabinet post had been filled.

The house was crowded inside as well. Mary Gallagher, Jackie's secretary, had been working full-time throughout the campaign from the small upstairs study. Now she had to share her miniscule office with Pierre Salinger, JFK's press secretary. Salinger's domain slowly spread. "It was so crowded," Jackie said, "that I could be in the bathroom, in the tub, and then find that Pierre Salinger was holding a press conference in my bedroom."

It's easy to see why Salinger would hold forth wherever he found some empty space. In addition to JFK and Jackie, Mary Gallagher and Salinger, the not-terribly-large house on N Street also had to accommodate Caroline and her nurse, Maud Shaw, and Providencia Parades ("Provie"), Jackie's personal maid. Evelyn Lincoln, JFK's secretary, came out every day. There was a steady stream of people to see JFK about appointments to government jobs. And a cook was usually on the premises.

Jackie, quite understandably in these last weeks of pregnancy, closeted herself in her bedroom much of the time. (After his impromptu press conference, Salinger no doubt heard one message loud and clear: in the future, Jackie's bedroom was off-limits.) Aside from the baby, soon to arrive, her major concern was the clothes she would wear to the Inauguration and to the various Inaugural balls, receptions, and parties.

Since they wore the same size, Jackie pressed Mary Gallagher into service as a model, and numerous letters were dispatched to Bergdorf Goodman in New York concerning the gown that Jackie would wear to the Inaugural Ball.

Stanley Marcus, owner of Neiman Marcus in Dallas, had sent some sketches and offered to make the Inaugural gown. Jackie turned him down with a polite note that said, in effect, that Texas was just too far away: "I think you can understand that it is more convenient for me to pick someone nearer home, as I will have to have it very soon after the birth of my baby. There will not be much time for fittings, etc."

Finally, after numerous fittings and design changes, Jackie had a gown to wear to the Inaugural Ball. But the details were not released to the press until January 19, the day before the Inauguration. Sketches of the gown and cape were given to reporters along with a brief description:

"The dress is a full length sheath of white silk peau d'ange veiled with white silk chiffon. The hip length bodice is richly embroidered in silver and brilliants. It is covered by a transparent overblouse of white silk chiffon. The back of the bodice is similar to the front.

"The floor length cape is made of the same white silk peau d'ange and completely veiled in silk triple chiffon. Under the ring collar, the cape is fastened with twin embroidered buttons. The shape of the cape is an arch from shoulder to hem with soft waves in back. It is also lined with white silk peau d'ange and has two arm slits.

"With the ensemble Mrs. Kennedy will wear 20 button white glace kid gloves and carry a matching white silk peau d'ange tailored clutch purse. Mrs. Kennedy's shoes will be matching white silk opera pumps with medium high heels."

The following November, Jackie presented the gown to the Smithsonian Institution for their collection of costumes worn by First Ladies. Hers was the fourteenth Inaugural gown in the collection and almost immediately became one of the most popular items in the entire Smithsonian.

Clothes were a problem. Jackie enjoyed beautiful clothes but didn't enjoy all the attention her wardrobe got. "I am determined that my husband's Administration—this is a speech I find myself making in the middle of the night—won't be plagued by fashion stories," she said. But of course it was.

Nearly two months before the election, the New York *Times Sunday Magazine* ran a story which discussed the fashion influence, often unintended, of former First Ladies and the impact that Jackie would be sure to have on current styles should her husband win in November:

"When Jacqueline Bouvier Kennedy, five days the wife of a Presidential nominee, stepped aboard a boat at Hyannis Port wearing shocking pink Capri pants and an orange sweater, reporters knew that they were witnessing something of possibly vast political consequence."

Jackie was not pleased. A friend said that she would have to tone down her individualistic fashion ways once she got to the White House. "Oh, I will," Jackie said. "I'll wear hats."

After a long story about Jackie's clothes appeared in *Women's Wear Daily,* she decided to try to stop the speculation by appointing a single designer. She chose Oleg Cassini, whose brother, as it happens, was society columnist Cholly Knickerbocker, and he had named Jackie "Queen Deb of the Year" when she made her debut in 1947.

Shortly after the election, Jackie wrote to Oleg Cassini: "What I need are dresses and coats for daytime; dresses suitable to wear to lunch. I don't know if you design coats, but I now see that will be one of my biggest problems as every time one goes out of the house, one is photographed in the same coat.

"Then, for afternoon, cocktail dresses suitable for afternoon receptions and receiving lines—in other words, fairly covered up. Also a couple of silk coats to wear over them when I go out in the late afternoon. Any suggestions for accessories you have to wear with these would also be appreciated.

"Then some pretty, long evening dresses suitable for big official dinners. You know the kind I like: Balenciaga covered-up look. Even though these clothes are for official life, please don't make them dressy as I'm sure I can continue to dress the way I like— simple and young clothes, as long as they are covered up for the occasion."

In spite of Jackie's expressed concern to Cassini about always being photographed in the same coat, the official policy was that she would wear the same outfit again and again. Jackie wrote a letter that was sent to *Women's Wear Daily* over the signature of her newly-appointed social secretary, Tish Baldridge, whom she had known at Vassar. The letter read, in part: "Mrs. Kennedy realizes that the clothes she wears are of interest to the public, but she is distressed by the implications of extravagance, of over-emphasis of fashion in relation to her life, and of the misuse of her name by firms from which she has not bought clothes.

"For the next four years Mrs. Kennedy's clothes will be made by Oleg Cassini. They will be designed and made in America. She will buy what is necessary without extravagance. You will often see her photographed in the same outfit."

In spite of her efforts to keep a low fashion profile, however, Jackie's clothes continued to be an endless source of news, comment, and speculation. She regularly turned up on the "Ten Best Dressed" lists. The minutiae that garnered attention frequently astounded her. "What difference could it make to anyone whether I wore two or three strings of pearls?" she once asked a friend.

In the weeks immediately after the election, Jackie also supervised the many details involved in moving from the N Street house to the White House. One of her chief tasks was to see that all the household possessions were inventoried. Jackie had to decide which pieces would go to their living quarters at the White House, which would go to their week-end retreat, Glen Ora, in the hills of Virginia, and which would be put into storage.

The new baby was due late in December. The plan was for Jackie to stay in Washington until it was time to fly to New York where the baby would be delivered by Caesarean section at New York Hospital on December 12. Jack would go to Palm Beach right after Thanksgiving to continue the process of putting his new Administration together. Jackie's mother would accompany her to New York. Jack would fly up the day the baby was born.

The President-elect and Jackie spent a quiet Thanksgiving Day together. Just before 8 P.M., JFK left for Palm Beach on the *Caroline*. Shortly after he left, Jackie began having labor pains. She called her obstetrician, Dr. John A. Walsh, at 10:15 P.M. He rushed to the N Street house and examined her. Walsh saw right away that this was no false alarm. He ordered an ambulance and took her to Georgetown Medical Center.

Jackie was afraid the campaign and election would again cause her to lose a child. Tears in her eyes, she asked Walsh, "Am I going to lose the baby?"

He assured her, as doctors always do, that everything would be all right.

And, in this instance, it was. Jackie was taken to surgery and given a general anesthetic, and Walsh performed the Caesarean delivery. At 12:22 A.M., John Fitzgerald Kennedy, Jr., was born. He weighed in at six pounds, three ounces.

At this point, JFK was on his way back to the capital. Just as the *Caroline* was about to land in Florida, the news came over the plane's radio that Mrs. Kennedy had been taken to the hospital. JFK ordered the plane back to Washington and tried to get more details on what had happened. It was another three hours, however, before he knew for sure that mother and baby were doing fine.

At about 1:30 A.M., he briefly visited Jackie, who was still coming out from under the anesthetic, then went down the hall to take a look at his son. JFK stayed in Washington, visiting Jackie and the baby twice a day. On December 2, he took Caroline to Palm Beach, but returned to Washington within a few days.

On December 9, Jackie and the new baby left the hospital. After a brief stop at their Georgetown house, Jackie, at the invitation of Mamie Eisenhower, made an impromptu visit to the White House. Reporters didn't find out about the visit until it was already underway. Photographers arrived just as Jackie and Mrs. Eisenhower emerged onto the north portico, murmuring goodbyes and thank-you's. The two women had toured the thirty rooms in the private quarters as well as the rest of the second and third floors. Mamie had arranged to have a wheel chair on hand, but it wasn't visible when Jackie arrived and she was "too embarrassed" to ask for one.

"I had come straight from the hospital," Jackie told a friend. "I had only walked about my room and a little bit down the hall since I had had John. I really shouldn't have gone. . . . Mrs. Eisenhower took me around three floors and showed me everything. That afternoon we took the plane for Florida. There I collapsed—I had to stay in bed five days!"

Jackie spent most of her Palm Beach sojourn in bed reading, writing long memos on yellow legal pads, or dictating letters to her secretary, Mary Gallagher, who had been installed in a room at the Palm Beach Towers Hotel on New Year's Day. Gallagher spent her days working at a desk that had been set up in Joe Kennedy's living room, just a few feet down the hall from Jackie's bedroom.

Gallagher sensed a certain lack of rapport between JFK's mother, Rose, and Jackie. Rose perhaps found it difficult to understand why Jackie spent so much time in her room. One day Rose stopped by Mary's desk.

"Do you know if Jackie is getting out of bed today?"

Mary didn't know.

"Well, you might remind her that we're having some important guests for lunch. It would be nice if she would join us," Rose said.

As soon as Rose departed, Mary hurried in to give Jackie her mother-in-law's message. Jackie laughed and, imitating Rose's high-pitched Boston twang, repeated her words, "You might remind her we're having important guests . . ."

Jackie remained in bed for the rest of the day and did not show up for the luncheon that Rose considered so important. It was Mary Gallagher's belief that "things were never the same between Jackie and her mother-in-law after that."

Even though Jackie seldom left her room, however, she was almost constantly busy with the last minute details of pulling her Inauguration wardrobe together and planning for the momentous change that would occur in her life when she officially became First Lady.

Bergdorf Goodman sent two women to Palm Beach for the fittings of Jackie's Inaugural gown. The final adjustments were not completed until the day before the Inauguration. In addition to the Inaugural gown from Bergdorf Goodman, Oleg Cassini was making another gown for her to wear to the Gala that would be held at the Armory the night before the Inauguration. The Gala was a fund-raising event sponsored by the Democratic National Committee. The master of ceremonies would be Frank Sinatra.

Cassini's Gala gown turned out to be Jackie's favorite and she offered it to the Smithsonian instead of her Inaugural gown. She would rather be remembered in the Gala gown. The Smithsonian, however, remained traditionalist to the end and insisted they would rather have the Inaugural gown for their collection of clothing worn by various First Ladies.

Then there was the outfit she would wear to the Inauguration. Cassini was working on a coat, and "Miss Marita," a hat designer for Bergdorf Goodman, was doing the famous Jackie pillboxes. Several were ordered: black velvet, red velvet, beige jersey.

Jackie did not want to wear a fur coat when her husband was sworn into office. "I don't know why," she said to a friend, "but perhaps because women huddling on the bleachers always looked like rows of fur-bearing animals."

Her strategy worked perfectly. Cassini made her a beige coat with large, cloth-covered buttons and a ring collar made of sable. She did not carry a handbag. Instead, she had a small sable muff. When the big day finally arrived, Jackie stood out elegantly among all the fur coats, busy hats, and large handbags.

For the Inaugural Ball, Jackie wanted to wear a diamond pin and diamond pendant earrings borrowed from Tiffany's. Jack was against such a plan. Jackie got around his opposition by getting Tiffany's to agree to say that she had borrowed them from her mother-in-law, Rose Kennedy. These obviously delicate negotiations were carried out by social secretary Tish Baldridge, who had been Tiffany's public relations director before coming to the White House.

Jackie ordered Tish to tell her former employers that "if it gets in the newspapers, I won't do any more business with Tiffany. If it doesn't, we'll buy all State presents there."

It didn't, and she did.

While in Palm Beach, Jackie also sent instructions to George Thomas, their butler-valet, who was still in Georgetown preparing for the move from N Street to 1600 Pennsylvania Avenue. Jackie told him to put together a box of assorted liquors plus several bottles of Dom Perignon champagne. She wanted the liquor and champagne waiting at their White House living quarters on Inauguration Day so she could be sure drinks would be available for family and friends. She knew that JFK would undoubtedly continue his practice of asking people over on a moment's notice. Jackie had no idea what supplies, if any, would await them in the White House living quarters. And it simply wouldn't do for her to have to send out for liquor as soon as they moved in.

Jackie flew back to Washington on the *Caroline,* arriving a scant forty-four hours before JFK's noon inaugural on Friday, January 20, 1961. Caroline and the new baby stayed in Palm Beach with their nurses. Of course, Jackie's traveling clothes were minutely described by reporters. One wire service description read: "The slim, young Jacqueline wore a black and white plain tweed suit for her trip. It was styled with slim skirt and short, loose jacket and worn with long, black kid gloves, a shiny new black alligator bag and high-heeled alligator pumps. A red suede beret perched atop her bouffant brown hair." There was simply no way that Jackie Kennedy could stop the endless flow of comment on her wardrobe.

The house on N Street, when Jackie arrived, was the scene of far more activity than it could easily handle. Hundreds of letters and dozens of packages had been arriving daily and were stacked up everywhere. Secret Service men were posted all around the house and inside the front door. JFK was seeing a steady stream of visitors, all of whom had to have their identification and credentials checked. In the kitchen, Pearl, the Kennedy cook, made endless pots of coffee. Valet George Thomas served it to the President-elect and his guests.

Jackie retired to her second floor bedroom. The very last stitches were put in her Inaugural and Gala gowns. Provie, her maid, began organizing and assembling each outfit that Jackie would wear for the various events, both public and private, of the Inauguration and the week-end following.

Jackie went to bed early that Wednesday night, knowing that she was facing several days that would be exhausting as well as exhilarating. Her obstetrician had told her, shortly after John, Jr., was born, to take it easy for at least six months. A Caesarean section is, after all, major surgery.

She awoke to a steady, relentless snowfall that, by late afternoon, would paralyze Washington. Her hairdresser, Jean Louis, came in the morning. Luckily, she had not made that appointment for later in the day. If she had, he would never have made it.

From three to six P.M. the Governors' Reception was held at a Washington hotel. JFK, putting in a brief appearance, was somewhat surprised to find himself suddenly shaking hands with former President Harry S. Truman. Jack promptly invited him back to N Street for a chat. When they arrived, Jack called upstairs and told Jackie they had a guest: Harry Truman. But Jackie was in her robe and couldn't come downstairs. She leaned over the bannister and waved. "Hello, Mr. President."

While Jackie continued her preparations for the evening ahead, the former President and the President-elect closeted themselves in the library, complete with wood-burning fire, for over a half-hour. When JFK finally emerged on the front stoop with his famous guest, reporters wanted to know if Truman had given JFK any advice.

"Advice is the cheapest thing in the world," Truman said, "but I let him know that I would do anything officially that he wants me to do." Truman added that he thought JFK was "brilliant."

The Kennedys had a crowded schedule on that Thursday evening before the Inauguration. After dinner with Philip and Katherine Graham, owners of the Washington *Post,* they would attend the Inaugural concert at Constitution Hall and then go on to the star-studded Gala at the National Guard Armory.

When the Kennedys, accompanied by long-time friend Bill Walton, arrived at Constitution Hall, only a few hundred people had managed to get there through the snowdrifts. Members of the audience and members of the orchestra continued to straggle in throughout the concert which began, more or less, on time. Many of them had simply abandoned their cars and walked to the hall.

Next stop for the Kennedys was the National Guard Armory. Because of the weather, the Gala got underway nearly two hours late. It was a dazzling show. Sinatra and his co-producer, Kennedy brother-in-law Peter Lawford, had selected an all-star cast from a horde of eager Hollywood and Broadway volunteers. The line-up of performers included Harry Belafonte, Bette Davis, Jimmy Durante, Mahalia Jackson, Fredric March, Ethel Merman, Sir Laurence Olivier and perhaps the biggest star of all, Eleanor Roosevelt.

There were numerous parties around town after the Gala, but Jackie decided she was not strong enough for such a late night— not with the long Inauguration day facing her. She went home right after the Gala, which didn't end until 1:40 A.M. It would be the last night she would spend in the old colonial house on N Street, the house that JFK had bought for her after Caroline was born.

Jack continued on to a party given by Joe and Rose Kennedy for the Gala cast and the members of Jack's new Administration. It was nearly 3:30 A.M. when the presidential limousine pulled up to his door in Georgetown. Later in the morning, he would become the thirty-fifth (and youngest) President of the United States.

JFK was up at 8:00 A.M., had breakfast with Jackie, and then attended nine o'clock mass at Holy Trinity, a Jesuit church four block away. When he got back, it was time to start dressing for the Inauguration. They would leave a bit earlier than planned. The Eisenhowers had invited them for coffee before they all proceeded to the Capitol for the swearing in.

When they arrived at the White House, Mrs. Eisenhower greeted them in the Red Room. Lyndon and Lady Bird Johnson, Richard and Pat Nixon, and several members of the Congressional Inaugural Committee were already there. It was not a happy occasion. The atmosphere was tense and strained. Jackie, wanting to save her strength, looked for a place to sit down. There was only one sofa in the room, and Pat Nixon was sitting on it with one of the Congressional wives. Jackie greeted the two women and sat down. Pat Nixon, who felt the election had been stolen from her husband, turned away and did not talk to Jackie. Mercifully, the ghastly affair was soon over, and they all left the White House for the rites of the Inauguration.

The snow had stopped, but it was a bitterly cold day, and Jackie felt it right away. She had always hated official functions and had avoided them whenever she could. The only thing that made this one bearable was that her husband was being sworn in as President of the United States. But Jackie undoubtedly wished that she could dispense with everything except watching Jack take the oath of office and listening to his Inaugural Address.

She had never heard Jack's Inaugural speech in its entirety. "I had heard it in bits and pieces many times while he was working on it in Florida," she said later. "There were piles of yellow paper covered with his notes all over our bedroom floor. That day, when I heard it as a whole for the first time, it was so pure and beautiful and soaring that I knew I was hearing something great. And now I know that it will go down in history as one of the most moving speeches ever uttered—with Pericles' Funeral Oration and the Gettysburg Address."

After the ceremony, everyone on the platform was escorted to the Capitol for a luncheon in the old Supreme Court Chamber. In all the confusion, Jackie had just a moment to touch her husband's cheek and say, "Jack, you were so wonderful." After the hurried luncheon President and Mrs. Kennedy sat in an open car in the Inaugural Parade. In addition to the freezing temperatures, there was a stout wind blowing most of the day, and the car moved slowly down Pennsylvania Avenue. Jackie was badly chilled by the time they finally took their seats on the reviewing stand. At 3:30 P.M, she knew she could not bear the cold any longer and went back to the White House.

The parade should have been over at five P.M. But it was after six when the last marchers passed by the reviewing stand. JFK had stayed until the very end, along with a few others: Lyndon and Ladybird Johnson, Bob and Ethel Kennedy, Phyllis and Douglas Dillon.

Inside the White House, Jackie had lain down for a nap in the Queen's Bedroom. Then she realized how tired she really was.

"When it was time to get ready for dinner—I couldn't get out of bed," she recalls. "I just didn't have one bit of strength left and felt absolutely panicked. What could I do? Somehow I managed to get in touch with Dr. Travell."

Janet Travell was still on the reviewing stand with Kennedy. When she got Jackie's message, she hurried to her bedside. Dr. Travell ordered her to have dinner in bed. Then she gave her a small, triangular-shaped, orange pill to take. It was Dexedrine.

Later, there was a rumble of criticism over Jackie leaving the reviewing stand so early. Once again, Janet Travell came to her rescue. "A Caesarean is major surgery and, combined with the sheer physical drain of creating a baby, would knock out most women for a long time," she told reporters. "And don't forget that Mrs. Kennedy also flew down to Palm Beach and lived in a house which was not her own, through which visitors constantly paraded. Actually, she had moved out of her own home and had very little time to plan a new and much more taxing life in the White House. . . . Added to all this," Dr. Travell continued, "the tensions of the presidential campaign still remained while she was faced by the burden of vast, new responsibilities. It was fantastic that she was able to accomplish what she did."

While Jackie was recuperating from the parade, her relatives and Jack's were downstairs in the State Dining Room milling about a huge punch bowl filled with caviar. The reception for their families was the first social event in the Kennedy White House, but Jackie never showed up.

When Jack finally arrived, Jackie allowed her godfather, Michel Bouvier, to come up to their rooms for a half-hour before she and Jack began dressing for the evening's five Inaugural balls. Her cousin, John Davis, wrote that later in the evening the Bouviers all had dinner together. He concluded that "it was probably easier for Jackie, who had always been shy with her relatives, to face the entire nation on TV than it was to confront her four families on that momentous day. To America she was the new First Lady. To the Bouviers, Lees, Auchinclosses, and Kennedys she was just Jackie. To play both roles required impossible shifts of emotional gear. Michel, who had seen Jackie upstairs, agreed with the interpretation."

But by the time she left the White House for the Inaugural balls, Jackie was once again her radiant self—even if some of that radiance was an amphetamine high. First there was a ball at the

Mayflower Hotel. They made it their first stop, out of courtesy to Harry Truman, who was staying there. Then they were whisked to the National Guard Armory again, site of the previous night's Gala, where the Main Inaugural Ball was being held. Orchestra leader Meyer Davis, who had played at the wedding of Jackie and JFK as well as at the marriage of Jackie's parents, was on hand to provide lilting dance music that nobody danced to. They were too busy looking at the stars in the presidential box.

The television cameras were there in force, along with the blinding lights that shown directly in the Kennedys' faces throughout the evening. No one seemed to notice. All the Kennedys seemed to come alive when there were operating television cameras in the vicinity. Jacqueline Bouvier, a Kennedy by marriage, was no exception. She fairly glowed.

But when they were leaving a couple of hours later for yet another ball, Jackie asked to be taken back to the White House.

"I just crumpled," she said later. "All my strength was finally gone! So I went home and Jack went on with the others."

What are we to make of these stories of Jackie's fragility? This, after all, was a woman whom subsequent events would show to have immense reserves of physical and emotional stamina. Was she really as easily exhausted as she claimed? Or did she use the Caesarian birth of her son to avoid those responsibilities she found distasteful? The answer to both questions might well be yes.

There is quite possibly a third and quite mundane reason for her early departures from the Inaugural events. It took hours for her to get ready for these affairs. Even though Jackie without make-up or elaborate hair-dos was a beautiful woman, she could not appear that way in public. Her make-up had to take into account what a news photographer's flashbulbs would do to her facial structure. Her hair was usually "done" in an elaborate coiffure that required rollers, back-combing or "teasing," and hair spray for the final effect. These hair-dos of the early sixties had rather short lifespans. A woman was lucky if they lasted out the evening. And every woman knows that the most careful make-up job starts to disintegrate within two or three hours.

The gowns Jackie wore were gorgeous, but did not lend themselves to eating, drinking, or dancing. And although she was a chain smoker, she would not light a cigarette in public. Jackie, especially at the Gala and the Inaugural balls, was hardly more than a mannikin, expected to look ravishing, expected to beam her dazzling smile at television cameras, Congressmen, and faithful party workers alike. And that is exactly what she did. When she felt that her make-up and hair-do were past repair, and having fulfilled her role as the handsome young president's beautiful young wife, she went home.

And what better excuse could she offer than a difficult child-birth?

Her much publicized dislike of politics served a similar purpose. It allowed her to play the role of wife and helpmate while pursuing her own goals and spending her time the way she wanted to. Shrewdly, Jackie screened her independence behind statements like this:

"I think a wife's happiness comes in what will make her husband happy. The most important thing for a successful marriage is for the husband to do what he likes best and does well. The wife's satisfaction will follow."

Even the President got in on the act of trying to explain why Jackie would not show up at many of the events where Presidents' wives were traditionally expected to put in at least a token appearance. "A man marries a woman, not a First Lady," Jack told a reporter-friend. "If he becomes President, she must fit her own personality into her own concept of a First Lady's role. People do best what comes naturally.

"I don't have to fight the day's political battles over again at night. She creates a different kind of atmosphere in my home life and I enjoy it."

Jackie's tastes for art, horses, and privacy even drew a comment from brother-in-law Bobby, now U.S. Attorney-General: "What husband wants to come home at night and talk to another version of himself?" Bobby asked rhetorically. "Jack knows Jackie will never greet him with, 'What's new in Laos?' "

In those first months after the Kennedys moved into the White House, Jackie poured her energy, intelligence, and taste into making their new home a warm and comfortable place to live. She had found the White House a drab and dreary place. Most of its 132 rooms were cold and uninviting. With the exception of the Lincoln Bedroom, which she loved, most of the thirty-odd rooms in the White House living quarters were furnished in what Jackie called "early Statler."

Within a week after the Inauguration, Jackie's New York decorator, Mrs. Henry ("Sister") Parrish II, had made the first of many visits to the White House. Her primary responsibility was to help Jackie make the living quarters warm, inviting, and "cozy." It would not be an easy task. She could hardly believe her eyes when Jackie took her into the Oval Sitting Room. It was depressing almost beyond description. "The only furniture in the room was a center table, two chairs and two television sets," Mrs. Parrish said. "Everything was spotlessly clean, as if no one had entered the door."

Within weeks the Oval Sitting Room had become one of the White House's most successful rooms. Jackie had ordered it refurbished in Louis XVI style. From the beginning, she had envisioned it as a place where JFK could meet important visitors in an elegant and relaxed setting, away from the inevitable cares and responsibilities of the President's oval office.

The family dining room presented another, almost insurmountable, problem. It was one floor below the rest of the living quarters and was not an inviting place to have a meal. The Eisenhowers had taken to eating their dinner on trays upstairs. That solution did not appeal to Jackie.

"When we had lived in the White House a few days," she wrote to a friend, "and I had seen what it was like eating off trays with four butlers hovering around—or descending to the first floor to that dark private dining room—I realized that we must have our own dining room."

Two weeks after the Kennedys moved in, the new dining room, along with a new kitchen and pantry, had been installed in their second floor apartment. This miracle was accomplished by the thirty-five skilled maintenance men on the White House staff.

By spring, most of the work on their living quarters had been completed—in spite of Jackie's having her bedroom painted twice within a few days. She had first ordered the walls to be done in pale green with white woodwork. The job was done during one of the week-ends she spent at Glen Ora. Extra men were used in order to do the painting and have all her furniture in place when she returned from the Virginia retreat. But when Jackie saw the results of the week-end's labors, she realized it wasn't *quite* what she'd had in mind. She ordered the room to be repainted in an off-white shade.

Later that day, one of the painters showed up in the office of Jackie's secretary, Mary Gallagher. "You know, it's not that we mind the work so much—after all, it *is* all in a day's work. But tell me, Mrs. Gallagher, you've been with Mrs. Kennedy now longer than any of us here—does she *always* go around changing her mind like this?"

Mary Gallagher was hard put to come up with an answer.

"Well, I think you'll find as time goes on," she said, "that Mrs. Kennedy has definite ideas and tastes when it comes to decorating and furnishing her rooms. So, I guess it's really just a matter of trying to accept things like this as they come along."

When the painter did not seem visibly cheered by Gallagher's response, she told him how Jackie had once changed the wallpaper in the study of their Georgetown house three times in just a few months. That story didn't produce a smile, either.

The restoration of the public rooms in the White House naturally took much longer than the decoration of the private rooms. The White House was public property, a kind of national historical museum and was not run by the President's staff but by the Fine Arts Commission which was ultimately responsible to the Congress.

JFK had considerable doubts about undertaking any extensive renovation. Advisers reminded him of the furor it had caused when Harry Truman had added a balcony to the South Portico.

Jackie, however, refused to be deterred. "I always loved beautiful houses; all the time I was in Europe I had gone out of my way to see so many. So I suppose that when I knew I would be living there, it wasn't a matter of wanting to restore it or not, it was something that had to be done. . . ."

She asked Henry Francis du Pont to head a committee that would be responsible for the White House restoration. Du Pont, the creator and owner of the Winterthur Museum near Wilmington, Delaware, was considered a top authority on American furniture and decorative objects in the 1640-1840 period. His participation seemed crucial. "Without him on the committee I didn't think we would accomplish much," Jackie said, "and with him I knew there would be no criticism. The day he agreed to be Chairman was the biggest red letter day of all."

Jackie had read everything the Library of Congress had—about forty books and numerous articles—on the White House. Her research led her to form very definite ideas about the changes that should be made. "Everything in the White House must have a reason for being there," she said. "It would be a sacrilege merely to 'redecorate'—a word I hate—It must be *restored* and that has nothing to do with decoration. That is a question of scholarship."

Within a month after the Inauguration, Jackie had her committee established. She was the honorary chairman, du Pont was the working chairman and there were fourteen committee members, most of whom were wealthy enough to make sizable contributions of furniture, paintings, and cash, in addition to their artistic expertise. The committee members included: Mrs. C. Douglas Dillon, Mrs. Charles W. Engelhard, Mrs. Henry Ford II, Mrs. Albert Lasker, Mrs. Henry Parish, Mrs. George Henry Warren, Mrs. Paul Mellon, Mrs. Charles Wrightsman, Charles Francis Adams, Leroy Davis, David Finley, John L. Loeb, Gerald Shea, and John Walker.

Shortly after the formation of the committee was announced, Jackie's press secretary, Pam Turnure, said, "She's enthralled and engrossed by this job of making the White House the showplace it ought to be. She is going to build it up to what it should be. She wants to be remembered for having done this."

Having transformed the White House living quarters and having set a small army to work on the restoration of the public rooms, Jackie began preparations for a trip to Europe with JFK. It would become, in Paris, her own personal triumph.

Aside from a brief trip to Ottawa in mid-May, this was the Kennedys' first trip out of the U.S. as President and First Lady. On the morning of May 31, 1961, the roads from Orly airport were jammed with an estimated 200,000 French men, women, children and teenagers all screaming, "Vive Jacqui! Vive Jacqui!"

All day long, wherever she went, there were enormous crowds waiting for a glimpse of "la jolie Jacqui." That night General de Gaulle and his wife held a reception for the Kennedys at the Elysee Palace. Jackie wore a gown by Oleg Cassini reminiscent of a Greek toga.

The next night she wore a white satin Givenchy gown, embroidered with rhinestones, to the state dinner at the Galerie des Glaces (Hall of Mirrors) at Versailles. With a diamond tiara in her Alexandre hairdo, she looked every inch the queen that night. Perhaps she knew even then that this glorious evening at Versailles would be the high point of her public life as First Lady.

The next day at lunch when JFK addressed a group of foreign correspondents, he made what became one of the most widely reported quips of his presidency. When Jack got up to speak, he said, "I do not think it altogether inappropriate to introduce myself to this audience. I am the man who accompanied Jacqueline Kennedy to Paris . . . and I have enjoyed it."

But the Paris sojourn was not all wine and roses. At a press conference set up for Jackie, the American reporters were enraged that Jackie totally ignored them, speaking only in French to their Gallic counterparts. It seemed to the American newswomen—virtually all the attending journalists were women—that her contempt for them was almost tangible.

At least one of them decided to fight back. Syndicated columnist Inez Robb filed a scathing report from Vienna, the next stop after Paris. Robb's angry words appeared on the front page of the *World-Telegram & Sun* in New York:

"Fresh from her triumphs in Paris and doubtless facing new ones here, Jacqueline Kennedy arrives in Austria at the termination of at least one honeymoon.

"That is the honeymoon between herself and the American press, as represented by the Washington corps and other newsmen on the President's first European tour since his election.

"On Broadway it always is regarded as fatal for an actor to believe his own press notices. The American press on this trip is convinced the First Lady had begun to believe the unstinting paeans of praise for her youth, beauty and intelligence that have appeared in American news media in the last six months."

After describing Jackie's contemptuous behavior toward the American reporters, Robb continued:

"This snub-direct to the American press has brought to a head the ballooning dissatisfaction with the inept press liaison between Mrs. Kennedy and the reporters who are assigned to cover her activities—not because they particularly enjoy the assignment, but because this is a task given them by their editors.

"The American press swells with pride that the First Lady is glorious in public. But it finds it difficult to understand the wife of a politician who must stand for re-election who models herself, it is reported, on Queen Elizabeth II.

"The press, having created a lovely legend, now finds it hard to be hoisted on a petard of its own creation."

Inez Robb may have been the first journalist to realize that Jackie Kennedy had a dark side to her nature, that she had certain most unattractive personality traits. On occasion, she could be inordinately selfish, insensitive, and stubbornly insistent on getting her own way no matter what others might want. In other words, Jackie sometimes behaved like a spoiled brat, like a little girl who had been taught by a too-indulgent father that the world existed for the sole purpose of pleasing her and meeting her demands, no matter how outrageous they might be. But it would be years before most people saw that aspect of Jackie.

In Vienna, Jackie again stopped traffic. Extra police were on duty to clear a path for her through the crowds that gathered whenever she appeared in public. The Vienna visit was also a summit meeting. JFK met face to face with Khrushchev for the first time. The encounter took place at a state banquet at the Shoenbrunn Palace. When photographers asked JFK and Khrushchev to pose together, Khrushchev indicated that he would prefer to have his picture taken with Jackie, resplendent in an elegant white gown, sewn with tiny pink beads, her Alexandre hairdo still intact. (The hairdresser had come to her Paris hotel room at seven that morning, before the flight to Vienna, to re-comb and restore her coiffure. It already had a name: La Parisienne.) The Soviet leader also insisted on escorting Jackie into the dining hall and sitting next to her on a sofa when the after-dinner coffee was served.

England was no different. Invariably, it was Jackie's car that got the loudest, most enthusiastic cheers. Kennedy was in the lead car with Prime Minister Harold Macmillan. Jackie followed in the car with Lady Dorothy Macmillan. Normally, the wives' limousine got only token applause. Jackie had changed all that.

The trip to England was not a formal state visit. The Kennedys were there for the christening of Lee Radziwill's daughter, Anna Christina. (Several years earlier, Jackie's sister had divorced Michael Canfield and married Stanislaus Radziwill, a former Polish nobleman turned London businessman. He was considerably older than Lee and everyone commented on his astonishing physical resemblance to "Black Jack" Bouvier.)

In spite of the personal nature of their visit, Queen Elizabeth and Prince Philip hosted a dinner at Buckingham Palace for the Kennedys. "It was just an informal affair," a spokesman for the queen said. "Fifty guests. None of the formality of a state dinner. No speeches. No serious conversation. It isn't done." Queen Elizabeth, bejeweled and beruffled, looked even dowdier than usual next to Jackie who was wearing a long sheath of pale, blue satin and long white gloves. Her hair was pulled up in a puffy chignon.

The next day, Jack and Jackie attended the christening of the Radziwill's daughter in Westminster Cathedral. Anna Christina's godfather was the President of the United States.

Just as there had been a huge crowd waiting for the Kennedys to arrive at Buckingham Palace the previous night, the streets outside the cathedral were packed with cheering well-wishers when the Kennedys and Radziwills left the ancient church.

At the end of their stay in London, the President flew back to Washington. Jackie, with the Radziwills, went on to Greece for a cruise in the Aegean aboard the *North Wind,* a 123-foot yacht owned by shipping magnate Markos Nomikos.

The Greek interlude was almost a complete change of pace from the rigid formality and adherence to protocol that had marked the earlier part of the trip in France, Austria, and England. Here in Greece, Jackie could—and did—go barefoot if she felt like it, could let her hair down both literally and figuratively.

During a stop at Hydra, she went ashore and danced with the patrons of the local taverna where they all dined on simple Greek food. At Delos, legendary birthplace of Apollo, she went swimming and waterskiing.

Even though this was an "unofficial" visit, the Greek government provided round-the-clock protection for the First Lady's party. While she was waterskiing in Cavouri Bay near Athens, five small Greek Navy patrol boats kept away sightseers. They also had orders not to let anyone photograph Jackie in her swimsuit.

The trip to Greece was originally set for five days, but Jackie was having such a good time that it was extended to eight days—in spite of news reports that JFK's back once again had him on crutches. When Jackie cabled for details, Jack told her it was not serious, that she should not cut her vacation short. He had strained his back during their Canadian visit in mid-May while taking part in a ground-breaking ceremony.

Her last night in Greece, Jackie had dinner with Prime Minister Constantine Caramanlises and his wife. Then Jackie, the Radziwills and the Caramanlis went dancing at a nightclub overlooking the Saronic Gulf. Jackie told reporters that she had been so charmed by Greek hospitality and spontaneity that she was planning to vacation there the following year. The next time she came, Jackie promised, she would bring her children.

There had been talk about Jackie waterskiing and dancing in Greece while her husband was ailing. So Jack met the *Caroline* when it landed at Washington's National Airport. Photographers were present to record the family reunion.

Back in Washington, Jackie supervised the preparation for what would be one of the grandest—and most criticized—state dinners of the Kennedy era.

The controversial affair was in honor of Pakistan President Ayub Khan. Inspired by the state dinner that de Gaulle had given for them at Versailles, Jackie decided that they should entertain the Pakistanis at Mount Vernon, George Washington's house overlooking the Potomac.

The logistics for the July 11 dinner were staggering. In addition to the Presidential yacht, the *Honey Fitz,* three other Navy vessels were required to transport the guests down the river. A marquee was set up on the lawn as well as tables for 150 guests. The National Symphony Orchestra played after dinner—so a special bandstand had to be built on the rambling Mount Vernon grounds. Special silver cups for the mint juleps had to be found; colonial costumes were ordered for the waiters; some way had to be found to eliminate insects; and last but definitely not least, portable toilets were required.

Jackie's new chef, Rene Verdon, prepared the food in the White House kitchens and then shipped it to Mount Vernon in Army field kitchens. Tiffany's and Bonwit Teller's decorated the tables and the Mount Vernon interior.

What on earth did this lavish display cost?

JFK's press secretary, Pierre Salinger, was bombarded with questions at the next morning's briefing for reporters. He was ready for them. In fact, he took the initiative.

"Since some discussion has arisen in the press about the cost of this dinner, I shall make a short statement. . . .

"This dinner was carried out under a plan which has been initiated by Mrs. Kennedy since she has been in the White House and a substantial—in fact the bulk of the special items for the dinner were donated by public-spirited citizens as a way of helping the White House in extending welcome to President Ayub Khan.

"For example, the tents, the decorations, the music were all donated—and the only costs involved were the costs of the food, which came within the normal State Department allocation for such entertainment.

"It would be impossible, under our budget, to entertain at State Dinners or to put on a function such as was put on last night—without the help of these public-spirited citizens."

Reporters wanted to know why. Salinger's answer was brief and to the point: "Because of the cost involved."

He then mentioned some of the more substantial donations to the Mount Vernon dinner: The National Symphony Orchestra provided the after-dinner music and paid the construction costs of the stand on which they were seated; Lester Lanin contributed a trio which played during the dinner; Tiffany and Co. of New York provided the decorations and John Vanderherschen Inc. of Philadelphia, the tent.

Salinger concluded his statement by saying, "I think Mrs. Ken-

nedy will continue her policy of calling from time to time on
various people for assistance in having our country put its best foot
forward—in meeting some of the famous people who come to visit
us."

The mystery in all this is how Jackie was able to get so many
people to provide their services *gratis* for her pet projects. She certainly never let there be any doubt as to who was ultimately responsible for all those grand White House entertainments. It was
Jacqueline Bouvier Kennedy, that's who. She even managed to per-
suade aging virtuoso cellist Pablo Casals to perform at a dinner for
the U.S. Nobel Prize winners. Formerly, Casals had vowed he
would not perform here as long as the United States supported the
Franco regime in Spain.

Getting other people to implement her own ambitions is a skill
that Jackie apparently developed at a very young age. Her cousin,
John Davis, recalls that "she possessed a mysterious authority,
even as a teenager, that would compel people to do her bidding.
Once, at the Maidstone, she asked her cousins the name of a song
she was humming, and those cousins spent the entire day trying to
find out . . . for Jackie."

Her efforts with regard to the Ayub Khan dinner did not go un-
noticed by the Pakistani chief of state. He invited her to visit him in
Pakistan.

With the Mount Vernon dinner behind her, Jackie took Caroline and John-John (JFK had begun calling his son by the double
name and it was soon taken up by everyone) to Hyannis Port for
the rest of the summer. It was mid-October before she returned to
Washington, although she kept in touch with the restoration project and other official matters via courier mail and long-distance
telephone calls to her personal secretary, Mary Gallagher.

All that summer there were rumors that Jackie was pregnant
again. JFK's assistant press secretary, Andrew Hatcher, repeatedly
told reporters that Mrs. Kennedy was not expecting another child.
Finally, it was discovered that the story had begun making rounds
after several correspondents had lunched with former Vice-President Richard Nixon at the National Press Club.

Jack Kennedy, in mock seriousness, asked some friends: "Nixon says we're having a baby; Andy Hatcher says we're not. Which
one do you think I ought to believe?"

Early in November, the U.S. Ambassador to India, John Kenneth Galbraith, brought an invitation from Prime Minister Nehru
for Jackie to visit India. Because of the tension between India and

Pakistan, she could hardly visit one country without visiting the other. Which was just fine with Jackie: she'd visit them both.

She decided to leave a few days before Thanksgiving. The President decided she wouldn't. He reminded her that in spite of her triumphant state visit to Europe earlier that year, she was the wife of the President—a politician's wife—and you did not leave your family at Thanksgiving to go on a personal junket to the other side of the world. Especially not when Thanksgiving coincided with the birthdays of your children: Caroline would be four years old on November 25, John-John would celebrate his first birthday on November 27.

And you certainly did not leave at Christmas time.

A few days after her original announcement, Pierre Salinger had an update: the trip had been postponed until early in 1962. The delay would give her time to "pay a more leisurely visit" and would also allow her to be in India for the celebration of their Republic Day on January 26.

Salinger also said the new schedule would give the First Lady "a less hurried and more comprehensive visit to Pakistan than would have been possible" had she not changed her plans.

Instead of the Far East, Jackie traveled with JFK in mid-December on a state visit to Puerto Rico, Venezuela, and Colombia. For several weeks before the trip, she had been brushing up her Spanish, never as good as her quite fluent French. Everywhere they went Jackie made a pretty little speech in Spanish. The crowds loved it.

JFK and Jackie went to Palm Beach for Christmas with Joe and Rose Kennedy as usual. On December 21, while playing golf, Joe Kennedy suffered the stroke from which he never fully recovered. Jackie spent incredible amounts of time at his bedside, reading to him and bringing the children for visits, even after he had been transferred to New York University's Institute of Medicine and Rehabilitation.

Jackie is splendid when dealing with tragedy and disaster. Terrible events seem to bring forth the nobility in her character as nothing else does: the letter of forgiveness she wrote her father after his humiliation at her wedding, the manner in which she handled his funeral, and the way she tried to amuse Joe Kennedy and take his mind off the devastating paralytic effects of his stroke. And there would be other, far more disastrous, events in the not-too-distant future.

In February, the $2 million White House restoration was nearly complete. Jackie very professionally served as hostess with Charles Collingwood of an hour-long CBS television special that took an estimated 56 million viewers through the restored public rooms. In her low, sultry voice, Jackie provided historical background and descriptions of all the changes that had taken place since the project began.

JFK, appearing strangely uncomfortable, joined her at the end of the show. He might have been the leader of the Western world and the most powerful man in history, but that night he looked like a man who had somehow stumbled into a ladies' tea party and couldn't find his way out again. House tours—even a tour of the White House to which he had so long aspired—were definitely not Jack Kennedy's metier.

Still, in spite of his earlier doubts about the political feasibility of the project, he was truly pleased with the results. After the Congress passed a law making the restoration permanent, JFK issued this statement:

"Through a wise provision of the Congress at its last session, the. White House, which had become disfigured by incongruous additions and changes, has now been restored to what it was planned by Washington. In making the restorations, the utmost care has been exercised to come as near as possible to the early plans and to supplement these plans by careful study of such buildings as that of the University of Virginia which was built by Jefferson.

"The White House is the property of the Nation and, so far as is compatible with living therein, it should be kept as it originally was for the same reasons that we keep Mount Vernon as it originally was.

"The stately simplicity of its architecture is an expression of the character of the period in which it was built and is in accord with the purposes it was designed to serve. It is a good thing to preserve such buildings as historic monuments, which keep alive our sense of continuity with the Nation's past."

What may have prompted JFK to publicly endorse his wife's efforts was when Alice Roosevelt Longworth, the outspoken daughter of President Theodore Roosevelt and a long-time arbiter of the Washington social scene, stopped by to see what had been done and gave her enthusiastic approval to the results of Jackie's year-long effort.

In order to further protect the restoration, Jackie had managed to create a new job through the Fine Arts Committee—that of

White House curator. Named to the post was Lorraine Pearce, a former staff member of du Pont's Winterthur Museum. Jackie immediately put her to work writing an over-sized pamphlet that would be called *The White House: An Historic Guide.*

Jackie had expressed amazement that such a guidebook had never before been written. It was one of her pet projects. In addition to working very closely with Ms. Pearce, Jackie personally supervised the *National Geographic* photographers, telling them exactly what camera angles she wanted.

The White House guidebook, which continues to sell briskly to this day, finally ran to 132 illustrated pages. Jackie wrote the Foreword:

> This guidebook is for all of the people who visit the White House each year.
>
> It was planned—at first—for the children. It seemed such a shame that they should have nothing to take away with them, to help sort out the impressions received on an often crowded visit. It was hoped that they would go over the book at home and read more about the Presidents who interested them most. Its purpose was to stimulate their sense of history and their pride in their country.
>
> But as research went on and so many little-known facts were gleaned from forgotten papers, it was decided to make it a book that could be of profit to adults and scholars also.
>
> On the theory that it never hurts a child to read something that may be above his head, and that books written down for children often do not awaken a dormant curiosity, this guidebook took its present form.
>
> I hope our young visitors will vindicate this theory, find pleasure in the book, and know that they were its inspiration.
>
> To their elders, may it remind you that many First Families loved this house—and that each and every one left something of themselves behind in it—as you do now by the effort you have made to come here.

The White House restoration and the publishing of the White House guidebook are certainly the major accomplishments of Jackie's adult life. This is not to say that she performed these tasks single-handedly. She had many knowledgeable and dedicated people to turn to for advice and expertise. There were many others who

spent their working days implementing her plans and decisions.

But it was Jackie's unique vision of what the White House ought to be and her persistence in pursuing it that were the indispensable factors in its transformation. She knew how the President's House ought to look and she knew that the White House should, as a matter of presidential policy, give formal recognition to the arts. It was a way of saying to the entire world: *This is what we stand for.*

And let's face it: all those glittery affairs were an awful lot of fun.

Many of the things we remember with pleasure and affection from John F. Kennedy's thousand days are actually Jackie's accomplishments: the elegant dinners; the New York City Center Ballet performing Jerome Robbins' *Ballets USA;* Basil Rathbone performing Shakespeare and reading from other Elizabethan poets; Pablo Casals.

When author and French Minister of Culture Andre Malraux visited Washington, Jackie put together a guest list that included Anne and Charles Lindbergh; poet Robert Lowell; playwrights S.N. Behrman, Arthur Miller, and Tennessee Williams; director Elia Kazan, actress Geraldine Page; painter Andrew Wyeth; and George Balanchine, guiding genius of the New York City Ballet. And after dinner, violinist Isaac Stern, cellist Leonard Rose, and pianist Eugene Istomin performed Shubert's Trio in B Flat Major.

Malraux was dazzled, as he quite properly should have been. But then, so was everybody. "If our mothers could see us now!" Tennessee Williams said gaily.

After the traditional toasts to Malraux and the other talented guests, JFK couldn't help wisecracking, "This is becoming a sort of eating place for artists—but they never ask *us* out!"

Another marvelous affair, the dinner for the American Nobel Prize winners, completely shattered the image of scientists and intellectuals as being stuffy, pompous, and rigid. As the guests arrived that night, the U.S. Marine Orchestra was playing dance music in the spacious hall outside the State rooms. The best brains in America may not have known that the President and First Lady were waiting to receive them in the East Room, but they knew what to do with a bare marble floor and lively music: they danced.

Later that evening, JFK made yet another of his eminently quotable statements: "I think this is the most extraordinary collection of talent that has ever been gathered in the White House—

with the possible exception of when Thomas Jefferson dined alone."

The third American President was a particular Kennedy favorite. Jackie, therefore, was especially delighted when her friend, Mrs. Paul Mellon, tracked down the famous Rembrandt Peale life portrait of Jefferson and donated it to the growing White House collection of superb American paintings. Jefferson sat for the painting in 1800 and liked it so much that a year later he asked Peale to make a copy for him.

"It is one of the finest male portraits ever painted," Jackie said. "You can look at it for hours, because it is so alive. His expression seems to be changing as if he were not only alive but actually looking at you. Everything Jefferson was is there: aristocrat, revolutionary, statesman, artist, sceptic and idealist. Compassionate but aloof. The Stuart portrait of Washington is so remote in comparison. Allegorical and not human. You can't feel what Washington was like from looking at it.

"The spirit of the eighteenth century is in Jefferson's face. I remember that Uncle Lefty once said to me when I was at Farmington that the eighteenth century had three geniuses and two of them were Americans: Jefferson, Franklin, and the third was Voltaire." ("Uncle Lefty" was Wilmarth Lewis, brother-in-law to Hugh Auchincloss. He and his wife lived in Farmington, Connecticut, during Jackie's years at Miss Porter's School. She visited them often. She recalls they served excellent chocolate cake and had an unusually well-stocked library.)

* * * * *

Finally, after three postponements, the long-discussed trip to India and Pakistan actually got underway. What was to have been a personal and private tour, however, turned into what was, for all practical purposes, a semi-official state visit. Accompanying Jackie was not only her sister, Lee Radziwill, and the inevitable contigent of Secret Service personnel, but social secretary Tish Baldridge, assistant White House press secretary Jay Gildner and, of course, Provie, Jackie's maid.

First stop was Rome, where Jackie attended a reception given in her "honor" by Italian President Giovanni Gronchi at the Quirinale Palace. Gronchi did not exactly roll out the red carpet. Jackie's reception committee was composed entirely of wives of

Italian government officials. Gronchi showed up briefly, proposed a toast, and then left.

A writer covering Jackie's trip for the New York *Herald Tribune* offered this analysis of the strange event: "Mrs. Kennedy's reception was friendly, but could not be called triumphal, one of the reasons being the Italian attitude towards the wives of celebrities. It can be summed up crudely as one housemaid did by saying that fundamentally Italians feel that wives should be home with the children and can in no sense stand in for a chief of state."

The next day Jackie met with Pope John XXIII for 32 minutes—it was the longest private audience he'd ever granted. St. Peter's Square was jammed with 15,000 Italians hoping to catch a glimpse of her.

Jackie said later that Pope John had "centuries of kindness in his eyes. I was determined to curtsy three times on the way in, as you're supposed to do. I did once, and then he rushed forward, so I barely got in one more curtsy."

Provie saw Pope John, also. Tish Baldridge had arranged for her to be included in one of the small group papal audiences. Further proof of his kindness: Pope John had a Rosary for Provie, a special gift for her alone.

Then they were off to India, where Indian Ambassador John Kenneth Galbraith was running the show. Though nearly fifty reporters were covering the trip, Jackie did not give interviews, nor did she say anything in public that could be turned into a decent news story. She confined her public statements to comments like: "How sweet!"—when she saw some trained camels dancing—or "How magnificent!"—when she saw the Taj Mahal, a legendary monument to love. (She asked her hosts if they would take her back so she could see it in the moonlight. They were happy to grant her wish.)

In desperation, the reporters started to interview Galbraith about—what else?—Jackie's clothes.

"What did she wear when she went riding?" they asked.

"What do you mean, what did she wear?" As an economist-author-diplomat, Galbraith had no doubt never been subjected to a fashion interview before.

"Did she wear boots?"

"I don't know. Sure, I guess she wore boots."

"Did she wear a hat?"

"Yes, I think it was a sort of hunting cap." Obviously the lanky ambassador was getting the hang of it.

"How does she like India?"

"Why, I don't know. She seems to love it."

Jackie later told a reporter that Prime Minister Nehru was "terribly good to us. He spent an hour or so each day walking in the gardens with Lee and me. We never talked of serious things, I guess because Jack has always told me the one thing a busy man doesn't want to talk about at the end of the day is whether the Geneva Conference will be successful or what settlement could be made in Kashmir or anything like that."

Jackie, who was in India behaving like a head of state and being treated like a head of state, continued to throw up her smoke-screen of wide-eyed, girlish innocence. The fact is that she enjoyed Galbraith's wit, intelligence, and erudition so much that during all the time he was Ambassador to India, she had copies of his reports and dispatches sent to her at the White House. Jackie was probably as well informed on Indian affairs as anyone in government.

In Pakistan, President Ayub Khan took her to see the Shalimar Gardens, built by the same Mogul Emperor who had created the Taj Mahal. "I only wish my husband could be with me and that we had something as romantic to show to President Ayub when he came to our country," she said.

And she especially enjoyed her visit to the historic and much-fought-over Khyber Pass. Eighteen of the mountain tribes had sent their chiefs to greet her with gifts of sheep, daggers, and blankets. "Of all the good things I was going to see [on this trip]," she told them, "this was what my husband wanted to see the most—the Khyber Pass. And me, too."

Later, she told writer Joan Braden that she'd been disappointed because "Adlai Stevenson had told me there would be men with swords and flying horses and, when I asked, I was told there never had been any horses. I adored the bagpipes and the officers' mess, though, and it was exciting when all the reporters were behind us and I walked alone up to the border and thought of Alexander of Macedon and all the people after him who had fought through the pass to reach the subcontinent, and how all we'd seen was because of him."

Before she left Pakistan, President Ayub Khan gave her a $100,000 emerald, diamond, and ruby necklace and a thoroughbred stallion, Sardar, that was flown back to the States aboard an Air Force plane and then trucked to Glen Ora. Sardar became one of Jackie's favorite horses. She was often photographed while riding him.

On the plane coming back to Washington, Jackie, who had just spent two weeks receiving the most extraordinary attentions from the Indian government, the Indian people who thronged to see her wherever she went and from the American press which covered her trip with a planeful of reporters and photographers, once again began singing her sweet, little "I'm just a wife and mother" tune.

Speaking to her friend Joan Braden, who covered the trip for the *Saturday Evening Post*, Jackie said, "Jack was so nice to let me come. He says I'm young and ought to do things like this that I want to.

"I just pray that I was all right and that the trip did some good. I'm glad I went, but I'd never take a trip like this again without Jack. There were moments like that time in Lahore at the governor's house, when I sat at the window and looked at the fantastic lighted trees reflected in moonlight pools, and wondered what I was doing so far away alone, without Jack or the children to see them.

"Jack's always so proud of me when I do something like this, but I can't stand being out in front. I know it sounds trite, but what I really want is to be behind him and to be a good wife and mother."

It is easy to be cynical about such statements, but more difficult to imagine the frustrations involved in being a woman of high intelligence, energy, and ambition locked into the essentially decorative role of an upper-class wife.

When Jackie was growing up in the thirties and forties, the only women she saw were either privileged wives like her mother or schoolteachers or servants. She saw no active, assertive, achieving, and independent women because, except for actresses and entertainers, there weren't very many of them in those days, and none of them were in her line of vision.

When she was married to Jack Kennedy, Jackie obviously tried to do and be all the things that a "good wife" is supposed to do. She saw that the home was pleasant, that the food was good, that the children were cared for. But she just as clearly loved the suddenly enlarged scope that being First Lady gave to her life. (The White House switchboard, however, was ordered to route her messages to "Mrs. Kennedy" rather than to the "First Lady," which she thought sounded like the name of a Kentucky Derby winner.)

Jack Kennedy had been conditioned from birth to perform like a thoroughbred. Joe Kennedy believed that life had one purpose and that was to win. Horse breeders and trainers have the same philosophy and the products of that philosophy are nervous, restless animals. JFK apparently drained off much of this excess energy via sex, a not uncommon habit among driven, neurotically ambitious men.

For a number of years—and many of them included the nine years of his marriage—Jack Kennedy was a compulsive womanizer. Jackie may not have known all the details of who, when, and where, but she knew that JFK was not sexually loyal to her. And it hurt. But what could she do about it?

Several things, as it happens. She was a brilliant First Lady and by the time of her trip to India had become an obvious political asset to JFK, whose New Frontier did not seem to be breaking much new ground after all. Jackie's triumph in Paris, for example, did much to divert world attention from the disastrous Bay of Pigs incident, which had occurred less than a month before the European tour.

Jackie's cousin, John Davis, observes that "most Bouviers who saw Jacqueline during her years as First Lady felt that she had blossomed in the White House as never before. As a senator's wife she had often seemed restless and vaguely dissatisfied. The rough and tumble of congressional politics was not at all to her taste, the small-time politicians she had to entertain often bored her, and she frequently felt frustrated because she could not be herself. But in the White House she came into her own. Above the vulgar contentions and ambitions of politics, she could finally call her own tune, be herself and get away with it."

Jackie very much lived her own life, as the long summers in Hyannis Port and the trips abroad without Jack clearly showed. She certainly wasn't hanging around the White House trying to keep an eye on him.

Her responses to Jack's numerous infidelities were not, of course, all constructive. Jackie's inability to keep her spending, especially on clothes, within reasonable limits, can be viewed as her reaction to Jack's inability or unwillingness to honor his marriage vows.

There has been much speculation in recent years on the Kennedy menage. What was the rock-bottom, unvarnished truth regarding this historic marriage? It is always assumed that Jack's philandering left Jackie angry and irate, furious at her husband's repeated betrayals.

And while she no doubt preferred that Jack be faithful to her, she also knew that the compulsive philanderer is not a happy and fulfilled human being. She had to look no further than the example her own father had given her throughout his long career as a ladies' man. For all his women and for all his sexual conquests, Jack Bouvier was neither contented nor self-assured. The simple truth was that all the women in the world could not fill the abyss of failure that lay at the core of Jack Bouvier's personality. He was a man who grew up knowing that everyone expected him to achieve unusual success . . . and achieve it early. As Grampy Jack's oldest son, he was also expected to one day take over the leadership of the entire Bouvier clan. Quite simply, he wasn't capable by nature for the kind of success his father expected of him. And Grampy Jack let him know it, over and over again.

For Jack Bouvier, seducing a woman provided a fleeting moment of success in a life that was otherwise burdened with an almost unbearable sense of failure. He spent his last years alone and would no doubt have eagerly traded the memories of all his conquests for regular visits and phone calls from his beloved daughters, Jackie and Lee.

Jack Kennedy's father, too, had enormous expectations of success by his son, and Jackie was well aware of their extent. On several occasions during the 1960 campaign she told friends that even though she found the prospect of losing her privacy "frightening," she still prayed that Jack would win the presidency because otherwise he would be impossible to live with. "How could you fill his life?" she said to an interviewer after the election. "If he had lost, he'd have been around the world three times and written three books. But it wouldn't have been the same."

Unlike Jack Bouvier, however, Jack Kennedy was within sight of that elusive goal: success. Merely being elected President did not assure success. He would have to be re-elected. And once re-elected, he would have to do whatever was necessary in order to be a great President, right up there with Jefferson, Lincoln, Wilson, and FDR.

In the early sixties, JFK's goal seemed attainable. Who could know the disastrous events that would follow the CIA-assisted overthrow of the Diem regime in South Vietnam? Who could foresee that placing a handful of American military "advisers" in that hapless land would result in one of the most disastrous and costly events in U.S. history, the quagmire of Vietnam?

All that horror was still to come.

Jack Kennedy's concerns then were closer to home. He tried to retrieve the Bay of Pigs fiasco with the Cuban missile crisis of 1962 and largely succeeded. The country, for the most part, saw the blockade of the Russian ships and the Soviet agreement to withdraw their missiles from Cuban soil as our serving notice on the Russians that we meant business: they were to stay out of the Western Hemisphere. Only later did reassessment suggest that those thirteen days had been a futile exercise of macho brinkmanship: a minor victory had been achieved at the risk of the unthinkable—nuclear war.

One substantial and lasting success of Jack Kennedy's was the Nuclear Test Ban Treaty, which was signed after months of hard negotiations with the USSR in October, 1963.

Jackie may have believed that the Test Ban Treaty, re-election in 1964, and other expected successes in civil rights and domestic economic progress would eventually provide a measure of peace and serenity for Jack Kennedy. Perhaps this new tranquility would obviate his need to constantly prove his ability to succeed by means of sexual conquests.

Remembering her father's sterile life, Jackie may even have felt a kind of pity for her husband's restive philandering while at the same time hoping that he would someday outgrow his need to play Don Juan.

In the meantime, she had attained world fame in her own right. In spite of continued lamentations over her lack of privacy, Jackie was enjoying her role as First Lady considerably more than she had thought she would.

And everybody knows that a guilty husband is a soft touch. Jack complained about the bills from time to time, but in practice she was free to spend whatever she wanted. According to Mary Gallagher, Jackie's personal secretary in those years, "Her total expenditures for 1962 came to $121,461.61—against $105,446.14 for her first year in the White House.

"It always amazed me," Gallagher wrote, "that Jackie spent more in a year on family expenses than the President's salary of $100,000!"

* * * * *

Jackie recuperated from her trip to India and Pakistan by spending the Easter holidays at Joe Kennedy's house in Palm Beach. After the spring social season ended in Washington, she accompanied JFK on a state visit to Mexico in June and then headed for Hyannis Port. In August, with Caroline in tow, she met Lee and "Stash" Radziwill for a vacation in Ravello, Italy.

There were "Welcome, Jackie!" banners all over town when they arrived, the usual crowds gathered wherever she went. There were rumors of sharks in the Mediterranean waters just off Ravello, and a Rome newspaper advised her to ignore them. "The sharks have never eaten anyone in Ravello," she was assured.

Waiting for her that first day on the beach, however, were sharks of a different variety: seventy-five *paparazzi* from Rome were ravenously clicking away. The world had an apparently insatiable appetite for pictures of Jackie—especially Jackie in a swimsuit. She allowed ten minutes of picture-taking, then the Italian police and the Secret Service cleared the beach of photographers.

She appeared to be having a marvelous time. There was a midnight dinner on the Isle of Capri, romantically bathed in the bright southern moonlight. There was sailing aboard Italian auto tycoon Gianni Agnelli's eighty-two foot yacht. There was dancing in a trendy little cellar nightclub and red wine with the Radziwills and Agnelli at a sidewalk cafe.

The dominant rumor on this trip was that Jackie was in Italy attempting to get her sister's first marriage, to Michael Canfield, annulled. Jackie was said to be meeting with a special Vatican emissary, these top secret enclaves purportedly being held on Agnelli's yacht. What the rumor-mongers apparently did not take into account was the fact that Radziwill, also a Catholic, had already been divorced two times when he married Lee. Getting three marriages annulled was probably more of an ecclesiastical coup than even Jacqueline Kennedy could manage.

After Italy, Jackie spent the rest of the summer dividing her time between Hyannis Port and the Auchincloss farm in Newport. When she finally returned to Washington in October, she told Tish Baldridge that she wanted her social schedule cut as much as possible.

It was too late to do anything about the rest of the year, but during the first four months of 1963, Jackie showed up at only three White House dinners and two receptions. The reason why was announced when she was in Palm Beach for Easter. Jackie was expecting JFK's third child in August. Her obstetrician, Dr. John Walsh, had advised her to cancel all official activities and public appearances. Therefore, the White House noted, she would be unable to accompany the President on state visits to Italy, Germany and Ireland.

After the news of her pregnancy was announced, Jackie appeared in public only twice. There was a state dinner for the Grand Duchess of Luxembourg in May and shortly after that, Jackie made a surprise visit to the Metropolitan Opera House in New York for a performance of England's Royal Ballet.

In June, she retired to Hyannis Port for the last months of her pregnancy. It was a quiet summer. The Kennedys had rented their house in the famous compound to a Kennedy sister. For themselves, they had rented an isolated and lovely house on Squaw Island, about thirty minutes' driving time from the compound. Jackie adored the Squaw Island house for its sense of being surrounded by the ocean and completely away from civilization. She loved the house so much she hoped they could build one exactly like it. She went so far as to have the house measured and drawings made for their architect to copy.

The baby was due at the end of August, but on August 7, Jackie began having labor pains. A helicopter was quickly ordered and took her and Dr. Walsh to Otis Air Force Base, which had a suite of rooms prepared for just such an emergengy. The premature labor was an old story for Jackie, but it's not the sort of thing any woman ever gets used to. "This baby mustn't be born dead," she kept saying.

But this time Walsh's assurances that everything would be all right came to nought. He delivered a baby boy, by a Caesarean section, as soon as Jackie was prepared for surgery. The child weighed four pounds, ten and a half ounces.

They saw immediately that something was wrong. The child was quickly baptized by Father John Scahill, the Roman Catholic chaplain at Otis. The baby was named Patrick Bouvier Kennedy. Then an ambulance, sirens screaming, took him to the Children's Hospital Medical Center in Boston.

That night in Washington, Pierre Salinger told reporters that the baby was suffering from "idiopathic respiratory distress syndrome." Later reports identified the ailment as "hyaline membrane disease."

Jackie was not told that the baby was having serious breathing difficulties and by 10 A.M. the next day was asking her secretary to bring the day's newspapers. She continued dictating memos regarding various White House social affairs planned for the fall. She made an appointment with Kenneth to have her hair done later in the month, and she asked Mary Gallagher to buy some new lipsticks for her.

Jackie didn't know anything was wrong until Walsh told her, early on August 9, that little Patrick had died at 4:26 A.M. that morning.

She had probably thought that even though the baby had arrived early, he was bound to get, as the son of the President, the very best medical care in the world. And in the mid-twentieth century, American medical research had produced a medical technology that could literally perform miracles.

But there were none available for Patrick Bouvier Kennedy.

She took it very hard. Walsh ordered her sedated.

* * * * *

Jack and Jacqueline Kennedy were terribly depressed by Patrick's death. JFK had the awesome responsibilities of the presidency to take his mind off the loss of his second son. What could Jackie do to recuperate emotionally from her third disastrous pregnancy? (There had been the miscarriage in 1955, the stillborn daughter in 1956, and now this.) Patrick's death may have hit them especially hard because there had been signs of renewal in the Kennedy marriage: Patrick had been a symbol of new beginnings, of a new phase in their relationship.

Maybe Jack was finally beginning to settle down. For Jackie's part, she had begun to accept that being First Lady involved certain political realities. She accepted the fact that she would be required to do some real campaigning in 1964. She accepted it and understood the reasons for it and was resolved to do a good job.

For perhaps the first time in their marriage, there was a growing awareness that they had a real partnership. They were a team. The White House press corps was the first to notice this new springtime in the Kennedy marriage. And the death of Patrick only served to bring them closer together.

But in those weeks after Patrick's death, Jackie did not look well. She had lost weight and her color was wan and pale. She obviously needed a long rest and a change of scene. But where to go that would be truly different and yet not expose her to the harassment of the usual crowds?

The perfect solution came in the form of an invitation from Greek shipping magnate Aristotle Onassis. Through Lee Radziwill, he offered Jackie the use of his sumptuous yacht, the *Christina,* for as long as she wanted it.

Onassis said he would stay in Athens while she was on board. Jackie wouldn't hear of it. As a compromise, Onassis said he would stay out of sight whenever they were in port. The press would be told that he was not on board. Jackie's companions on the cruise, in addition to the inevitable Secret Service agents, would be Franklin D. Roosevelt, Jr., and his wife, the Radziwills, and Onassis's sister, Artemis.

Where would the cruise go?

"The ship will go wherever Mrs. Kennedy wants it to go," Onassis said. "She is the captain."

The 303-foot *Christina* dwarfed all other yachts on which Jackie had been entertained. (She had been on board the *Christina* once before. In the fifties, when Jack was still a Senator, they had visited Joe and Rose Kennedy who were vacationing in the south of France. Onassis invited them on board to meet Winston Churchill, one of Jack's heroes. While JFK and Churchill talked, Onassis showed Jackie around the *Christina.)*

In preparation for the cruise on which he would host the First Lady of the United States, Onassis, one of the greatest and most successful social climbers in history, ordered thousands of dollars worth of caviar, fresh fruits, vintage wines, and other delicacies. It took three days to load the ship. He hired two hairdressers, a Swedish masseur, and a dance band.

They stopped at Lesbos and Crete, then proceeded to Turkey where they docked at Smyrna, Onassis's birthplace. Everyone insisted that he come ashore and act as their guide. The photographers materialized immediately. Next was Istanbul. More photographers. After a few days' exposure in the tabloid newspapers, the Congressional criticism began. It was more serious than usual: FDR, Jr., was Under Secretary of Commerce, and Onassis had frequent dealings, often abrasive, with the U.S. Maritime Administration.

But who could have guessed that the real story of the cruise had nothing to do with political wheeling and dealing?

After a few days, it was clear that Onassis was smitten by Jackie. He turned on his considerable charm and literally showered her with attention, concern, witty stories, and a constant stream of gifts, some inconsequential, others breathtaking.

When the cruise finally ended, several weeks later, Onassis gave

Jackie a diamond and ruby necklace. To Lee, he gave a string of pearls. If Onassis was smitten, Jackie was impressed. She made sure that Onassis's various addresses were entered into her address book. Then she ordered a silver cigarette box from Tiffany's and sent it to him with a warm letter of thanks for his hospitality.

Early in November, shortly after Jackie had returned to Washington, she and JFK had several old friends, including Benjamin Bradlee and his wife, Toni, over for a small dinner party.

According to Bradlee, who was then head of *Newsweek's* Washington bureau, the talk turned to who JFK's successor would be in 1968. (Kennedy believed he would win the 1964 election.) Everyone agreed it wouldn't be Lyndon Johnson, then vice-president.

"Well, then who?" Jackie asked.

"It was going to be Franklin [FDR, Jr.]" Kennedy said, "until you and Onassis fixed that."

JFK told Jackie that he wanted Onassis to stay away from the U.S. until after the 1964 election. He obviously believed that the cruise had attracted far too much negative attention. But he was willing to use Jackie's guilt feelings to his own advantage.

"Maybe now you'll come with us to Texas next month," he said.

Jackie readily agreed: "Sure I will, Jack."

* * * * *

The purpose of the trip was to assure a Democratic sweep in Texas at next year's election. In 1960, JFK had barely won the state. Vice-President Lyndon Johnson and his wife, Ladybird, would accompany the Kennedys on their Texas itinerary along with governor John Connally.

The presidential party left Washington on Thursday, November 21, and flew directly to San Antonio, where JFK dedicated the new $16 million aero-space medical center at Brooks Air Force Base. Then the party flew to Houston. That evening, with Jackie sitting close by, JFK spoke at a dinner sponsored by the United Latin American Citizens. Later that night, they flew to Fort Worth, arriving at the Texas Hotel shortly after 11 P.M.

The morning of November 22 began with JFK addressing a breakfast gathering of the Fort Worth Chamber of Commerce. Explaining Jackie's absence, Kennedy said, "Jackie and Lady Bird may take a little longer to dress but then, they always look much better than Lyndon and me."

Upstairs, Jackie had about finished dressing for what she knew would be a very long day. After all the political visits and speech-making, she and JFK would spend a few days with the Johnsons at their Austin ranch.

Jackie had chosen to wear a Chanel suit of shocking pink wool with navy blue trim. There was a matching "pillbox" type hat on the back of her head and short, white kid gloves. Later that morning, when they landed at Dallas' Love Field, she was given a bouquet of deep pink roses. She put them on the seat between them after they had got into the back of the open car—Jack didn't like the "bubble top" designed to protect him and had ordered it removed—for the motorcade to the Dallas Trade Mart where JFK would speak at a luncheon. Governor and Mrs. Connally sat in the jump seats in the middle of the long limousine. Two Secret Service men were in the front seat, one of them at the wheel.

Shortly before they passed an undistinguished red brick warehouse known as the Texas School Book Depository, Mrs. Connally turned to JFK and said, "No one can say Dallas doesn't love and respect you, Mr. President."

"You sure can't," Jack agreed.

Then they were approaching a triple underpass and Jackie thought that there would be at least a brief respite from the glaring sunlight as they drove under it. She was waving to the crowds on the left; JFK was waving to the crowds on the right. The pink roses lay on the seat between them.

And then there was what sounded like firecrackers and she turned to Jack and saw that her life had been blown apart. She must have instantly known and instantly recoiled from knowing that nothing would ever again be quite the same. Her life had suddenly and tragically and drastically changed course in a place and time she would never have guessed: a sunny November day in Dallas, Texas.

* * * * *

There were moments during the next few hours of that long and unbelievable day that Jacqueline Kennedy was dazed and uncomprehending. At other times, she understood only too well what had happened and the sorrow written on her face was terrible to see.

But, slowly, a kind of controlled fury took hold of her. It cleared her head. She knew what she had to do. It would be her last official task as First Lady: she had to bury the President.

The first evidence of this fury was the refusal to change her blood-drenched clothing. "I want them to see what they've done to Jack," she said fiercely.

Shortly after 2 P.M., Jackie was in the back cabin of Air Force One kneeling beside JFK's coffin and waiting for the plane to take off. Then Mrs. Johnson came back and asked her if she could bear to come to the presidential cabin and witness Lyndon Johnson's swearing-in as thirty-sixth President of the United States. The official White House photographer positioned himself so that the bloodstains didn't show. There was no way, however, that he could hide her ravaged face.

The next photographs were taken when Air Force One set down at Andrews Air Force Base and a yellow forklift slowly lumbered up to the rear door of the plane. Bobby Kennedy had boarded the plane by its front entrance and made his way to the cabin where Jackie sat with JFK's coffin. They are shown hand-in-hand, following the coffin out of the plane. And what she wanted the world to see is plainly visible: her skirt and her stockings are caked with the blood of the dead president.

A Navy ambulance was waiting to take Kennedy's body to Bethesda Naval Hospital, where an autopsy was to be performed. A limousine was waiting for Jackie, but she would not leave JFK. Instead, she sat on the floor in the rear compartment of the ambulance with Bobby and Godfrey McHugh, a Kennedy aide.

While she waited in a seventeenth-floor suite for her husband's body to be prepared for burial, Jackie began planning the funeral. Calls went out to their old friend Bill Walton, to Arthur Schlesinger, Jr., and to Richard Goodwin. She wanted information on the lying-in-state and funeral of Abraham Lincoln, who had also been cut down by an assassin's bullet.

While they waited, Bobby received word from Dallas that a likely suspect, Lee Harvey Oswald, had been arrested. It was said that Oswald was a Communist.

"He didn't even have the satisfaction of being killed for civil rights," Jackie said bitterly. "It had to be some silly little Communist."

It was nearly 4:30 on Saturday morning when Jacqueline Kennedy came home with her husband for the last time. The white and gold East Room had been prepared with black mourning crepe to receive him. JFK's coffin was placed on a black-draped catafalque in that same room where Lincoln's had lain nearly one hundred years earlier.

By this time Jackie had been awake continuously for nearly twenty-four hours. Finally, with a last look at the honor guard at attention around Jack Kennedy's coffin, she slowly made her way to her own bedroom.

Mercifully, she slept for several hours.

* * * * *

It was bleak in Washington that Saturday. A cold and relentless rain came down most of the day. At ten o'clock, Mass was said in the East Room with the Kennedy and Auchincloss families and a few friends in attendance. A mahogany table placed at the foot of the president's casket served as an altar. Two prie-dieux were placed in front of it. Jackie and Caroline knelt at one of them. Bobby used the other. Everyone else knelt on the East Room's oak floor while Father Robert Cavanaugh, a former president of Notre Dame, said a low Mass.

Jackie spent most of that day greeting the various officials who came to pay their final respects to the slain president. They included former Presidents Eisenhower and Truman, Chief Justice Earl Warren, General Maxwell Taylor and the rest of the Joint Chiefs, New York Governor Nelson Rockefeller, and virtually all the members of the Cabinet, the Supreme Court, the Congress, and the diplomatic corps.

She also continued planning the funeral and settled various disputes that had arisen among the Kennedy family and its advisers. The Catholic hierarchy, for example, wanted the funeral held at the Shrine of the Immaculate Conception, Washington's huge new cathedral. It was the largest Catholic church in the country.

Jackie refused. The funeral Mass would be held at the smaller and less grand St. Matthew's because JFK had often attended Mass there and because it was only eight blocks from the White House and she intended to walk to the funeral behind the caisson bearing her husband's body. She had originally wanted to walk to the funeral from the Capitol, but she was finally persuaded that some of the world leaders who would be walking with her were simply too old for such a long walk.

The Kennedy family and the President's long-time political aides—the famed Irish mafia—wanted him to be buried in Brookline, Massachusetts, in the family plot where his brother, Joe, Jr., and his infant son, Patrick Bouvier, were buried.

Jackie said no. She wanted him to lie in a hero's grave at Arlington National Cemetery. She felt that JFK belonged to the country and to history. His family and his native state could no longer claim him. Defense Secretary Robert McNamara vigorously supported her position.

Early Sunday morning, accompanied only by Secret Service agents, Jackie was driven across the Potomac to inspect the gravesite at Arlington. It was on a gentle slope that rolled away from the pillared Custis-Lee mansion. As she had ordered, the Army engineers had marked off JFK's grave along a direct line to the Lincoln Memorial. The gravediggers were already at work.

This day had dawned clear and sunny. Standing under the bare trees, Jackie could see the dome of the Capitol etched against the blue November sky. In a few hours, her husband's body would be taken to the Capitol to lie in state under that very dome. He had spent eight years in that building as a Congressman and Senator. He had been inaugurated in front of that building. And now thousands of people were waiting for his coffin to arrive so that they could silently walk past it and say goodbye.

It seemed unreal, impossible, grotesque.

Jacqueline got back in the White House limousine and told them she was finished with her inspection.

That afternoon, hand-in-hand with Caroline and John, she was first in line to follow the nine military pallbearers as they carried the heavy casket up the marble steps into the Capitol.

The lack of sleep and the grief showed. Her face was drawn, her eyelids puffy. But during all the eulogies delivered at the Rotunda service, she did not weep. Her eyes filled with tears several times, but, with an obvious effort of will, she held them back.

At the end of the service, she took Caroline with her and knelt briefly at JFK's bier. Leaning forward, she kissed the coffin. Caroline reached out and touched it.

John had been restless, and a nurse had taken him into Speaker John McCormack's office. The child saw a tiny American flag sitting on a desk.

"I want to take that home to my Daddy," he announced.

He carried the little flag back to the White House. There were two events scheduled for the following day: his father's funeral and his third birthday party.

* * * * *

Aristotle Onassis was in Hamburg, Germany, the day Jack Kennedy was assassinated. Less than six weeks had passed since Jackie and Ari had been cruising the Mediterranean together on the *Christina.* An aide gave him the news as he was about to have dinner, and Onassis immediately called Lee Radziwill in London. She urged that he come to the funeral with her and her husband. Then, a few hours later, Angier Biddle Duke, the Chief of Protocol, called Onassis and invited him to stay at the White House. He accepted the invitation and was one of the few house guests that week-end who was not a member of the family.

In his book, *Death of a President,* William Manchester mentions in passing one of that week-end's lighter moments: "Rose Kennedy dined upstairs with Stash Radziwill; Jacqueline Kennedy, her sister, and Robert Kennedy were served in the sitting room. The rest of the Kennedys ate in the family dining room with their house guests, McNamara, Phyllis Dillon [Mrs. Douglas Dillon], David Powers and Aristotle Socrates Onassis, the shipowner who provided comic relief, of sorts. They badgered him mercilessly about his yacht and his Man of Mystery aura. During coffee, the Attorney General [Bobby] came down and drew up a formal document stipulating that Onassis give half his wealth to help the poor in Latin America. It was preposterous (and obviously unenforceable), and the Greek millionaire signed it in Greek."

Monday was the longest day.

At 11 A.M. on November 25, 1963, the funeral cortege began as the caisson bearing JFK's coffin departed from the Capitol. A half-hour later, it had arrived at the White House. Jacqueline Kennedy, veiled in black, took her place just behind the horse-drawn caisson. Senator Edward Kennedy was on her left. Attorney General Robert Kennedy was on her right.

Following behind her was the rest of her husband's family. And behind them was Lyndon Johnson, the President, and his wife, Lady Bird, the First Lady.

The rest of John F. Kennedy's funeral procession is best described in *The Torch Is Passed,* an account of that week-end put together by Associated Press writers and photographers:

"There came then the strangest of all sights, in large shapes and small, in cadence and out, the princes and kings, the foreign presidents and prime ministers, marching up an American street past American drugstores and American cafeterias and Americans mourning an American President. De Gaulle of France in olive gray, Selassie of Ethiopia heavy with medals, Baudouin of Belgium in khaki, Philip of England in Royal Navy blue, Frederika of Greece in a fur coat, Mikoyan of Russia in a black coat and striped trousers; in all two hundred and twenty marching symbols from ninety-two nations.

"There came then, from the government, from the government of law, the Justices of the Supreme Court and the men of the Cabinet and the men of the Congress and, perhaps saddest of all, the tiny group of close friends and advisors who had followed him all the way and were still following him; Pierre Salinger, who worried about his image, and Ted Sorenson, about his rhetoric, and Kenny O'Donnell, about his appointments and much more than that."

Richard Cardinal Cushing, in black vestments, met Jacqueline and Rose Kennedy at the door of St. Matthew's. Then Cushing, who had married Jack and Jacqueline Kennedy, baptized their children, prayed at Jack's inauguration, and conducted infant Patrick's funeral began intoning another requiem Mass.

After the funeral service was over, the final journey to Arlington began. The line of cars was so long that some were still leaving St. Matthew's as those leading the procession were entering Arlington, three miles away.

Many of those who attended the St. Matthew's service were unable to get to Arlington in time for Cardinal Cushing's prayers at the grave, where the aging Boston prelate offered the soul of "this wonderful man" to God.

Fifty U.S. military jets flew over the grave in precise formation. When their roar had subsided, the traditional 21-gun salute shattered the stillness of that sunny autumn afternoon. Taps was played and the flag covering the coffin was tautly folded by the honor guard and presented to Jacqueline.

At 3:34 P.M., the body of John Fitzgerald Kennedy was lowered into the ground.

For Jacqueline, however, the day was not quite over.

As soon as the graveside services at Arlington were finished, she had planned a reception at the White House for the foreign heads of state, diplomats, and ambassadors who had attended her husband's funeral.

She had wanted to see four of the visiting statesmen in private: General de Gaulle, Prince Philip, Eamon de Valera, and Haile Selassie. When these brief visits were accomplished, she went downstairs, where a buffet had been served, and joined Ted Kennedy and Angier Biddle Duke to form a receiving line in the Red Room.

Her cousin, John Davis, had flown to Washington for the funeral from Naples. Most of the Bouviers had left Washington after the funeral without seeing her. But Davis did not want to return to Italy without tendering his sympathy in person. He got in line with all the foreign diplomats and waited his turn. When they finally shook hands, Davis was amazed at her continuing display of strength.

"I had expected her to look weary and oppressed. Under the eyes of the entire world she had marched from the White House to St. Matthew's, attended a long, emotionally draining funeral, presided over her husband's burial, received four of the strongest political personalities in the world, and was now greeting foreign emissaries by the score. Yet she was still radiant, enthusiastic, vital. It was astonishing to behold. Not a trace of fatigue, or concern, or fragility. The old charm was still there. Each visitor received a warm, personal welcome. Serene and confident, she gave of herself unsparingly."

After the reception, when the last official guest had left the White House, Jacqueline would return to the private quarters. Her mother would be waiting, along with Rose Kennedy and her other Kennedy in-laws, Lee and Stanislaus Radziwill, and a few others.

John-John had already opened some of his presents and, after dinner, there would be a cake with three small candles on it. He would have lots of help, if he needed it, in blowing them all out.

But none of them would make the wish that was in their hearts because they knew there was no chance at all of its coming true.

* * * * *

In recent years, Jackie has been much criticized for the way in which she planned and managed the lying-in-state and funeral of her husband. Her detractors hint that the events of that November week-end were carefully staged in order to feed the legend of John

F. Kennedy as fallen hero. The critics speak of an "excess of show-manship."

One reason for the criticism is that at least two of Jack Kennedy's successors in the White House have made us unrelentingly suspicious of the motives of politicians. We are ashamed to recall that not so long ago we were willing to believe anything they told us. The news media contributed to the illusion by automatically censoring reports on the occasionally scandalous behavior of the men who held public office. We feel we've been conned. So now we're willing to believe nothing, and every politician in living memory gets tarred with the brush of corruption and manipulation.

We shall never know what John F. Kennedy would have accomplished in a full eight years as President. But while he was alive he inspired an entire generation to believe that things could be different and better than we had known them to be. He—and Jacqueline—brought style and wit and grace and elegance to the White House. And Jack and his brother, Bobby, as Attorney General brought real and honest White House concern to the issue of civil rights.

In spite of the very human faults and shortcomings that he shared with the rest of us, Jack Kennedy, had he lived, had every chance of becoming the great President he wanted to be.

Many of us that week-end wept as if we had lost someone in our own families. The only consolation to be had was the magnificent manner in which he was laid to rest.

The cynics may call that showmanship.

The rest of us call it dignity.

Chapter Four

Building a New Life

Chapter Four

Building a New Life

Two weeks after JFK's funeral, Jackie moved into a Georgetown house that Under Secretary of State Averell Harriman and his wife made available to her. Her mother and stepfather, Janet and Hugh Auchincloss, were living in the same neighborhood and Ted and Joan Kennedy were just a few blocks away.

Inevitably, depression set in. Her cousin and godfather, Michel Bouvier III, visited her shortly after she had moved into the Harrimans' house and found her disoriented and shaken. Writing of their meeting, historian John Davis, another Bouvier cousin, said that "Michel was deeply moved by Jacqueline's disjointed account of the assassination and its aftermath and was repeatedly struck by how cruelly it had affected her. Both the clarity of her thinking and the stability of her emotions had been temporarily undermined. It was a wonder . . . that she had retained her sanity."

The "Irish mafia" visited her often, before she left the White House and after moving to the Harrimans' house. Kenneth O'Donnell, in his memoir of the Kennedy years, recalls that they did what they could "to ease her loneliness. She asked Dave Powers to come in every day to have lunch with John and to play games with the little boy. Bobby and I spent some time with Jackie almost every afternoon, both of us so troubled and uncertain about the future that she probably was more consoling to us than we were helpful to her."

In January, Jackie bought a house in Georgetown directly across the street from the Harrimans'. She was hardly settled in it before she got her first taste of what her life would be like in the future. Lee Radziwill had been staying with her since the funeral. Late in January, she and Lee had dinner at the Jockey Club with actor Marlon Brando and film producer George Englund. News reports had Brando "escorting" Jackie—as if he were her "date" instead of a casual dinner companion. Apparently, nothing she did could be considered "casual."

She felt stung and further depressed by the inordinate amount of media attention this non-event attracted. "The sad thing about that incident," said newsman and old friend Charles Bartlett, "was that Jackie didn't really want to go along in the first place. Her sister talked her into joining the party because she didn't want to have to dine alone at home."

In the meantime, the letters of sympathy and condolence continued to pour into Washington. By mid-January over 800,000 had been received and Jackie went on television to say "thank you." The appearance on CBS, her first public statement since the assassination, originated from Robert Kennedy's vaulted Justice Department office. With her were Bobby and Ted Kennedy. Her voice was lower than usual and a few times she resolutely blinked back tears.

"The knowledge of the affection in which my husband was held by all of you has sustained me, and the warmth of these tributes is something that I shall never forget.

"Whenever I can bear to, I read them. All this bright light gone from the world. All of you who have written to me know how much we all loved him and that he returned that love in full measure."

With flames flickering in the fireplace behind them, Jackie continued: "My greatest wish is that all of these letters be acknowledged. They will be, but it will take a long time to do so. I know you will understand.

"Every message is to be treasured, not only for my children, but so that future generations will know how much our country and peoples in other nations thought of him."

She said that all the letters of condolence would be placed with JFK's papers in Kennedy Library in Boston.

"I hope that in the years to come many of you and your children will be able to visit the Kennedy library. It will be, we hope, not only a memorial to President Kennedy, but a living center of study of the times in which he lived and a center for young people and for scholars from all over the world."

Jackie was not only amazed by the volume of letters, but touched by the sincere outpourings of grief that streamed into Washington from people in all walks of life, from every corner of the United States . . . and beyond. Nearly twenty percent of the letters came from foreign countries.

But not all the attention she received was so gratifying. Crowds continued to gather outside her Georgetown house, hoping to catch a glimpse of her. Washington tour buses had even taken to stopping so their passengers could get out and take snapshots of 3017 N Street.

By spring she knew she had been mistaken in imagining that she could live in Washington. It wasn't just the crowds. It was all the haunted and lonely feelings that assaulted her as she tried to create a new life in the same neighborhoods where she and Jack had started out. The memories were simply too powerful.

On trips to New York, she began looking at apartments, including one at 810 Fifth Avenue, the address of Nelson Rockefeller and Richard Nixon. Whether because of her prospective neighbors or for other reasons, Jackie decided that would not be a good place to live. She kept looking.

Spring brought near disaster and the painful re-opening of wounds that had scarcely begun to close. A small plane in which Ted Kennedy was a passenger crashed near Northampton, Massachusetts. The pilot and another passenger, one of Ted's administrative assistants, were killed instantly. Ted was critically injured, suffering a fractured vertebrae and several broken ribs. Indiana Senator Birch Bayh and his wife, Marvella, miraculously escaped with only minor injuries.

The Kennedy family had had to endure more grief than seemed humanly possible: Joe, Jr., and Kathleen dead in plane crashes, Jack brutally cut down in the third year of his presidency, and now this. Jackie flew to Ted's bedside along with Bobby and the rest of the Kennedys. She'd had her fill of tragic hospital scenes this year. First, there had been Patrick's death in August, then that lonely emergency room in Dallas, and now Ted devastated by injuries and two men dead.

She and Bobby had coffee in the hospital cafeteria. "We certainly have rotten luck," she said.

Back in Georgetown, she was visited by members of the Warren Commission who took her testimony concerning her husband's assassination: "I was looking this way, to the left, and I heard these terrible noises, you know. And my husband never made any sound. So I turned to the right and all I remember is seeing my husband, he had this sort of quizzical look on his face, and his hand was up. It must have been his left hand. And just as I turned and looked at him, I could see a piece of his skull and I remember it was flesh-colored. I remember thinking he just looked as if he had a slight headache, and I just remember seeing that. No blood or anything.

"And then he sort of did this (indicating), put his hand to his forehead and fell in my lap.

"And then I just remember falling on him and saying, 'Oh, no, no, no.' I mean, 'Oh, my God, they have shot my husband.' and 'I love you, Jack,' I remember I was shouting. And just being down in the car with his head in my lap. And it just seemed an eternity.

"You know, there were pictures later on of me climbing out the back. But I don't remember that at all."

Then they asked her if she could remember how many shots had been fired.

"Well, there must have been two because the one that made me turn around was Governor Connally yelling. And it used to confuse me because first I remembered there were three and I used to think my husband didn't make any sound when he was shot and Governor Connally screamed.

"And then I read the other day that it was the same shot that hit them both. But I used to think if I only had been looking to the right I would have seen the first shot hit him, then I could have pulled him down and then the second shot would not have hit him . . ."

The assassin's first bullet entered the President's neck, and while seriously injured, JFK conceivably could have been saved by quick and skilled medical attention had the neck wound been his sole injury. It was the second shot that killed him, the shot that shattered the skull. Believing that no useful purpose would be served by printing Jackie's descriptions of the President's wounds, the Warren Commission omitted them from its final report.

Jackie's testimony to the Commission shows that one of the lingering results of that awful day in Dallas was a feeling of guilt.

If only . . . she had been looking in his direction, she might have saved him.

If only . . . she had been willing to shake more hands at Love Field when they landed in Dallas, the timing of the motorcade might have been different . . . not tragic at all.

If only . . . she had insisted, demanded that the bullet-proof bubble top be in place on top of the presidential Lincoln convertible.

Many people close to Jackie believed that this perfectly ordinary and understandable guilt she felt over the assassination was fed by another, more insidious brand of self-blame that was a serious threat to her mental and emotional stability.

Jackie felt that she had let her husband down politically over and over again during his life. The long cruise on the Onassis yacht after Patrick's death was a case in point. And there were others—many others. She just wasn't a Bess Truman or a Mamie Eisenhower or a Pat Nixon. She was Jacqueline Bouvier Kennedy and she liked elegant things and she liked to travel and she needed those long, uninterrupted summers with the children on the Cape and some days, even in the White House—oh, God, especially in the White House—she would just cancel a whole day's schedule and spend the day in bed with a good book. Not for any good and sufficient reason but simply because she felt like it.

Now all these self-indulgences began to haunt her. She was determined that she would not fail her husband in death the way she had so often failed him in life. The first thing she did, even before she left the White House, was to go downstairs and see Lyndon Johnson.

It was awfully difficult to make this short trip because it didn't seem to her that he belonged in there. To visit Johnson in Jack's office was, in many ways, like losing him all over again. Still, it was something she knew she had to do: there was something she wanted Lyndon Johnson to do and she would be more likely to get him to co-operate if she spoke to him about it soon.

Johnson had plenty of guilt problems of his own to deal with. He had yearned to be President for years and years, wheeling and dealing and learning Washington as well or better than any man or woman alive had ever known it. But he had never wanted to be President on these terms. He had wanted to win it on his own.

So when Jackie came in that day and sat down and looked at him with those piercing brown eyes and asked him in her sweet little voice if he would change the name of Cape Canaveral to Cape Kennedy, he was almost relieved and didn't have to give the matter a second thought. He simply picked up the phone with her sitting there and got Florida Governor Farris Bryant on the other end and told Bryant the plan and said they'd surely appreciate his help in the matter.

British journalist Robin Douglas-Home, who had managed over the years to conduct several unusually candid interviews with Jackie, said, "I know from my talks with her that she had a very strong guilt complex, that she felt she had not supported her husband politically in life. She felt very strongly that she'd not given him the kind of political backing she should have done. . . . It became an absolute fixation that she would never fail him in his death."

Her memorializing activities of that first year were considerable:

—Through her press secretary, Pamela Turnure, Jackie announced that she planned to do everything in her power to assist in the creation of the John F. Kennedy Center for the Performing Arts, intended as a national cultural center in Washington.

—With Bobby, she appeared at an exhibit of JFK mementoes at the IBM building in New York.

—Again with Bobby and other members of the Kennedy family, she appeared in a tribute to JFK beamed via satellite to European television stations.

—She promoted the proposed JFK memorial library on numerous occasions, sometimes with Bobby, sometimes entirely on her own. She was especially pleased when she attended a luncheon given by the Pan-American Union in March. Virtually all the delegates assured her of Latin American support for the JFK library. Oil-rich Venezuela pledged $100,000. But when impoverished little Puerto Rico pledged an equal amount, Jackie was so moved that her eyes filled with tears.

* * * * *

With the ordeal of testifying before the Warren Commission behind her, Jackie left with the children for the traditional Kennedy summer in Hyannis Port. She interrupted the vacation several times to look at apartments in New York. She finally bought a fifteenth-floor, five-bedroom co-op on Fifth Avenue at 85th Street for approximately $200,000.

The news that she was leaving Washington broke on July 7. A month later, she flew to Europe for an Adriatic cruise on the *Radiant,* a yacht owned by old friend Charles Wrightsman and his wife. Also on hand were the Radziwills and Lord Harlech, British ambassador to the United States, and his wife.

When the *Radiant* dropped anchor off the small Yugoslav coastal town of Zadar, the usual crowd gathered on the docks, hoping Jackie would soon be coming ashore, but she didn't. Yugoslav President Tito had invited her to meet with him but she refused the invitation, saying that she was still in mourning. Instead, Tito sent a delegation of Foreign Ministry officials to the *Radiant* to welcome her to Yugoslav waters.

After the cruise, she spent several days with Lee at the Radziwill summer villa in Porto Ercole, a coastal resort north of Rome. The Dutch royal family also owned a villa there and Jackie was entertained by Queen Juliana and Princess Beatrix with a seagoing excursion to the Tuscan island of Giannuti.

Jackie flew back to the States, tanned and rested, just in time for the Democratic National Convention in Atlantic City. She had said that she would not attend the convention, but Jackie had been known to change her mind in the past. A film about JFK was scheduled to be shown as part of the convention program. There were many who thought that Jackie, after all she had done to perpetuate Jack's memory, would very much want to see the demonstrations of loyalty and affection that would undoubtedly occur.

And there was much media discussion about the role of Bobby Kennedy in Democratic politics. Would Johnson want him as a running mate? Would Bobby settle for the vice-presidential nomination? If he wanted second place on the ticket, Jackie could make sure he got it with a few words to the convention.

In spite of the columnists' speculation, however, Robert Kennedy knew that he would be consigning himself to four years of oblivion if he were successful in jamming through his nomination as Johnson's Vice-President. Johnson didn't want it to appear that he needed a Kennedy on the ticket to get elected, nor did he want in the second spot a man who was heir to a powerful political machine that owed Johnson nothing.

Bobby chose instead to run for the Senate from New York. Jackie chose not to attend any of the formal convention sessions. She appeared, instead, at a memorial reception for JFK at Atlantic City's Deauville Hotel. Incredibly, over 5,000 people showed up.

In November, Bobby was elected to the Senate and the first anniversary of John F. Kennedy's assassination inexorably rolled around. By this time, Jackie was not only settled into the Fifth Avenue apartment, she had also rented a place in the country, a four-bedroom fieldstone house in Glen Cove, Long Island.

Newspapers and magazines ran numerous stores and articles on the assassination, on "what might have been" had JFK lived and on how Jackie had fared during her year of mourning. She declined, however, to be interviewed for any of these stories. Nor would she go on television. Nor did she participate in any of the memorial services planned for November 22, 1964.

Instead, she spent that week-end at her Long Island house with her sister, Lee Radziwill, and her Kennedy sister-in-law, Jean Smith.

Jackie observed the first anniversary of her husband's death in her own way, on her own terms. *Look* magazine produced a special *JFK Memorial Issue* and Jackie agreed to contribute. Her tribute was brief, eloquent, and loving:

"It is nearly a year since he has gone.

"On so many days—his birthday, an anniversary, watching his children run to the sea—I have thought, 'But this day last year was his last to see that.' He was so full of love and life on those days. He seems so vulnerable now, when you think that each one was a last time.

"Soon the final day will come around again—as inexorably as it did last year. But expected this time.

"It will find some of us different people than we were a year ago. Learning to accept what was unthinkable when he was alive changes you.

"I don't think there is any consolation. What was lost cannot be replaced . . .

"Now I think that I should have known that he was magic all along. I did know it—but I should have guessed it could not last. I should have known that it was asking too much to dream that I might have grown old with him and see our children grow up together.

"So now he is a legend when he would have preferred to be a man . . ."

* * * * *

New York City is a much more sophisticated city than Washington, D.C. The capital remains, in essence, a small company town where everybody knows everybody else's business and living a private life is well nigh impossible, especially if your name is Jacqueline Bouvier Kennedy and your husband was once President of the United States.

New Yorkers, for the most part, welcomed Jackie and then left her in relative peace. In good weather, she would plop John, Jr., on the rear seat of her bicycle and give him a ride up Fifth Avenue to his nursery school. She took the children rowing in Central Park. She often walked Caroline to the Convent of the Sacred Heart School. Ex-New Frontiersmen often called on her. Bobby Kennedy continued—in spite of his Senate duties and his large family—to be available to her, to do what he could to be a father to Caroline and John, Jr.

She frequently went on skiing vacations with the other Kennedys and continued to travel on her own: in February, 1965, she went to Mexico with the Radziwills and Pierre Salinger—who had lost his Senate bid in California.

In May, accompanied by Pat Lawford, she took the children to England for the dedication of the JFK memorial at Runnymede, England. It was an impressive occasion. Both Queen Elizabeth and former Prime Minister Harold Macmillan spoke at the ceremony.

At first, it had bothered Jackie when her name turned up in a gossip column everytime she went out to dinner or attended the theatre or ballet. She was fearful that gossip about her life would hurt JFK's image. At some point, however, Jackie obviously realized that if she allowed such fears to rule her life, she would be practicing a form of purdah.

There is a certain simple-mindedness that underlies much public and media thinking. It is a view of the world painted entirely in black and white. No provision is made for shades of gray. Since real life is composed almost entirely of shades of gray, the disparity between this simplistic tabloid version of existence and reality is enormous. And when you try to explain your complex and textured self to the tabloid mentality, you only succeed in providing fresh material for distortion.

So Jackie stopped worrying about her image and Jack's image—since it was hopeless to think she could control them—and began to live in a manner she had always managed very well: she did precisely what she wanted to do, went wherever she wanted to go, and saw whomever she wanted to see.

Her decision not to become a professional widow may perhaps be dated to the party that Lee Radziwill threw for her in April, 1965, at the Radziwill's Fifth Avenue duplex. "It's just a teeny, tiny dance for less than one hundred," is how Lee diffidently described her sisterly soiree.

Director Mike Nichols was Jackie's escort and the guest list also included: Adlai Stevenson, Leonard Bernstein and his wife, Leopold Stokowski, Bobby and Ethel Kennedy, Franklin D. Roosevelt, Jr., and Pierre Salinger.

The dancing continued all through the night, and at five A.M. the next morning, Jackie was still going strong, along with a very few others. Most of the guests had long since departed.

Adlai Stevenson was her escort often enough for the gossip columnists to begin predicting marriage. Stevenson once sent Jackie one such column with his own comment—a jest—scrawled across the top: "Why don't we make these rumors reality?" (When Stevenson died of a heart attack in London that summer, Jackie, at Hyannis Port, told reporters she was "shocked and saddened" by the death of her "old and dear friend.")

In the fall, Jackie gave a party of her own. Following the opening of a North Indian art exhibit at Asia House, she hosted a bash for ex-Ambassador to India John Kenneth Galbraith at an East Side restaurant, the Sign of the Dove. Secret Service personnel were on hand to screen the guests and make sure that reporters didn't get in.

The entertainment was provided by "Killer Joe" Piro, discotheque dance teacher, whom Jackie hired to teach everybody how to do the Monkey and the Jerk. "All my nieces and nephews can do these dances so well," she told Piro. "I'd like to do them well, too."

Most of the guests at the party danced until well past midnight. But one man merely came in to the crowded, noisy room, caught Jackie's eye, smiled and waved to her, and left. The man who couldn't stay at what turned out to be one of the year's best parties, Aristotle Onassis, later told a friend, "For five years, after President Kennedy died until Jackie and I got married, I was, insofar as public exposure went, the invisible man."

From Onassis's permanent suite in New York's Pierre Hotel on Fifth Avenue at 61st Street to Jackie's apartment at 85th Street is a comfortably brisk stroll. Onassis was fond of walking in the world's large cities, especially at night. He visited Jackie at her apartment whenever he was in New York, and he was a guest at a number of small dinner parties she gave.

None of New York's professional Jackie-watchers realized that a courtship was being conducted. Meticulously, they kept track of Jackie's numerous escorts. There were a lot of them to keep track of. In the five years after Jack Kennedy's death, a partial list of the men Jackie was seen with includes (in alphabetical order): Spain's Duke of Alba, Leonard Bernstein, Truman Capote, Randolph Churchill, John Kenneth Galbraith, Roswell Gilpatric, Richard Goodwin, Averell Harriman, Alan Jay Lerner, Paul Mathias, Robert McNamara, Gian-Carlo Menotti, Mike Nichols, Andre Meyer, Anthony Quinn, Franklin D. Roosevelt, Jr., and Arthur Schlesinger, Jr. Many of these men were married. Jackie simply used them to accompany her to the theatre, the ballet, or wherever she wanted to go. One writer observed, "When Jackie wants to go out, she borrows other women's husbands as freely as the woman next door borrows a cup of sugar."

Most of her escorts could not be considered prospective husbands. One sharp-tongued Manhattan matron described Jackie's escorts as "very married, very old or very queer."

There were, however, exceptions. Director Mike Nichols was considered a "real" companion, as was Roswell Gilpatric, who had been JFK's Deputy Secretary of Defense. But impediments to either match were painfully obvious. Most important, neither had the money to support Jackie in the style to which the Kennedy money had accustomed her, and a vast abyss existed between her social status and theirs, between her celebrityhood and theirs. As the fallen queen of Camelot, Jackie couldn't marry just anyone. It would have to be someone who could be seen as sharing the same plane of existence as John F. Kennedy. Such men were rare. Certainly, a movie and theatre director, no matter how gifted he might be, did not approach JFK's status. Neither did Gilpatric, although Jackie chose him to accompany her on a trip to Mexico's Yucatan peninsula. (Gilpatric's wife later sued for divorce.)

When Jackie visited Spain and Italy in 1966, a storm of rumors linked her to Spain's Ambassador to the Vatican, sixty-one-year-old Antonio Garrigues y Diaz Canabate, whom she had first met when he was stationed on a tour of duty in Washington. Garrigues, a widower and father of eight, had asked Jackie if she could make a brief side trip during a skiing sojourn in Gstaad, Switzerland, and visit him in Rome. She said yes and, leaving Caroline and John, Jr., to their nurse and their skiing lessons, boarded a commercial airliner for Italy. Garrigues was waiting when she landed at Rome's Leonardo da Vinci Airport.

That evening, he gave a glittering dinner party in Jackie's honor. Most of the U.S. diplomatic corps in Rome showed up.

That was all it took to set the gossip factories running at peak output. Soon Italian newspapers were carrying front-page stories about the imminent announcement of their engagement.

Back in New York, when reporters called Jackie's office to check out the story, Nancy Tuckerman said, amazed, "They're just good friends and that's all there is to the matter."

A few months later, Jackie went to Spain as the guest of the Duchess of Alba, herself an outspoken and independent woman, at her fifteenth century palace in Madrid. Jackie attended Spain's biggest debutante ball and was a huge success at her first bullfight. When she arrived, wearing a mantilla, to take her seat at *La Maestranza* bullring, the 18,000 *aficionados* cheered her in a manner they usually reserved for their most favored *toreros*. One of them, Manuel Benitez, known to his fans as *El Cordobes,* after he had killed his bull that afternoon, cut off its ear and offered it to Jackie, this being a traditional gesture of respect.

After the death of the bull, Benitez, dragging his red cape carelessly behind him on the bare earth of the arena, majestically walked over to Jackie's ringside box. "It is a great honor," he said, "to dedicate the death of this bull to you and to the whole Kennedy family, for whom I have great admiration." The crowd went wild. Jackie, with a smile, accepted the tribute.

Back in the United States, Cleveland Amory, president of the Humane Society, had harsh words for Jackie's allowing herself to participate in such a bloody rite. "It is a sad and singularly ironic footnote to our modern age of violence that Mrs. Jacqueline Kennedy, of all people, who has seen the barbarousness of the present era at such tragic first hand, should now see fit to condone and even compliment the bullfight, which is one of the last relics of the barbarism of the past era," Amory said.

But Jackie, as usual, paid no attention to her critics and went to the bullfights the next day.

Escorting her during most of her public forays in Spain was Ambassador Garrigues. This served to revive all the stories concerning their imminent marriage, stories which had never completely died down after her visit to Garrigues in Rome earlier in the year. Finally, they reached such a level of intensity that Jackie's mother, Janet Auchincloss, spoke up. "Our family has known Senor Garrigues since he was Spain's Ambassador to Washington," Janet said. "I saw him in Rome recently and he is as upset as my daughter over this romance nonsense. Because of our family friendship, it was only natural for her to stay with him in Rome. . . . And why on earth should they not go out together. But romance? That is rubbish."

Even the U.S. Ambassador to Spain, Angier Biddle Duke, the Chief of Protocol during the Kennedy years, spoke to reporters with an official statement from Jackie herself: "On behalf of Mrs. Kennedy, I wish to make it crystal clear and completely understood that there is no basis in fact to the rumor of an engagement."

By far the most logical candidate to wed the widow of the President was Lord Harlech, Britain's ambassador to the United States during the Kennedy era. (Before Queen Elizabeth gave him a peerage, he was known as David Ormsby-Gore.) Jackie had traveled several times with Lord and Lady Harlech, who had died not long after President Kennedy's assassination. So Harlech was a widower—no divorce to complicate matters—the owner of a large and comfortable estate in Wales, and eminently presentable: tall, handsome, and distinguished.

When he and Jackie journeyed to Thailand and Cambodia together in 1967 to see the ancient ruins at Angkor Wat, it was widely assumed they would marry within a year or two. *Women's Wear Daily,* which has become the most indefatigable Jackie-watcher, regularly predicted that the engagement would be announced any day.

As a diplomat and English lord, Harlech was one of the few men alive who could qualify as a worthy successor to John F. Kennedy. Having been on good terms with JFK when he was President, Harlech, with his English public school diffidence, would be able to participate, without resentment or jealousy, in keeping the memory of Camelot alive. This was an especially important task now that Senator Robert F. Kennedy was in a close race with Senator Eugene McCarthy for the Democratic presidential nomination, a race from which President Lyndon Johnson had been forced to withdraw because of his escalation of the Vietnam War and the lies he had told his Cabinet and the American people in order to effect that escalation.

But Harlech and all the others, no matter the illusions they may have entertained, essentially served Jackie's convenience. Her central relationship was with Onassis. This is not to say they were lovers during this period. One of the things Black Jack Bouvier had stressed, over and over, was that the unattainable woman was the

most desirable. But Onassis was the central extra-familial relationship. She knew he was fascinated by her and was trying to win
her good opinion.

For her own part, Jackie had been fascinated by Onassis ever
since the cruise on the *Christina* in October, 1963. She had
returned to the White House full of praise for him: he was "alive
and vital." And the way life was lived by the handful of Greek shipping magnates who dominated the industry was far beyond anything her own comfortable, but genteel, upbringing had prepared
her for. Putting it baldly, no one in the history of the world had
ever lived on such a lavish scale: not the Roman emperors, not the
Persian kings, not the Chinese emperors, not the French aristoc-
racy of the eighteenth century. Only a born ascetic could remain
impervious to the lures and charms of such a life. And Jacqueline
Bouvier Kennedy was most definitely not an ascetic.

One of the reasons no one caught on to the burgeoning attraction between Jackie and Onassis, even though they were occasionally seen having dinner at various New York restaurants, is
that during the period from 1963 to 1968 Onassis was very visibly
involved with his long-time mistress, singer Maria Callas.

Christian Cafarakis, a former steward on the *Christina,* in
writing about Onassis and Jackie, says that Jackie spent several
days during the week preceding Christmas, 1964, in Ari's Paris
apartment. Onassis told the couple tending to his Avenue Foch
residence that a very important guest would soon be arriving—and
that this guest must remain anonymous.

"George and Helene were used to their employer's wild flights
of fancy, but this time he seemed to be asking the impossible. They
racked their brains to think of some way to wait on his friend
without ever seeing him—or her. Was someone going to blindfold
them and guide them in and out of the room? Eventually, they reported back to their boss to tell him they were stymied. After long
thought, Onassis found a solution. He had a revolving table placed
in the corridor between the kitchen and the dining room. Helene
could put out the meals, course by course, and Onassis himself
would serve them. Next, Helene was to clean the bedroom reserved for the VIP and make the bed while the guest was in the
bathroom; the bathroom could then be cleaned after the guest returned to the bedroom. Both servants were then to remain in the
kitchen for the rest of the day."

But of course the chauffeur immediately identified the famous guest, even behind her enormous sunglasses, when he and Onassis picked her up at Orly. And he lost no time in telling the perplexed George and Helene.

According to Cafarakis, Ari had told Maria Callas, who lived in Paris when she wasn't on board the *Christina,* that he would be out of town for several days. On Jackie's last day in Paris, Callas happened to drive by and, seeing Ari's Rolls-Royce pull into his building, assumed that he had arrived home early. She decided to drop in and welcome him back.

At this moment, Onassis was putting Jackie's luggage in the elevator and taking her down to the basement garage where the Rolls was waiting to take her to the airport. When Onassis returned to his apartment, Maria Callas was watching television in the living room.

* * * * *

There was a second reason why reporters were thrown off the Jackie-Ari trail. Late in 1966 Jackie became embroiled in a series of legal efforts intended to stop publication of William Manchester's *Death of a President,* the authorized version of the assassination and its aftermath.

Jackie had first approached Manchester in February, 1964, and asked him to write the official account of JFK's death. She had done so because, in 1962, Manchester had written a profile of Kennedy called *Portrait of a President.* The adoring tone of this book was a recommendation—at least to Jackie—that qualified Manchester for the much more complicated assignment of writing about the assassination.

The Kennedys undoubtedly also believed that Manchester, as an ex-newspaperman turned college professor, would be more tractable and easily controlled than a better-known professional writer would have been. Manchester, for example, quickly agreed, and generously, to share the book's profits with the Kennedy library in Cambridge and to give Bobby and Jackie final approval rights. Shortly after agreeing to the terms set by Jackie and Bobby, he signed a contract with Harper & Row, which published many books by Kennedys, and set to work conducting the dozens of interviews on which the book would be based.

Meanwhile, writer Jim Bishop, author of such bestsellers as *The Day Christ Died* and *The Day Lincoln Was Shot,* also wanted to write an account of JFK's death. His book, to no one's surprise, would be called *The Day Kennedy Was Shot*. Bishop wrote to Jackie, told her his plan, and asked for an interview. She turned him down: "The idea of it is so distressing to me, I can't bear to think of seeing—or seeing advertised—a book with that name and subject, one that my children might see or someone might mention to them." Jackie told Bishop that she had *hired* William Manchester to "interrogate everyone who had any connection with those days—and if I decide the book should never be published—then Mr. Manchester will be reimbursed for his time. Or, if I decide it should be known—I will decide when it should be published."

Bishop didn't take this first no as final. He wrote to her again, no doubt making his case by saying that he was a responsible writer and journalist and that history and her husband's memory could only be served by any honest effort to chronicle those dark days in November, 1963. Jackie wrote back: "None of the people connected with November 22nd will speak to anybody but Mr. Manchester. That is my wish, and it is theirs also."

Bishop refused to put his plan aside. He wrote his book without the sanction of Jackie or the Kennedy family. In spite of Jackie's orders that no one talk to Bishop, a great many people did—some of them Kennedy friends.

Bishop had a contract for his book with Random House, which was then still headed by its founder, Bennett Cerf. One day Cerf attended a luncheon where Jacqueline Kennedy was also a guest. In tears, she begged Cerf not to publish the book. Robert Kennedy also let it be known that he was against the project.

Still Bishop persisted. Using the twenty-six volumes of the *Hearings Before the President's Commission on the Assassination of President Kennedy* as the primary source, and gaining numerous interviews, he produced a highly readable account of JFK's assassination.

Even as Bishop was completing his book, however, the cosy relationship that Jackie had with Manchester was falling apart. The conflict had been building all through 1966 as rumors about Manchester's *Death of a President* bounced between Washington and New York. While there was much concern over the harsh manner in which Manchester had dealt with Lyndon Johnson, portraying him as a crude and boorish man, Jackie was primarily upset about the way that Manchester had handled the material she had given him in ten hours of taped interviews.

Before their first session early in 1964, Jackie had only one question for Manchester: "Are you just going to put down all the facts, who ate what for breakfast and all that, or are you going to put yourself in the book, too?"

Manchester replied that he didn't see how he could keep himself out of it.

"Good!" she said emphatically.

She then proceeded to pour out her very soul to Manchester as if he were a father-confessor who could exorcize the tormented obsession with the assassination that was consuming her in those days.

Instead, Manchester, a sensitive and emotional man, seems to have been deeply affected by the heart-wrenching grief and touching intimacies that Jackie candidly revealed to him in their two taping sessions.

She apparently believed he would not write about her feelings and perceptions in quite so direct a fashion. Manchester no doubt saw that the material she had given him was overwhelmingly powerful—the raw clay of which definitive history is made. As a historian, he must have been awed by the responsibility he had to render Jackie's feelings and reactions accurately.

Manchester, in an incredible feat of authorship, completed his 1400 page manuscript early in 1966 and gave it to Harper & Row editor Evan W. Thomas II. Neither Jackie nor Bobby wanted to read it—or at least that was their official statement. They gave copies to five former New Frontiersmen, including two who had become professional journalists: John Siegenthaler, formerly of the Justice Department and now editor of the Nashville *Tennesseean,* and Edwin Guthman, an aide to Bobby who had become national news editor of the Los Angeles *Times.* They felt that Manchester "had used bad judgment and even bad taste in places," and suggested changes. Manchester agreed to the changes, but his health was beginning to suffer from wondering whether the book would ever be published.

At this point—it was July, 1966—Bobby sent him a telegram which said that "members of the Kennedy family will place no obstacle in the way of publication." Not unreasonably, Manchester interpreted the telegram as saying that the book was approved, that

Harper & Row could start setting the manuscript into type, that he could begin negotiations for the magazine rights.

While Jackie was enjoying a seven-week vacation in Hawaii, Manchester engineered a deal with *Look*. They would print excerpts from *Death of a President* in seven consecutive installments. For these exclusive magazine rights, *Look* would pay Manchester $665,000.

Jackie did not like the idea of the *Look* serialization. She did not want the children—especially Caroline, who would be nine years old in November—to be subjected to seven weeks of newspaper and television stories about the book's revelations. Nor did she herself want to be constantly reminded for nearly two months about those devastating days in November, 1963.

And she was astonished at the money Manchester was making. She had been given to believe when she and Bobby had signed their Memorandum of Understanding with Manchester that he would realize no more than $150,000 from subsidiary rights. Jackie felt strongly that no one should make money from Jack Kennedy's death. There was nothing, however, that she could do about the money. *Look* paid Manchester $365,000 in August, the rest to come in five installments ending in 1971.

The waters were further muddied when former Kennedy speechwriter and Peace Corps head Richard Goodwin, who was Manchester's neighbor in Middletown, Connecticut, saw a copy of the *Look* contract. He was startled to see that it did not give the Kennedys final copy approval.

In other words, *Look* was free to excerpt only the more sensational portions of the book. These pages, appearing out of context in a mass circulation magazine, could present a grossly distorted version of the events in Dallas and of the people involved in them.

Goodwin relayed this information to Jackie, who decided it was time, at last, to read the manuscript herself, no matter how painful it might be. In fact, she read it several times. The result of her study was a three-page list of passages that she objected to. She demanded they be cut or substantially rewritten. Bobby met with editors of *Look;* they refused to make any changes.

Manchester and Harper & Row, however, indicated they were anemable to revisions. Late in November, page proofs were sent to Jackie and Bobby. Jackie immediately claimed that the changes and cuts had not been made. The book still contained fifteen pages of her personal reactions. "That's all she has left—her personal life," said a member of her family. "She wants to protect that."

Goodwin tried to work out a final compromise with Manchester, but he seemed impatient with further negotiations. Commenting on Jackie's objections, he said, "I'll go think about them—and talk with my lawyer."

Later, Manchester was quoted in a small Manhattan monthly, *Books,* as saying, "Let's get out the book as I wrote it—and to hell with the Kennedys."

When both Harper & Row and *Look* refused to let Jackie or the Kennedys see the next set of galleys, she decided to sue in order to stop publication. "I have to try," she told friends. "We might lose this, but I have to try. I can't lose all that I've tried to protect for these years. We have to do what is necessary. We have to sue."

She called a news conference at her Park Avenue office and then sent JFK's chief speechwriter Ted Sorenson to appear in her behalf. He read her statement to the reporters who had packed the three small rooms. It said that Manchester's book was "in part both tasteless and distorted." Then she got down to the issues:

"Its inaccurate and unfair references to other individuals [an obvious reference to Lyndon Johnson] in contrast with its generous references to all members of the Kennedy family, are perhaps beyond my prevention; but to expose to all the world at this time all the private grief, personal thoughts, and painful reactions which my children and I endured in those horrible days does not seem to me to be essential to any current historical record . . .

"To the author and publishers this book will only be another transient chapter in their works; but my children and I will have to live with it for the rest of our lives.

"As horrible as a trial will be, it now seems clear that my only redress is to ask the courts to enforce my rights and postpone publication until the minimum limits of my family's privacy can be protected."

She had left them an opening, but Manchester, Harper & Row and *Look* did nothing, hoping that Jackie's statement was a bluff. It wasn't. Two days later, she asked the New York State Supreme Court to stop publication on grounds of breach of contract. Her petition stated, "I have never seen Manchester's manuscript. I have not approved it, nor have I authorized anyone else to approve it for me."

Publication, she said, would not only be a "violation of my rights, but will cause me great and irreparable injury. It will result in precisely the sensationalism and commercialism which we— Robert Kennedy and I—sought so strenuously to avoid. The threatened publication is in total disregard of my rights and, if it goes forward, will utterly destroy them."

According to *Time,* she asked the court for five remedies:

1. That Manchester, *Look*, and Harper & Row be barred from publishing the manuscript until she approved the text and publication date;

2. That they be permanently enjoined from using any of the letters from herself and Caroline that might be in Manchester's possession;

3. That they be prohibited from using material from Manchester's taped interview with her and that they return all the tapes;

4. That *Look* be prevented from using her name in advertisements, as it had been doing;

5. That she be granted punitive and compensatory damages and court costs.

Manchester replied that he had not "broken faith with Mrs. Kennedy" but that subsequent events had left him unable "to feel any sense of joy or even of genuine achievement" over the book. He added that even though he had made substantial changes requested by the Kennedys, "in the last analysis, this is my book. Neither Mrs. Kennedy nor any member of the Kennedy family nor anyone else is in any way responsible for my research or the content of my work. It is my responsibility."

Having dropped her bombshell, Jackie cancelled plans to spend Christmas and New Year's at Sun Valley with Bobby and his family. Relations between Jackie and Bobby were said to be strained. Bobby had told friends that the entire affair was a mess and that he wished he could wash his hands of it. He was surprised that things had gotten so completely out of hand. And, it was further said, he had been completely unable to reason with Jackie. She had, after all, freely given Manchester all the material that she now objected to and was trying to stop in court.

No matter that they had the right to review the final copy. Bobby knew that for Jackie to offer her thoughts and reactions to Manchester at the beginning and then insist on taking them back at the end would strike most people as capricious and unfair.

Instead of skiing with Bobby, Jackie took her children to Antigua, where she stayed in seclusion at a friend's estate. (At least that was the official statement as to her whereabouts. It is difficult not to speculate that when Jackie was out of public view on these various "secluded" estates, she was in fact with Aristotle Onassis aboard the *Christina.*)

In her absence, *Look* had agreed to delete 1600 words—about seven manuscript pages—and Jackie returned to New York on January 8 to the first newspaper accounts of what would be published in *Look* on January 10.

An example of the kind of editing Jackie demanded can be illustrated with a letter she had written to JFK during her cruise on the *Christina* in October, 1963. A West German magazine, *Stern,* had purchased German magazine rights. *Stern's* editors refused to make the cuts that *Look* had agreed to. Legally, of course, they were not required to, and they simply ignored Bobby's demands that they print the final *Look* version.

Jackie's letter read, in part: "I miss you very much—which is nice though it is also a bit sad—but then I think how lucky I am to be able to miss you—I know that I always exaggerate—but I feel sorry for everyone else who is married—I realize here so much that I am having something you can never have—an absence of tension—I wish so much that I could give you that—so I give you every day while I think of you everything I have to give."

By the time the lawyers got through with it, Jackie's warm and affectionate letter to her husband had been boiled down to this: "She told him how much she missed him—of her sorrow that he could not share with her the tension-free atmosphere of the Mediterranean."

Less than a week after *Look's* first installment of *Death of a President*—there would be four, not seven as originally planned—Harper & Row agreed to delete 4200 words. This amounted to about seventeen pages of manuscript copy. Most of their content consisted of the unguarded statements that Jackie had given Manchester as they talked in her Georgetown living room three years earlier. Based on what she had told him, Manchester had written:

"During her three years in the White House, she had learned much about Lyndon Johnson. Their rapport had been excellent, but she knew how skillful he was at manipulating people. She intended to make certain she was not manipulated now [as Air Force One approached Washington from Dallas]. A great deal depended on what the press was told when they landed.

"She sent for [White House Press Secretary Mac] Kilduff and said, 'You make sure, Mac—you go and tell the President—don't let Lyndon Johnson say that I sat with him and Lady Bird and they comforted me all during the trip. You say—you say that I came back here and sat with Jack."

. After this telling passage had been treated with the Kennedy blue pencil, it read like this:

"During her three years in the White House, she had learned much about Lyndon Johnson.

"Their rapport had been excellent, but a great deal depended upon what the press was told when they landed. She sent for Kilduff and said, 'You make sure, Mac—you go and tell them that I was not up front, but that I came back here and sat with Jack.' "

Technically, Jackie had "won" in her battle with Manchester, Harper & Row, and *Look*. But it was a costly victory. The contretemps had dragged on for months. When it was finally over, she was exhausted and had given up hope that she would be able to preserve JFK's memory the way she wanted to. It was an impossible burden. She was somehow expected to live up to an image that had been false to begin with. No one could have had the idyllic marriage that she and JFK supposedly shared—at least in the media during the days of Camelot.

As time went by, more and more people would write about what they knew. In fact, the books were already appearing. Maud Shaw had written about her years as nanny to Caroline and John, Jr. Evelyn Lincoln was planning a book on her twelve years as secretary to JFK. And Paul Fay had written about Jack.

Fay had first known Jack Kennedy in the Navy—they were both PT-boat commanders—and had served as Under Secretary of the Navy during the Kennedy presidency. His memoir of a twenty-one-year relationship with JFK was personal and occasionally irreverent. When Fay completed the manuscript, he showed it to five old Kennedy friends, including former Ambassador to India John Kenneth Galbraith. They all approved. Then he asked Bobby and Jackie to read it. Jackie wanted 30,000 words cut—nearly half the book.

Fay refused. After the book came out, he sent a check for $3,000, a portion of the royalties, to Jackie for the Kennedy Memorial Library to be built in Boston. She angrily refused the donation and returned Fay's check, calling his gesture "hypocritical." "Although she found nothing in the book that was unkind to Jack," Fay said, "I believe that she felt it was an invasion of privacy."

The steady stream of headlines engendered by the Manchester affair and all the books Jack's old friends were writing made Jackie feel vulnerable and exposed. The more she became the official widow of Jack Kennedy, the more their life together seemed to slip away from her. And there had been many, many good moments between them, in spite of the politics, the ambition, Jack's often poor health, and the other women. Her role as Camelot's dowager queen was, in many ways, like a prison. She felt limited and constrained, always expected to live up to the image people had of her as some sort of uncanonized saint. She knew she could not spend the rest of her life fighting these battles on behalf of Jack's memory.

Quite simply, she needed a protector. Jackie began to think seriously about Onassis, who had often hinted that he would propose if he felt she would be receptive to him.

Onassis understood how truly difficult her position was, behind all the glamour and glitter and gossip column gushings. Once, at a cocktail party in Paris, he had told a reporter: "She's a totally misunderstood woman. Perhaps she even misunderstands herself. She's being held up as a model of propriety, constancy and so many of those boring American female virtues. She's now utterly devoid of mystery. She needs a small scandal to bring her alive. A peccadillo, an indiscretion. Something should happen to her to win our fresh compassion. The world loves to pity fallen grandeur."

The Kennedys had known all along that she and Onassis were very close, but they never imagined she would consider marrying him. It did not seem possible that this short, crude, Greek wheeler-dealer, no matter how rich he was, could be considered an appropriate stepfather to the children of President John F. Kennedy.

Months went by. Jackie had not made up her mind what to do. Certainly, if she married Onassis it would be the end of Camelot. She knew that's what everyone would say. In fact, she would be lucky if that was all they said. Whenever her mind started filling up with thoughts like this, she decided, like Scarlett O'Hara, to think about it tomorrow.

Then it was New Year's Day again, the first day of 1968, one of the most painful and chaotic years in American history. Early that year, she discussed her attachment to Onassis with Bobby. He had asked her, if she eventually decided to marry Onassis, to at least put off the wedding until after the November election. She agreed to wait.

But public events only served to increase her uneasiness. She was not a political person. Her response to life was primarily aesthetic. But the long, drawn-out, brutal Vietnam war had managed to impinge itself on her awareness. The Tet offensive had been disastrous for the American forces, and she had heard, via the literary grapevine, that David Halberstam was working on a book in which he blamed the entire Vietnam mess on Jack, Dean Rusk, and Robert McNamara.

You could not turn on the television set without having the war right there in your living room: the shooting, the ghastly flame-throwers, the Vietnamese children, wide-eyed and battered, the wounded young American soldiers with their exhausted faces and blood-stained bandages. And she knew enough about politics to know that Johnson, having announced he would not be a candidate, was powerless. The war was out of control. The men would go right on dying until after the inauguration of the new President in January, 1969.

And yes, she hoped that it would be Bobby. Once she had been telling a friend about the way Bobby had stood by her during those terrible days and months after Jack was killed. "I'd go to hell for him," she said. And she meant it.

Then Martin Luther King, Jr., was killed, and there were riots in black ghettoes all over America. From the windows of her apartment, she could look uptown and see the smoke rising from the burning buildings of Harlem.

For his part, Onassis had made so much money and had outwitted, even destroyed, so many business opponents that there were few challenges left to arouse his interest. His pursuit of Jacqueline Kennedy could totally absorb his prodigious energies. To make her his wife would be a final, triumphant achievement to crown his career. To acquire the world's most celebrated woman—the widow of an American President—was no small thing. Besides, she was elegant and beautiful and could be incredibly charming when she felt like it. In addition to all that, he truly liked her. She was a good match for him: her imperiousness matched his own. She expected to be treated like a queen and she was.

Onassis, fanatically loyal to his family (as is customary in Greece), discussed the marriage with his sister, Artemis. She was enthusiastic about the match. Then Onassis told Lee Radziwill that he was ready to propose to her sister, but he didn't know if Jackie would welcome an offer of marriage from him. He knew, of course, that Lee would immediately call Jackie and give her a complete report on their conversation. When he called Jackie later and invited her for a cruise in the Caribbean on the *Christina* in May, he told her there was something he wanted to discuss with her. She accepted his invitation quite eagerly and he assumed that she would accept his proposal just as readily.

But she didn't. They discussed the possibility of marriage for hours, day after day. She was terribly fond of him, but there were so many obstacles.

She was concerned about religion, her children, and the Kennedys. Onassis was divorced. If she married him, she might well be excommunicated from the Catholic Church. She did not care to have an ecclesiastical scandal in her life. The children were an even graver concern. Caroline was six years old when her father died. She remembered him. Toward Onassis, she was sometimes withdrawn, at other times openly hostile. It was different with John, Jr. He was friendly toward Onassis, as he was toward all his uncles and the men who had been close to the father.

Onassis wooed the children as he had wooed Jackie. Every time he saw them, he had presents and gifts to pass around. But could he play a fatherly role to these two children, one of whom bore the scars of remembering her father's violent death?

Jackie didn't know.

And she did not want to cut herself off from the Kennedys. She owed Bobby an immense debt, and she knew it. More importantly, she *felt* it. And she wanted the children to always feel part of the clan. It was good for children to belong, to have roots like that, to have cousins and aunts and uncles and grandparents they regularly saw. Somehow, if she were going to marry Onassis, she would have to get their approval.

Onassis, for all his former trepidation, was amazed when Jackie did not immediately set a date. (Callas had been badgering him to marry her for years.) She told him that nothing could be done until after the November election. She would not damage Bobby's bid for the presidency. Onassis had no choice but to wait out the election.

And then, unbelievably, tragedy struck the Kennedys once more. On June 5, the night of his victory in the crucial California primary, Robert F. Kennedy was assassinated.

The news of Bobby's death did not shatter Onassis. On the contrary, his reaction to it was selfishly blunt: "It's a tragedy for

America, but for Jackie . . . she's finally free of the Kennedys."

He immediately flew to Los Angeles and found Jackie in a state of profound emotional disorientation. He stayed with her there and accompanied her to Bobby's funeral at St. Patrick's Cathedral in New York.

According to Onassis biographer Frank Brady, "She was in a state of panic and disbelief, occasionally lapsing into dialogue that indicated that she was confusing both assassinations, at one point even temporarily believing that she was still First Lady."

Onassis feared that this latest blow might make her unwilling to go through with the marriage. She could easily become a sort of glamourous hermit, constantly secluded in her New York apartment, her house in New Jersey, or Hyannis Port. But Jackie's reserves of strength pulled her through again. And Onassis was quick to learn that what she craved was not seclusion but escape. Another Onassis biographer, Willi Frischauer, described her feelings after the assassination of her brother-in-law: "Bobby's death filled her cup to the brim leaving no more room for suffering; . . . anger was replacing sorrow and turning her against the violent society which she held responsible for her own bereavement. If America ever had a claim on her after Jack's death, that claim was now forfeited. If she ever had any doubt or obligation to consider the impact of her action on the political prospects of the Kennedys, they were resolved by the shots that ended Bobby's life. For her, escape was the only way out. Jackie was shedding the Kennedy shackles . . . her decision to marry Onassis was made at the grave of Robert F. Kennedy."

A psychiatrist in Boston, the Kennedy home base, substantially agreed with this assessment: "When Bobby was killed, she lost someone who was very close to her. It might have been the crucial factor in her decision to marry Onassis. It would seem that she once again felt acutely alone and unprotected, that her fear of a hostile world was re-ignited, and that she sought a new protector. Running to a land other than her own may also have been an attempt to escape the country that, unfortunately, represented so much pain and sorrow to her."

In July, Onassis visited Hyannis Port. The remaining Kennedys were edgy about the relationship. Rose, especially, was concerned about Onassis having been divorced. But he turned on his considerable charm, began regaling them with one intriguing anecdote after another—many of them bawdy—and soon had won them over.

Onassis had stories to tell from his childhood in Turkey, his emigration to Argentina after the Greeks were driven out of Smyrna, his early days in the tobacco business, and, of course, tales from several decades about his encounters with the great, the near-great, and the would-be great: Winston Churchill, Eva Peron, Princess Grace and Prince Rainier, Greta Garbo, Elizabeth Taylor and Richard Burton.

Later, describing his visit to the Kennedy stronghold, he said, "They're so talkative, they could amost be Greeks."

Finally, Rose decided that it would be all right for Jackie to marry Onassis. In her autobiography, *Times to Remember,* she wrote: "And with contemplation, it seemed to me the first basic fact was that Jackie deserved a full life, a happy future. Jack had been gone for five years, thus she had had plenty of time to think things over. She was not a person who would jump rashly into anything as important as this, so she must have her own good reasons. I decided I ought to put my doubts aside and give Jackie all the emotional support I could in what, I realized, was bound to be a time of stress for her in the weeks and months ahead. When she called I told her to make her plans as she chose to do, and to go ahead with them with my loving good wishes."

The only things that remained to be done were to work out the pre-nuptial contract and to make the plans for the wedding. They still hadn't set a date. Before they did that, Teddy, as the only surviving Kennedy brother and head of the clan, would have to "talk things over" with Onassis, who suggested they meet in Skorpios.

"As I did not expect a dowry," he said, "there was nothing to worry about."

Chapter Five

An Island of One's Own:
Marriage to Onassis

Chapter Five

An Island of One's Own:
Marriage to Onassis

The first thing Teddy did was to try to convince Onassis that the marriage was a mistake. He pointed out that public opinion of the match would undoubtedly be negative and that Onassis would no doubt find it awkward to be stepfather to such young children.

When these arguments brought no reaction, Teddy said, "We love Jackie."

"So do I," Onassis said, a bit annoyed, "and I want her to have a secure and happy future."

Teddy then said that Jackie would lose her $150,000 annual income from her Kennedy trust if she remarried.

Onassis shrugged.

Then they got down to specifics.

In 1972, Christian Cafarakis, a former steward on the *Christina*, claimed in his book, *The Fabulous Onassis*, that Jackie and Ari had signed a 173-clause pre-nuptial contract spelling out, in detail, various financial and connubial matters.

It is extremely doubtful this contract ever existed. Onassis always denied it, no copy of it has ever turned up, and subsequent events would seem to discredit the Cafarakis claim.

This mythical contract, however, received so much attention that it may be worth listing some of its more famous provisions. They may tell us nothing about Jackie and Onassis, but they tell us a great deal about what is at the core of the tabloid mentality: sex and money:

—Jackie gets $3 million outright in tax-free bonds.

—If Onassis ever leaves her, she gets $10 million for each year of their marriage.

—If Jackie leaves him before they've been married five years, she gets $20 million. If she departs after they've been married five years, she gets the $20 million plus an additional yearly allowance of $180,000 for the next ten years.

—If they are still married when Onassis dies, she will receive $100 million.

—If Jackie dies before Onassis, all her property and money would go to Caroline and John, Jr. In addition, Onassis would support them until they are twenty-one years old.

—If Jackie and Ari both die before Jackie's children reach age twenty-one, their guardians would be the Radziwills.

—Jackie gets $5,000 a month *each* to pay for Caroline and John, Jr.'s education, governesses, clothing, medical bills, and pocket money.

—Jackie gets all the costs of her New York apartment and the maintenance of her cars paid by Onassis. These expenses average $10,000 a month.

—Jackie gets all her personal bills paid by Onassis. These would include her hairdressers, masseuses, doctors, manicurists, etc.

—Jackie gets $10,000 a month as a clothing allowance.

—Jackie gets $6,000 a month to pay her staff of personal bodyguards.

—Jackie does not have to bear Onassis a child.

—Jackie and Onassis are to have separate bedrooms.

—Jackie need spend only Catholic holidays and summer vacations with Onassis.

Cafarakis goes on to describe a complicated clause dealing with Jackie's life as a peripatetic jetsetter: "When Jackie doesn't travel on Olympic Airways or in her husband's private plane, she's entitled to purchase six first class tickets, since she insists on the following arrangements: the seat beside her, plus the seats directly in front and in back of her, must always be empty; the two seats across the aisle to her right must always be occupied by the two detectives. This would mean that each time Jackie flew from New York to Athens, for example, on an airline other than Olympic, she would spend a total of $6,996 in first-class round trip tickets."

The actual document that Jackie and Onassis signed was far simpler and considerably less generous to Jackie than the much-publicized Cafarakis version. Onassis required her to give up the rights she would have to share in his estate under the Greek law which obligates a husband to leave at least 12.5 per cent of his wealth to his wife and 37.5 per cent to his children. Thus it was impossible for a Greek to disinherit his family. If he died without a will, the law required that all of his estate be divided by his wife (25 per cent) and children (75 per cent).

In return for giving up her legal right to a minimum of 12.5 per cent of Onassis' estimated assets of $500 million, Jackie received immediately an outright gift of $3 million and $1 million each for her two children. After his death, she would receive $150,000 a year for life.

As the London *Sunday Times* investigative team describes the Onassis-Kennedy financial arrangements in their biography of Onassis: "It was a businesslike agreement, but it did give some indication of Onassis's attitude toward Jackie. He was prepared to protect her financially, meet her considerable expenses, and make sure that in the case of his death she would be significantly better off than when he had married her. But he was not prepared to make her part of his family at the expense of those he considered his rightful heirs."

In spite of this pre-nuptial agreement, which thoroughly protected their interests, both of Onassis' children, Alexander and Christina, made no secret of their contempt, dislike, and possibly even hatred for Jackie, whom they perceived as an interloper and a fortune hunter.

They had felt the same way about Maria Callas. Both children hoped that their father would remarry their mother, Tina Livanos Onassis, who had married an English aristocrat, the Marquess of Blandford, a year after she and Onassis were divorced in 1960. After several years, when that marriage appeared to be in trouble, both children urged their father to settle his differences with her and re-establish the Onassis family. Onassis apparently kept their hopes alive that a reconciliation might one day occur.

Alexander was twenty years old in 1968, a precociously adult young man, which is not to say that he had achieved maturity. He was romantically involved with the Baroness Fiona von Thyssen-Bornemisza, daughter of an English rear admiral and former fashion model. When the liaison between Alexander and Fiona was established late in 1967, she was thirty-five and he was nineteen. Fiona said that for the next five years, she was "his mistress, mother, and priest confessor."

Alexander desperately needed someone to fill these roles for

him because his relations with Onassis were strained, even tor-
tured. Onassis simply overwhelmed the boy. When he didn't do
well at his studies, Onassis put him to work in one of his offices in
Monaco. Alexander dreaded his father's phone calls, and dreaded
even more those occasions when he was summoned to appear in
Athens or Skorpios in person. He had been known to bribe doctors to say he was too ill to make the trip.

Still, Alexander knew that one day he would take over one of
the world's greatest fortunes and a complicated, far-flung shipping
empire. This knowledge gave Alexander a patina of arrogance and
swagger, totally at odds with the frightened and father-dominated
boy he was in his deepest self.

Christina was eighteen when her father announced that he
planned to marry Jackie Kennedy. An indifferent student, she had
attended various expensive boarding schools in New York,
London, and Switzerland. Her upbringing was not conducive to a
feeling of rootedness. Her life had been lived in Athens, Paris,
Monaco, London, and New York.

Onassis treated her like a pet—to be indulged but also to be
brought to heel whenever he thought it appropriate. Above all, she
was not to be independent. Once, without asking him, she bought
herself a color television set. Onassis was enraged, supposedly by
the extravagance. A few weeks earlier, however, he had bought her
an emerald necklace which was worth the television set many times
over.

Christina referred to Jackie as "my father's unhappy compulsion."

News of the impending marriage broke in the Boston *Herald-
Traveler* on October 15, 1968. The story was probably responsible
for advancing the wedding date. Jackie knew that reporters would
have her apartment staked out constantly until there was a formal
announcement. She called Onassis—by then she was back in New
York—and said they should get married quickly. It would have
been more convenient for both of them to marry late in December
when Caroline and John, Jr., would be on vacation from school. As
for Onassis, he was engaged in delicate negotiations with Greek
dictator George Papadopoulos concerning a proposed ten-year,
$400 million industrial development project. Nothing like it had
ever before been attempted in Greece.

Two days after the story was front-paged in Boston, Janet
Auchincloss announced her daughter's impending marriage

through former White House social secretary Nancy Tuckerman, Jackie's old roommate from Miss Porter's.

Ms. Tuckerman's statement was brief: "Mrs. Hugh D. Auchincloss has asked me to tell you that her daughter, Mrs. John F. Kennedy, is planning to marry Mr. Aristotle Onassis sometime next week. No place or date has been set for the moment."

That night Jackie and her children were quickly whisked past the reporters and photographers who were camped outside her Fifth Avenue apartment and taken to John F. Kennedy Airport, along with two of her Kennedy sisters-in-law, Jean Smith and Pat Lawford, Janet and Hugh Auchincloss, and a few other relatives. Ninety passengers were booted off a scheduled Olympic Airways flight to Athens so that Jackie and her entourage could have the privacy they needed for (1) their pre-nuptial festivities or (2) uninterrupted sleep.

Reporters were waiting for Onassis the next morning at the Athens airport. He did not try to avoid them. "I am going to marry her tomorrow or within three days at most," he said grandly. I can't say exactly because I must see and talk to her." They would honeymoon on Skorpios, he added, "unless Jackie wants to make a tour of the Mediterranean on the *Christina*."

Then Onassis begged off answering more questions by saying, "I have so many family problems to settle on my head. Please leave me alone and give me your blessing."

Then he got into a smaller plane and flew to Andravida, some two hundred miles west of Athens, where Jackie's 707 had been diverted in an attempt to avoid reporters. Ari's plane then took them to a nearby military base where a helicopter was waiting to take everyone to Skorpios.

Also making their way to the lavish little island were several hundred reporters and photographers. The closest most of them got was the fishing village of Nidri on the nearby island of Lefkas, where they immediately tried to hire fishing boats to take them across the two miles of Ionian Sea that separated them from one of the biggest stories in years.

It was one of the most unsuccessful invasions in history. In addition to his regular security forces, Onassis had hired two hundred guards for the wedding. And his friends in the Athens junta generously provided Greek naval vessels and helicopters to defend Skorpios.

In spite of these precautions, a small fleet of fishing boats, loaded with journalists, tried to rush the island. A couple of men actually made it, only to be punched and roughed up by Onassis' guards. In order to prevent an ugly and potentially dangerous melee (FOUR REPORTERS SHOT DEAD ON EVE OF JACKIE'S WEDDING was a headline that would not promise the best of luck to the newlyweds) Jackie agreed to a brief news conference—no photographers allowed—and made what she hoped would be such a touching statement that they would all leave her and Ari alone on their wedding day. She said: "We know you understand that even though people may be well-known, they still hold in their hearts the emotions of a simple person for the moments that are the most important of those we know on earth— birth, marriage and death. We wish our wedding to be a private moment in the little chapel among the cypresses of Skorpios with only members of the family present, five of them little children. If you will give us those moments, we will so gladly give you all the cooperation possible for you to take the pictures you need."

The reporters weren't buying it. Finally, after threats and counterthreats, a compromise was reached. A "pool" of four journalists attended the wedding of Mr. Aristotle Onassis and Mrs. Jacqueline Bouvier Kennedy. It began at 5:15 P.M. on October 20, 1968, in the tiny chapel of Panayitsa, the "little virgin."

Only about 25 persons could fit inside the small chapel. In addition to Jackie's children and the people who had flown in from New York with her, attending the wedding were the Radziwills, the Onassis children, his sisters and their husbands, and a handful of his closest friends and business associates, including the inevitable bodyguards.

Jackie wore a two-piece dress of ivory chiffon lace. Designed by Roman dressmaker Valentino, it had long sleeves and a short, pleated skirt. A matching ribbon of ivory silk was in her hair. Ari wore a blue business suit with a white shirt and dark red tie. Caroline stood at Jackie's side with a lighted candle throughout the simple Greek Orthodox ceremony.

Artemis, Onassis's sister, acted as sponsor and placed the traditional wreaths of lemon buds on their heads, exchanging them between the bridal pair three times while the priest chanted the marriage liturgy. Then the rings were placed on their fingers and exchanged three times, and Jackie and Ari first kissed, then drank from a ceremonial goblet of red wine.

The priest, a chaplain at Athens University, chanted the final

words of a Greek wedding: "The servant of God, Aristotle, is wed-
locked to the servant of God, Jacqueline, in the name of the Father,
the Son and the Holy Ghost, Amen."

The priest held out his hands and Jackie and Ari joined him for
the traditional dance of Isaiah: they circled the altar three times
while all the guests showered them with flower petals.

One of the pool reporters was Mario Modiano, the Athens
correspondent of *The Times* of London. His report is worth
quoting because it is probably the best eyewitness account we shall
ever have of this famous and unlikely match.

Modiano said that Jackie looked "drawn and concerned" and
that during the ceremony her "glance kept turning anxiously to
Caroline. The Onassis children seemed grim."

After the ceremony, there was no kiss or embrace by the couple. "Jackie seemed oblivious of her second husband but terribly
aware of Caroline." There was a gentle autumn rain falling when
she left the chapel, not with Ari, "but clinging to John Kennedy's
daughter.

"Showered with flower petals, they headed in the wrong way
and had to be brought back to the open-sided mini jeep. She got
into the front seat and put Caroline on her lap and held her tightly.
Her sister Lee and her own daughter sat in the back with a sullen
John who never smiled, and never lifted his head. Onassis took the
wheel and drove away towards the *Christina* in the harbor one mile
away.

"The quiet wedding was often marred by shouts and screams
from scores of journalists aboard hired fishing boats who were not
allowed to land. A few of them jumped into the sea and were finally
allowed to join—in soaking clothes—the group of tolerated 'pool'
journalists and cameramen flown in by Olympic, who came to be
known as the 'champagne pool.' Otherwise the press was kept out
of the church (an earlier attempt to confine them to another part of
Skorpios while the wedding was taking place, having been defeated
by Alexander who shepherded the pool to chapel in his jeep).
Jackie, who seemed terrified of the photographers, insisted that
there should be no pictures inside the church. Later, aboard the
Christina, they agreed to pose for photographers while the journalistic fishing boats came alongside and there were screams of 'O-
na-sis, O-na-sis' until the ship-owner and his bride agreed to pose
for them, too.

"The pool journalists were invited for pink champagne in the yacht. The couple responded to good wishes with a laconic 'Thank you.' They did not know what their honeymoon plans were. Jackie had a blank look and a fixed smile on her face. The only time she reacted was when AP photographer Jim Pringle introduced himself. She looked startled and said: 'Are you Irish?' and giggled. Then getting impatient with the press, they returned to the drawing room where relatives and friends had gathered. As the reporters glued cameras and noses on the windows, the curtains were drawn abruptly."

It does not appear to have been a totally happy occasion. Alexander's seemingly malicious ploy of personally chauffering the reporters and photographers to the chapel may provide at least a partial explanation for Jackie's "drawn" look. For her soon-to-be stepson to display such open hostility to her at the very moment she was marrying his father must have been incredibly upsetting.

Later, Alexander said, "My father needed a wife but I certainly didn't need a stepmother. ... I do not understand my father's fascination for the Kennedy woman. He's been in love with her for ages. She's beautiful, intelligent and quite formidable, in the best European sense. But she can be so alarmingly exigent. She could undermine everything. She could jeopardize a whole epoch."

The world press reacted as if Jackie had married a man who combined the qualities of Henry VIII, Savanarola, and Nero:

—Sweden's *Stockholm Expressen:* "Jackie, How Could You?"

—Italy's *Il Messagero:* "John Kennedy Dies Today for the Second Time."

—Italy's *La Stampa:* "Jackie, Why?"

—Germany's *Bilt-Zeitung:* "America Has Lost a Saint."

In Paris, *Le Monde* editorialized: "Jackie, whose staunch courage during John's funeral made such an impression, now chooses to shock by marrying a man who could be her father ... and whose career contradicts—rather strongly, to say the least— the liberal spirit that animated President Kennedy."

In Italy, *L'Espresso* commented on the inappropriateness of a marriage between "this grizzled satrap, with his liver-colored skin, thick hair, fleshy nose, the wide horsy grin, who buys an island and then has it removed from all the maps to prevent the landing of castaways; and, on the other hand, an ethereal-looking beauty of 39, renowned for her sophistication and her interest in the fine arts, and a former First Lady at that."

The official Vatican newspaper, *L'Osservatore della Domenica*, said that Jackie was "a public sinner . . . and was therefore barred from receiving the sacraments."

Only in Greece did media and public opinion favor the match. One newspaper, *Acropolis*, declared: "The wedding will bring Greece to the forefront in a manner no one could have dreamed." Some Greeks actually believed that Jackie's arrival on Skorpios would herald the return of democratic parliamentary rule which had been absent from Greece since the military junta had seized control of the government eighteen months earlier.

The reaction in the United States was mostly shock and disappointment, leavened by humor. Comedian Bob Hope cracked, "Richard Nixon has a Greek running mate—now everybody wants one." Former President Dwight Eisenhower observed, "Those Democrats will stoop to anything to get the Greek vote."

Maria Callas, who had not known about the impending marriage until a few days before it occurred, said acidly, "She did well to give a grandfather to her children."

* * * * *

Three days after the wedding, Jackie phoned New York decorator Billy Baldwin and summoned him to Skorpios. She wanted him to decorate the main house: Onassis had given her *carte blanche* to do with it as she liked.

"This house I want to be a total surprise," Ari said. "I trust you and I trust Jackie and I don't want to know anything about it." The only thing he insisted upon was a long sofa in front of the fireplace, "so I can lie and read and nap and watch the flames."

Baldwin found the *Christina* to be "the epitome of vulgarity and bad taste." His stateroom was swathed in pink taffeta. The bathroom was solid pink marble. Still, in spite of the manner in which the room's gaudiness assaulted his fragile sensibilities, Baldwin had to admit that the accommodations on the *Christina* were "fantastically comfortable."

Jackie took Baldwin on walks around Skorpios, and once, when they had climbed to a beautiful clearing in the trees near the highest point on the island, she confided that Onassis planned eventually to build a villa on the spot. "I think he has in mind something like the Trianon at Versailles or some kind of domesticated

Acropolis," Jackie said. "As far as I'm concerned, there will never be a house here."

But in spite of her low opinion of Onassis's taste in architecture, Baldwin felt there was a strong bond between them. One night when she heard Onassis's seaplane approaching, Jackie paused in mid-sentence until she heard the splash of the Piaggio's amphibious landing. "Thank God he's safe," she said.

After Baldwin left, she and Ari went for a brief cruise in the Aegean, and then Jackie flew to London to visit her sister, Lee. Onassis continued his negotiations with the junta concerning the industrial development scheme for several more days (the plans were eventually abandoned by both parties), then flew to Paris where he was photographed having dinner with Maria Callas at Maxim's, thus generating the first rumors of divorce less than a month after the wedding. He then proceeded to England, joining Jackie at Turville Grange, Lee's country house outside London, and promptly caught a cold and took to his bed. Jackie amused herself by taking walks in the woods with Lee's other guests, Rudolf Nureyev and Margot Fonteyn.

Jackie returned to New York alone. Onassis flew to Paris. Except for brief trips to Greece with Caroline and John, Jr., at Christmas and Easter, Jackie spent most of the school year in New York. On weekends she went to her rented country house in New Jersey, and she occasionally visited her Kennedy in-laws in Hyannis Port and Palm Beach.

Onassis was in and out of New York regularly but erratically. They were both seen with other escorts, although Onassis found himself the target of reporters' questions more often than Jackie did. He told one gossip-columnist, "Jackie is a little bird that needs its freedom as well as its security, and she gets them both from me. She can do exactly as she pleases—visit international fashion shows and travel and go out with friends to the theater or anyplace. And I, of course, will do exactly as I please. I never question her and she never questions me."

Because Onassis kept his suite at the Hotel Pierre, the word got around that he and Jackie didn't live together when he was in New York, thus keeping all the rumors of their impending break-up alive.

According to Onassis biographer Frank Brady, Onassis's suite at the Pierre provided substantial tax benefits as well as a convenient place to do business: "If his 'permanent' address were the same as Jackie's, he would have made himself vulnerable to some enormous tax problems, and avoiding taxes was almost a religion to Onassis. It was important, therefore, not only that he disclaim Jackie's apartment as partly his own, it was equally important, for financial reasons, that he not 'live' there. Since he paid not one penny in U.S. taxes, his name could not appear on any leases and therefore arrangements were made for Jackie to be the leaseholder in an apartment atop Onassis's Olympic Towers on Fifth Avenue."

He lived in Jackie's apartment when he was in New York and stayed at the Pierre only when he had business to conduct—he had always been fond of working until 3 or 4 A.M.—or when he went nightclubbing. Jackie didn't enjoy nightlife and went to bed rather early. Rather than disturb her sleep in the middle of night, Onassis would stay at the Pierre.

In the early years of their marriage, Jackie and Ari struck most observers as happy and contented, occasionally even joyous. Ari displayed Jackie like a jewel. Publisher Gardner Cowles remembers Onassis's deference to Jackie at a dinner given in their honor by David Rockefeller. "He was happy to stay in the background," the former publisher of *Look* said. "One had the sense of a man who felt he had accomplished something prodigious and was proud of it."

Ari's pride in her, his frequent and lavish gift-giving, especially of jewelry, and his obvious desire to please her duplicated and, in a sense, re-established the central relationship of Jackie's life. Aristotle Onassis was the kind of flamboyant business success that Jack Bouvier had always wanted to be. In those first years after they were married, Onassis's money provided not only absolute financial security but a very real emotional security as well. Psychologically, Jackie was able to re-create her most intense girlhood experience: the adoration of a father who attempted to guarantee his daughter's love by means of gifts. and other material indulgences.

Jackie plainly thrived on this kind of attention. A friend of Ari's, the wife of a British diplomat, remembers seeing her in Athens. "Jackie doesn't show emotion easily or readily; yet she would lift the curtain now and then, and one could get a quick but revealing glimpse of her real feelings. Once we were lunching at the Grand Bretagne in Athens. . . . She had ordered a salad and yogurt— and she was gushing like a young girl."

In spite of her nearly constant dieting, Jackie was in superb spirits that day—and it was all due to Ari. "He makes me come alive," she confided. "He's so considerate. His constant attention and ingenuity are wonderful. Last Thursday morning, for example, he told me I looked quite pale and needed a bit of a change. He suggested we fly to Paris and have dinner at Maxim's.

"He's always doing things like that," Jackie continued. "He notices things others fail to see. He has such a brilliant mind and can pick up things and completely analyze them and be right."

Jackie paused for a moment and her luncheon companion says she'll never forget the exuberance of Jackie's next statement or the way her eyes shone. "It's a delightful feeling to be in love," Jackie said.

Onassis was equally extravagant in his praise of Jackie. Once he was discussing tides with another fleet operator. Suddenly, Ari blurted out, "Jackie's tides go from high to higher. She always operates on a very high plain—she was the real brains behind Jack Kennedy. A remarkable woman!"

A particularly happy occasion was Jackie's fortieth birthday party late in July, 1969. It came in the middle of a long, relaxed summer, one of the happiest they were to know, their first long stretch of intimacy. Caroline and John, Jr., had ponies, horses, and small boats at their disposal. Ari took the children on long walks around Skorpios. Sometimes they all piled into a runabout and skimmed over to Nidri, two miles away, for a hearty Greek lunch of feta cheese, black olives, and stuffed grape leaves at the little restaurant there.

On Jackie's birthday, July 28, Ari had twelve dozen red roses flown in from Athens. He had wanted orchids, but none were available. He also gave her a diamond necklace, a bracelet, and earrings worth $1 million. That night there was a party on board the *Christina*. Two nights later there was another party at the villa in Glyfada. Among the guests were Christina, two of Onassis's sisters and their husbands, and assorted friends of both Jackie's and Ari's.

At midnight, Onassis announced they were all going to the Neraida, a waterfront bistro on the Saronic Gulf. Off they went in a caravan of black limousines. The Neraida is an open-air *taverna*, more lavish than most such establishments in Greece, and the soft summer night smelled faintly of the calm Aegean gulf, just yards away.

The *bouzouki* players outdid themselves for their famous guests, and Jackie clapped like everyone as the men did the *syrtaki*. They sat close together all evening—or rather, well into the morning. Ari had his arm around her and they whispered together and kissed each other like two high-school kids in the throes of first love. Ari taught her a Greek salute and Jackie stood and toasted first the band and then their guests. It was an exceptionally gay and light-hearted time.

The photographers finally managed to get past the guards at about 5 A.M. But Ari and Jackie were both in a good mood.

"Have you no God?" Ari said, laughing. He offered them champagne and food. "Why do you keep chasing us?"

"Why do you keep running away?" one photographer said, between clicks.

"Ah, but that is my trick," Ari said. "If it was too easy to take our pictures, none of you would have bothered."

But this truce with the *paparazzi* was short-lived. If Jackie thought that Ari's half-billion dollar fortune could buy her the privacy she could not have as JFK's widow, she was very much mistaken. Jackie's life before her marriage to Onassis was like a cloister compared to the media circus it became after they wed. Every move they made was scrutinized, analyzed, dissected, and usually misinterpreted. Every minor marital row was blown completely out of proportion. Ari could complain off-handedly to several friends that Jackie was "always reading," and a day later the comment would be the lead item in three (or more) gossip columns.

Jackie was reported to have used judo on a New York *Daily News* cameraman who tried to photograph her coming out of a theatre that was showing a Swedish sex movie, *I Am Curious (Yellow)*. Bystanders said the photographer in question, loaded with equipment, tripped over himself. Since Jackie weighed about 120 pounds and has never been known to study judo and the photographer weighed close to 200 pounds, it seems reasonable to trust the eyewitness reports.

Besides, had she known judo she would no doubt cheerfully have used it on Ron Gallela, a photographer who virtually lived in front of her apartment waiting for her to come out. Anytime it was announced in the papers that Jackie was expected at the theatre, a museum opening, or a party, Gallela would be waiting for her at the door. Gallela estimates that he earned about $50,000 a year from his photos of Jackie, with or without Ari, in the years after their marriage.

When he started pursuing the children as they were playing or riding their bikes in Central Park, Jackie was so enraged over what she called his "constant surveillance" that she went to court for an injunction that would keep him 200 yards away from her apartment and 100 yards away from herself, no matter where she was. Gallela countersued for $1.3 million in damages for "false arrest, malicious prosecution and interference with my livelihood as a photographer."

When the case finally got to court, Gallela claimed that Jackie was a public figure, "the number one cover girl in the world" and the epitome of "the American dream." Jackie's attorney, former federal judge Simon Rifkind, who had also represented her in the fracas with William Manchester, countered that Gallela had transformed her life from a dream to a nightmare.

Jackie said that she had developed what she called "the Ron Gallela smile" as a form of defense. "I try to keep smiling, to keep my head up . . . because I believe he wants to provoke me into an unusual position."

The lower court found for Jackie, but Gallela appealed and the higher court reduced the distance to twenty-five feet. That meant, in effect, that the photographer had won. In spite of her profound and understandable dislike for him, Gallela has taken some of the loveliest pictures of Jackie in existence. He further parlayed his troubles with her into a best-selling picture book called *Jacqueline* and a lecture tour.

By the time this entire scenario had been played out in the courts, the strains and tensions were beginning to surface in the marriage. Jackie was beginning to discover that Onassis, like her father, would draw the purse strings if he felt slighted. When Simon Rifkind's law firm billed Onassis for their legal services in the Gallela matter, Ari refused to pay. He told a reporter that he had had "nothing to do with the damned thing." So the law firm had to sue to get its money. Jackie was heard to complain that Onassis was "cheap." He was not cheap so much as he was erratic and impulsive. Eventually, he paid the $235,000 legal fee for Jackie's battle with Gallela. "Everyone is happy now," Onassis said.

They never agreed on how to handle the press. Jackie had always wanted any publicity she got to be on her own terms. When she discovered after Jack Kennedy's death that she could not control what was written about her, her contacts with reporters became limited to terse statements issued by a family spokesman. She never gave interviews or answered reporters' questions on the street. She kept the Ron Gallela smile on her face, kept her eyes ahead, kept walking. Her Secret Service guards would shoo away anyone who was too persistent.

Onassis, however, had a childlike fascination with seeing his name in print. When he first established a base in New York in the early 1940's, his name began to turn up in the gossip columns regularly. He freely talked with all the New York columnists as he made the rounds of Manhattan's poshest nightclubs. And when he began visiting Twentieth-Century-Fox head and fellow Greek Spyros Skouras in Hollywood, they started writing about him in the movie colony as well.

This was nothing out of the ordinary. Onassis was seen as just another rich businessman who enjoyed cafe society in New York and the company of starlets in Hollywood. He became much more visible and his uniqueness was emphatically underscored when, in 1953, he bought a controlling interest in the famous Monte Carlo casino in Monaco. The purchase instantly made him famous world-wide as "the man who bought the bank at Monte Carlo." He loved it.

Onassis once told a group of Greek reporters at an Athens hotel, "I always answer the phone, even if I have to get out of my bathroom. I am always accessible to the press. I am not like some people who sit on top of the Himalayas," he concluded with a sly dig at his arch-rival Stavros Niarchos.

The reporters, of course, were well aware that while Onassis might always answer the phone, getting his number in the first place was an impossible task. Journalists generally liked him, however, because, unlike Jackie, if they did manage to corner him, Onassis was friendly and often surprisingly candid. Journalists knew they could always count on him for a few good quotes.

* * * * *

In the beginning, Jackie's spending didn't bother Onassis. He was no doubt proud that he could afford the world's most expensive woman. Early in 1969, shortly after Jackie and the children had returned from a Christmas holiday in Athens, it appeared that she was trying to test the limits of either Ari's income or patience. In the spring, *Women's Wear Daily* dubbed her "the retailer's best friend."

"Jackie O continues to fill her bottomless closets," *WWD* said. "She is making Daddy O's bills bigger than ever with her latest shopping spree. She is buying in carload lots."

It is difficult to get accurate reports on what are essentially private transactions. Some estimates, however, based on interviews with Madison Avenue boutique owners, state that Jackie spent $1.25 million on clothes in the first year of her marriage to Onassis. This astonishing figure is put in perspective, however, when compared to the $5 million in gifts, primarily, jewelry, that Ari presented to Jackie during that first year.

When the stories about her shopping binges began appearing in the papers, reporters tried hard to get Onassis to complain. But his words indicated nothing but pride, generosity, and understanding. "God knows Jackie has had her years of sorrow," he told one writer. "If she enjoys it, let her buy to her heart's content."

On another occasion, chatting with a Paris journalist, Onassis explained, "There is nothing strange in the fact that my wife spends large sums of money. It would be abnormal if she didn't. Think how people would react if Mrs. Onassis wore the same dresses for two years, or went to second-class beauty salons, or rode around in a family-type automobile. They would immediately say that I am on the verge of bankruptcy and that soon my wife will be forced to work to earn a living."

Then he turned sentimental. "If women didn't exist," Ari declared, "all the money in the world would have no meaning." Or perhaps sentiment isn't totally accurate. Onassis' belief that women give meaning to money is reminiscent of one of the theses of nineteenth-century economic philosopher Thorstein Veblen, who maintained that one of the chief functions of rich men's wives was to serve as a vehicle for them to display their wealth. It was a wifely duty that Jackie performed with great diligence.

Onassis, however, gave little attention to his own wardrobe. It was hardly shabby, but it was nothing special, either. Ari had two trademarks: He nearly always wore sunglasses in public, and he never wore a top coat.

In the early 1940's, Ari began wearing sunglasses, even at night, even in dark nightclubs, because he believed that his eyes showed too much about what he was thinking and feeling. He was convinced that a shrewd business opponent could capitalize on this knowledge, so Ari began shielding his too-candid eyes with dark glasses. He would take them off to have his picture taken, but for little else.

His refusal to wear a topcoat, he said, was strictly a matter of thrift. Thrift? That's what the man said: "Since I have a chauffeur-driven limousine, I rarely have to be out in the cold for more than a few seconds. I also go to ten or more nightclubs or restaurants in the course of an average day. Since I am known as a 'rich' person, I feel I have to tip at least $5.00 each time I check my coat. On top of that, I would have to wear a very expensive coat, and it would have to be insured. Added up, without a top coat, I save over $20,000 a year!"

His extravagances went way beyond the latest fashions. He indulged himself with Skorpios and the *Christina*, his very own island stronghold and the world's most sumptuous private yacht.

From the air, Skorpios' four hundred acres take the vague shape of a scorpion, hence its name. In the late 1950's, Onassis had sent his agents all over the waters surrounding Greece looking for a suitable—and totally uninhabited—island. In 1963, they found Skorpios in the Ionian Sea off the western coast of Greece. When Onassis inspected the rocky and barren island, he decided instantly he wanted to buy it. He paid $110,000 and then began turning Skorpios into a sea-surrounded paradise. The transformation cost $3 million and includes reservoirs on the island's uppermost levels. There is no natural water supply and each day the reservoirs are replenished with water brought in by tanker.

After the roadbuilders and landscape architects departed, Skorpios had six miles of roads, and its once bare and wind-swept surface was covered with hundreds of trees—mostly cypresses and pines—shrubs, flowers, and other vegetation imported from all over the world.

The house that Ari constructed in the midst of this freshly created Utopia was a low, rambling fourteen-room villa, constructed primarily of cement on an unusually thick and deep foundation. Because nearby islands had suffered a severe earthquake in the mid-1950's, Onassis had ordered the architects to make the house impregnable to natural disasters.

When Jackie heard about the earthquakes, months after they

were married, she refused to sleep in the house anymore. She slept, instead, on the *Christina*.

Onassis's famous yacht had begun it sea-going life as an unpretentious Canadian frigate, the *Stormont*. After acquiring the ship for $50,000, he spent $4 million converting her into a floating palace. German architect Caesar Pinnau was put in charge of redesigning the ship, and the German shipyard Howaldt-Kiel handled the construction work. Normally, when Onassis had this same shipyard build a tanker for his ever-expanding shipping fleet, he scarcely noticed what they did. All he wanted to know was when the new tanker would be completed so it could start earning money for him. With the *Christina*, however, he fussed over every rivet. The bathroom in the master stateroom was a copy of the one that King Minos had built in his palace in ancient Crete. Ari insisted the marble bathtub be sunk below floor level. Presumably, this was the way King Minos had bathed; this was the way that Aristotle Onassis wanted to bathe. In order to accomplish this, the entire floor of that level of the ship had to be raised.

In addition to Ari's staterooms, there were nine guest suites, each named after a Greek island—Lesbos, Corfu, Ithaca, Rhodes, Andros, Crete, Chios, Santorin, and Mykonos—each composed of living room, bedroom, and bath.

A small hospital was built into the *Christina*, complete with operating room and surgical and X-ray equipment. A doctor was on board for every trip lasting more than a day.

There was an incredible amount of gadgetry on board: air conditioning, an elaborate alarm system that could be triggered by an open porthole (sabotage) or a sudden rise in temperature (fire). The water in the swimming pool was regulated to always remain a few degrees cooler than the current air temperature and the mosaic tile floor of the pool could be raised to deck level to provide a dance floor. There was a forty-line radio-telephone system and the latest in sophisticated radar. It took four diesel generators running around the clock just to keep the *Christina's* infrastructure operating.

After the *Christina* was launched in 1953, Onassis used the elegant yacht to attain and consolidate the sort of world-wide social prestige that had so far somehow eluded him. Taking incredible pains to be a perfect host—the best bread in Paris was flown to the ship every day, vintage wines were stored in its specially cooled "cellars"—Onassis lured on board and entertained Hollywood "royalty": Marlene Dietrich, Douglas Fairbanks, Greta Garbo, Ava Gardner, Cary Grant, Jack Warner, Darryl Zanuck. Then there was the hereditary royalty: ex-King Farouk of Egypt and his latest mistress; the Begum Aga Khan, the Maharani of Baroda; ex-King Peter of Yugoslavia and his wife; Prince Rainier and Princess Grace. There were guests from the world of the arts: Margot Fonteyn, Richard Burton and Elizabeth Taylor, and opera diva Maria Callas.

His most famous and unlikely guest was former British Prime Minister Winston Churchill, considered *the* grand old statesman of the western world. A stranger friendship can scarcely be imagined. What did Churchill, revered for his brilliant and courageous wartime leadership of embattled Britain and a Nobel Prize winner, have in common with Aristotle Onassis, a man who frequently, with great amusement, quite audibly displayed his flatulence in public, a man who had made a huge fortune by methods that were not always consistently ethical, a man who had never been seen reading a book in his life?

The chemistry remains mysterious, but after their first meeting, Churchill described him as "a man of mark." And after their meeting in Monte Carlo in the 1950's, Churchill spent all his vacations cruising with Onassis aboard the *Christina*. Somebody once asked Churchill why he spent so much time with Onassis. He replied, "I go cruising with Mr. Onassis, because nobody else ever asked me."

Including the sailors, maids, stewards, chefs, and bartenders, it took 65 people to run the *Christina* at a cost of a half-million dollars a year. In addition to all of Onassis's various residences and permanent hotel suites, it *does* help to put Jackie's spending in perspective.

Although Onassis would later complain bitterly about Jackie's spending, the first serious strains that developed in the marriage were based on that staple of male-female relationships: jealousy. Like most Levantine men, Onassis thought of women as possessions. His first serious liaison began when he was twenty-eight. For nearly twelve years, beginning in 1934 and continuing almost to the day he married Tina Livanos in 1946, Onassis virtually lived with Ingeborg Dedichen, the daughter of a Scandinavian shipowner.

Once she wore a pair of bright green slacks to a dinner party at the home of Stavros Niarchos. (This was during World War II when all the Greek shipowners were sitting out the hostilities in the United States. Many of them had rented houses on Long Island as both Niarchos and Onassis had done.) Ari felt shamed and humiliated by Ingeborg's outfit and beat her when they got home. The next day he told her, "All Greek husbands, I tell you, all Greek men, without exception, beat their wives. It's good for them. It keeps them in line."

But that beating was nothing compared to his reaction when she made him jealous. Once Ingeborg allowed a Yugoslav shipowner to drive her home from a party that Onassis had not attended. He beat her so badly that he gave the servants the rest of the week off so they wouldn't see her battered face.

Presumably, Onassis had given up beating women by the time he married Jackie. But he had definitely not overcome his tendencies toward jealousy in spite of all his brave statements about giving Jackie her freedom and how they both did what they pleased. If he was away from New York and saw in the papers that she had been escorted somewhere by another man—it didn't matter how old, married, or queer her squire happened to be—Ari would complain vigorously. He frequently quizzed her friends about the men that Jackie had been seen with after JFK's death and before her marriage to him. The topic seemed to cause him real pain.

One of Jackie's friends said, "I thought Ari was a man of the world, but at times he'd act like a jealous, heartsick kid and try to pump me about Lord Harlech or some other men he thought Jackie had once favored."

Where John F. Kennedy was concerned, Onassis put himself in a curious bind. The reason that Jackie had attained the world stature that made her a desirable wife to the celebrity-conscious Onassis was because she was the stylish and elegant widow of a stylish and elegant U.S. President. At the same time, he feared that Jackie had loved JFK more than she loved him. He imagined that Jackie considered JFK her "real husband" whereas he, Ari, was little more than a companion and reliable cornucopia of riches.

The same woman who recalled his quizzing her about Jackie's escorts said that "Ari would pretend to be asking political questions, but it was as if he hoped to trap Jackie into saying that she had preferred JFK to him."

The first blow-up came, however, over several letters that

Jackie had written to Roswell Gilpatric, considered by many to have been a possible marriage prospect in her pre-Onassis days. The letters turned up for sale in February, 1970. Gilpatric said they had been "purloined."

One of them had the *Christina* as its return address and was written within a month—it was dated November 13, 1968—of Jackie's marriage to Onassis. The brief note read:

Dearest Ros—

I would have told you before I left—but then everything happened so much more quickly than I'd planned.

I saw somewhere what you had said and I was very touched—dear Ros—I hope you know all you were and are and will ever be to me.

> With my love,
> Jackie

Onassis was deeply hurt by the publication of these few letters. He viewed them as undeniable evidence of Jackie's deep and possibly even continuing affection for another man.

He retaliated by rather cruelly using Maria Callas to make Jackie jealous. Knowing full well that reporters were always following him in Paris, he spent four consecutive evenings at Maria Callas's apartment on the avenue Georges Mandel. These trysts were naturally written about in the Parisian tabloids.

Still, Ari couldn't be sure that Jackie, back in New York, had gotten the message. He proceeded to invite photographers to shoot him and Callas having dinner at Maxim's. The photo appeared, as he had hoped, in an American newspaper. Jackie saw it and flew immediately to Paris. A few nights later, it was Jackie and Ari who were being photographed at Maxim's. No doubt he felt that he had taught her an important lesson: even before you marry him, never write letters that will humiliate a Greek husband.

Onassis's chief cruelty, however, lay in the brutal manner in which he used Maria Callas. Quite possibly, Onassis led her to believe that he was leaving Jackie and would one day marry her. Four days after Jackie turned up, Callas was admitted to the American Hospital in the Parisian suburb of Neuilly. The official story was that she was suffering from a sinus condition. In fact, she had arrived there in a coma caused by an overdose of barbiturates.

Parts of this unhappy scenario were re-played several months later. Callas was visiting another shipowning family, the Embiricos, on their Aegean island of Tragonisis. Onassis arrived by helicopter with a pair of antique earrings for the singer.

One day when they were both on the beach, Onassis spotted a photographer offshore in a small boat. Knowing they were all equipped with telephoto lenses, Ari passionately kissed Maria. The cameraman happily clicked away. So no one could possibly miss the point of his affection for Callas, Ari then proceeded to kiss her little dog. The shots appeared all over the world.

"I have great respect for Aristotle," Callas said cryptically. "And there is no reason for us not meeting here since Mr. Embiricos is a mutual friend."

Jackie was in New York when she saw them. Once again, she got on a plane and rejoined her husband although she must have been furious at his repeated—and successful—attempts to manipulate her. She must have felt especially degraded by the way *Time* magazine described the incident: "Responding like a dalmation to the fire bell, Jackie flew to Greece, to Onassis, to the yacht *Christina* and to squelch rumors."

It was a complicated situation. Onassis had reached a point in his life where he desperately needed intense affection and loyalty from his children and from Jackie. And yet it appears that the only way he knew to get these things was by antagonizing and provoking them almost beyond endurance.

No one could stand up to him. His children were afraid of his explosive temper, his abusive language when he was angry, and his ability, through his money, to control their lives.

To only a slightly lesser degree, these same factors held true for Jackie. But Onassis's circuitous methods of seeking affection and closeness were especially ineffective with her. She had been brought up to fear and repress strong outbursts of feeling. She had learned to keep her emotions under tight control. Her chain smoking—a standard method of "anchoring" anxiety—is a good example of her emotional repression. Of course, Ari was a chain smoker as well . . . and drank rather more than was good for him, too.

Psychologically, Jackie and Ari appeared to have much in common. The need each had to *acquire*—objects, places, people—gives further evidence of a certain insatiability of character that depth psychology attributes to oral dependence: a need to cling to certain habits and symbols of wealth, security, and status in order to allay unconscious fears of starvation and abandonment.

Their needs may have been similar, but their backgrounds and temperament were vastly different. The ways in which each behaved in order to feel secure often made the other's insecurity that much worse.

Ari's daughter, Christina, was the one who made the first move to get out from under her father's oppressive domination. In 1971, she met Joseph Bolker, a forty-eight-year old California building contractor, while both were sunbathing beside the swimming pool of the Hotel Metropole in Monte Carlo. Divorced and the father of four daughters, Bolker was also such a good listener and so attentive that Christina followed him to California. When he suggested that she should go back to Europe, she became hysterical.

Neither Bolker nor Christina was able to view their situation with detachment or clarity. Neither seemed capable of analyzing the cause of their decidedly strange behavior: at Christina's insistence, they were married on July 29, 1971, in Las Vegas, the day after, as it happens, Jackie's birthday.

Onassis was informed and was beside himself with rage. "He was furious," recalled a guest on Skorpios when the phone call came in. "He did not try to hide his anger. The news exploded like a bomb on the island."

Immediately, Onassis pegged Bolker as a fortune hunter and cut Christina out of the trust that he had established for her and Alexander. Onassis began to imagine that Tina, his first wife and Christina's mother, had somehow engineered the marriage in order to hurt him. And when Tina divorced the Marquess of Blandford and married his old enemy, Stavros Niarchos, Onassis was consumed by a devastating combination of rage, jealousy, and paranoia. He suspected that Tina, wealthy in her own right through her father, Stavros Livanos, had somehow made it financially feasible for Christina to marry Bolker. Onassis managed to have Bolker's phone tapped.

After six months of threats, counter-threats, accusations, and middle-of-the-night phone calls, it was finally becoming clear to Christina and Bolker that the marriage had been ill-advised. They were divorced in May, 1972, less than a year after the wedding.

Shortly before the decree became final, Christina said, "He may soon be just my ex-husband, but he will always be my best friend. I am too Greek and he is too Beverly Hills. That's really the trouble."

Jackie must have been horrified and repelled by the raw and powerful passions that surged in the Onassis clan, frequently merging with equally violent emotions in the Livanos and Niarchos families. It was like something out of Greece's gory and revenge-ridden past. A Sophocles or an Aeschylus was needed to do justice to the monumental disappointments, intrigues, and jealousies that Christina's brief marriage unleashed.

Jackie was very much the awed and frightened outsider. Onassis, unfortunately, interpreted her withdrawal as abandonment in his hour of great need. So Jackie also became a target of his paranoia and essential simplicity. More and more articles and books were appearing in which he was portrayed, directly or by innuendo, as a rich and foolish older man being taken for a ride by a greedy, remote, and much younger wife. He began to believe the stories. Maybe the writers knew something he didn't. Onassis began to discuss the possibility of divorcing Jackie with his son. Alexander, of course, was delighted to hear that his father was finally coming to his senses vis-a-vis "the geisha."

If 1971 was a disastrous year for Ari, it was equally so for Jackie, over and above the effects that Ari's troubles with his family had on her well-being.

Further proof that Skorpios was not the safe retreat she'd imagined it to be came when fourteen nude photos of her appeared in a nine-page layout in an Italian skin magazine. The editor boasted that a team of ten photographers with scuba equipment and waterproof cameras were responsible for the coup.

Such a gross invasion of privacy hardly seems imaginable. Rumor had it that Ari had offered a quarter of a million dollars for the negatives, but he refused to confirm these stories. Instead, when speaking to reporters, he tried to make light of the incident. "I have to take my pants off to put on my bathing suit," Ari said. "Well, so does Jackie."

But no matter how much Ari tried to make light of the incident, it upset him—perhaps as much as it angered Jackie. He was a Greek husband and one of the richest men in the world and, on his own island with his own security staff, he could not protect his wife from harassment. Four guards and two maids, suspected of cooperating with the photographers were fired, but the harm had already been done.

The continuing assaults of the media on Jackie, on Ari, on Skorpios, on the *Christina* and, to a somewhat lesser extent, on Jackie's Fifth Avenue apartment, put increasing strains on their relationship.

In the summer of 1972, Onassis was lunching in a Roman restaurant with Elizabeth Taylor. One of the *paparazzi* rushed forward to get a shot. Onassis threw a drink in his face. The incident made the columns and Jackie, in spite of her own profound dislike, possibly even hatred, of the *paparazzi*, told Ari she was "ashamed" of him. Her stiff upper lip was still in place. Ari, who still felt twinges of the social unease he'd known as a young man, felt stung and belittled.

Later that year, Jackie threw a party at the El Morocco in New York to celebrate their fourth wedding anniversary. Several of Jackie's more observant guests noticed that Onassis seemed exhausted and depressed. The storytelling Ari of former years had vanished. He seemed to be going through the motions of being the guest of honor at his wife's party, but it was obvious his heart wasn't in it.

No one could know he was only a few months away from the most shattering event of his life, the blow from which he would never recover.

* * * * *

Alexander Onassis had loved cars, boats, and planes from his earliest years. His poor eyesight kept him from becoming the commercial pilot he yearned to be, but Ari had given him a small Greek airline to run. Alexander made a success of it. And although he couldn't qualify for the big super jets, he was authorized to fly small planes and to instruct others in their operation.

On Monday, January 22, 1973, Alexander was scheduled to check out a new pilot for his father's seaplane, a Piaggio. The regular pilot was recovering from an eye operation and would be disabled for several months. At about three o'clock that afternoon, the three men—new pilot Donald McCusker, regular pilot Donald McGregor, and Alexander—were waiting to take off from Athens airport. McCusker knew how to handle amphibians but had never flown a Piaggio before. Alexander and McGregor would instruct him in the singularities of the plane during a series of practice landings and take-offs in the Aegean. They never got that far. The plane crashed into its right wing about one hundred feet into take-off and cartwheeled over 150 yards across the field.

Miraculously, McCusker and McGregor, though severely injured, survived. Alexander, however, suffered massive head injuries, and even though neurosurgeons were flown in from London and Boston, nothing could be done. He was placed on life support systems after a three-hour operation, but his brain was dead. About twenty-four hours after the accident, Onassis ordered that as soon as Christina arrived to say "goodbye" to her brother, Alexander should be allowed to die. The plug was pulled late that afternoon. At 6:55 P.M., Alexander's heart stopped.

For several days, Onassis was literally out of his mind with grief. He talked of freezing his son's body until brain surgery was advanced enough to heal him. Back in the villa at Glyfada, he wept constantly and inconsolably. Jackie was there and tried to comfort him, but he turned away from her. He left the house shortly after midnight and wandered the streets in a daze. He was unable to attend Alexander's funeral. His son was buried on Skorpios, outside the little chapel where Ari and Jackie had been married.

Onassis became convinced that Alexander had been murdered by his business enemies—vague and faceless men who had on several occasions taken a shot or two at him. An exhaustive investigation was ordered. The inquiry raised more questions than it answered. Though it was established that important controls had been reversed in the airplane, it appeared to be an unfortunate mechanic's error, not attempted sabotage. But Onassis could never admit that Alexander had died in a true accident. For the rest of his life, he believed that the real cause might yet emerge, the saboteurs and assassins found.

* * * * *

From the day of Alexander's death, the life force relentlessly ebbed from Aristotle Onassis. His grief over Alexander's death was exacerbated by guilt, one of the most destructively convoluted of human emotions. In the months after Alexander died, Onassis decisively turned away from Jackie. Eventually, he would turn *on* her. Alexander had despised her and had urged divorce. Now Onassis, engulfed in hopelessness, must have assuaged the guilt he felt over his frequent abuse of Alexander by blaming Jackie for his estrangement from the boy—who had opposed the marriage from the beginning. Onassis occasionally saw Callas, regretting perhaps that he had not married her when he could have. "The singer" was a violent and passionate person like himself, unlike "the geisha" who had her emotions under such tight rein.

Jackie knew it was an impossible situation, but she did nothing about it except to spend even more time away from him. When she was on Skorpios, primarily in the summer, he usually did not confer with her when inviting people to visit. So she frequently ignored his guests when they arrived.

In desperation, she proposed a trip to Egypt to distract him from brooding about Alexander. He went along, but it was clear his heart wasn't in it. Something in Ari had broken. He didn't want to be distracted anymore.

His increasing alienation from Jackie came to a head in January of 1974. She had suggested they vacation in Acapulco. Since she had honeymooned there with JFK and Ari was well aware of its memories for her, it was not a politic choice for a place to revive an ailing marriage. Then she made matters worse by suggesting they buy a house there. They looked at a number of villas but Onassis would not agree to buy one.

Waiting to board his private plane back to New York, Jackie and Ari began quarreling. It got worse once they were airborne. Finally, he moved away from her, sat by himself, and in an angry, bitter mood began writing out a new will. Although Jackie saw him filling page after page of a yellow legal pad with his careful script, she was unaware that a new will was taking shape.

When Alexander was alive, he had frequently urged his father to use some of his money for philanthropic purposes. But although Onassis was perfectly willing to help friends and relatives on a personal basis, he would never agree to give money away to strangers, no matter how deserving they might be. He would sometimes discuss various good works with Alexander but nothing ever came of it.

His previous reluctance to give to charity, as Alexander had advised, became fresh fuel for Onassis's burgeoning guilt. The first paragraph of the new will set up the "Alexander Onassis Foundation." Its purpose would be to "promote the Nursing, Educational, Literary Works, Religious, Scientific Research, Journalistic and Artistic endeavors."

Onassis did not attempt to cut Jackie out of his new will, nor did he reduce the $150,000 income she would get after his death according to the terms of their pre-marital contract. But he added an interesting provision: what it said, in essence, was that if, after his death, Jackie tried to contest his will, seeking a bigger share of his estate for herself, then his primary heir, Christina, should fight her in court *no matter what the cost.*

Jackie and Christina each got a half-share of Skorpios and the *Christina.* Onassis named his first wife, Tina, executor of the new will.

As the year 1974 wore on, Onassis, already in a weakened condition, was struck a series of devastating blows:

—The people of New Hampshire banded together and refused to let Onassis build an oil refinery on the state's brief stretch of Atlantic coast. Onassis had long wanted his own refinery, and when New Hampshire rejected him, he knew that he would never have one. It was a crushing defeat for a man who had once been one of the world's great wheeler-dealers.

—What he had at first thought was simply a profound exhaustion caused by grief, grew progressively worse. Forced at last to see doctors, whom he deeply mistrusted, Onassis was diagnosed as having myasthenia gravis, an incurable, though treatable, disease characterized by failing muscle control. He had to begin taking massive injections of cortisone in order to arrest the disease's progress.

—In September, Tina was found dead in her Paris hotel suite. Her demise was so sudden that Christina demanded an autopsy, which found that Onassis's first wife and the mother of his children had, indeed, died of natural causes. By this time, Onassis's condition had deteriorated so badly that he was unable to attend her funeral. The following month he was admitted to a New York hospital for intensive cortisone therapy.

Onassis and Jackie were virtually estranged during most of 1974. Occasionally, they would make a public appearance together but, for the most part, the pair went their separate ways. Onassis was obviously failing. He seemed to have aged twenty years almost overnight. The divorce rumors increased.

Jackie waited it out. She could no doubt have sued for divorce and received a much bigger settlement than the one called for in her pre-marital agreement, but she chose not to put the ailing and defeated Onassis through such an ordeal. Nor, it must be said, did she herself relish the thought of going through any sort of public trial, either in America or in Greece.

She had learned years before to take these difficult periods one day at a time. And that is what she did in 1974.

Journalist Liz Smith, who had written a number of perceptive articles on Jackie since her White House days, did a story that summer on the occasion of Jackie's forty-fifth birthday. Smith wrote: "Today she appears serene, sometimes almost tranquilized, as if living out the end of a dream."

It was an amazingly accurate description of Jackie's mental and emotional state. Whether she achieved her "tranquilized" state via Valium or her own incredible willpower hardly matters. As she had been called on to do before, she survived that difficult year intact.

* * * * *

Onassis's bitterness and paranoia reached incredible levels in the last year of his life, and virtually all of it was directed against Jackie, who had become a symbol to him of all the foolish things he had ever done. He complained about her constantly to his family and business associates. He said she was "cold-hearted and shallow." There were also the standard accusations of profligacy. But there was a strange remoteness about it all. Friends perceived that he was increasingly overwhelmed by a devastating sorrow, but found himself inarticulate in his misery. Instead, he would complain about Jackie. It was easier than facing himself.

He even went through the motions of initiating a divorce. According to the Onassis biography written by four London *Times* reporters, "he asked Roy Cohn, a lawyer who had earned a certain notoriety in the fifties as one of Senator Joe McCarthy's investigators, if he would represent Onassis in divorce proceedings. Cohn agreed, and Onassis secured the services of a private investigator. A 'blueprint' for the divorce took shape in the course of a number of meetings at the Onassis offices and at El Morocco."

It is difficult to imagine what Onassis believed his private investigator would come up with.

Helen Vlachos, a gallant Greek newspaper publisher who was imprisoned by the junta, once said of Onassis that he was "the top public relations genius in the world, and he concentrates on one client—himself."

Late in 1974, Onassis, visibly a very sick man, decided to turn public opinion against Jackie. He invited Washington columnist Jack Anderson to New York, took him to lunch at "21" and, amid a stream of inconsequential chatter, dropped several complaints about Jackie's spending. Then, having cast out the bait, he talked of other matters.

Onassis took Anderson back to his office, introduced the columnists to his closest aides, and left the premises. The aides promptly gave Anderson the reason for his day's excursion to New York—which turned out to be detailed stories about Jackie's lavish spending habits. They said that Jackie and Ari's marriage had broken due to "total incompatibility" and that Onassis would soon seek a divorce. They also told Anderson that it was Jackie who had relentlessly pursued Ari—not the other way around.

Onassis's overtures to Jack Anderson were probably his last attempt to manipulate the media for his own ends. In retrospect, the episode appears to be a bitter old man's attempt to humiliate a much younger wife who was once considered proof of his virility and who had never claimed that she was thrifty.

Anderson eventually used the material he got that day, but when it appeared in print, Onassis was already dead.

* * * * *

Late in January, 1975, Onassis was back in Athens, having recently lost Olympic Airways to Greek government control. He came down with what appeared to be the flu and stayed in bed at the Glyfada villa.

Jackie was in New York writing about Cornell Capa's newly opened International Center of Photography. The piece was published in *The New Yorker's* "Talk of the Town" section, and like all reports that appear there, it was unsigned.

In February, she flew to Athens. Onassis's condition was much worse. The flu had become pneumonia and he was having severe abdominal pain from an attack of gallstones. Medical opinion was divided. A French physician said the gallbladder should come out immediately. An American doctor said Onassis's heart was much too weak to withstand major surgery. Finally, it was decided to operate.

Jackie, Christina, and Ari's sister, Artemis, flew with him to Paris, where his gallbladder was removed at the American Hospital on February 10. There were severe complications. In addition to the myasthenia gravis that had weakened his heart, Onassis had developed hepatitis. His lungs were still laboring under the pneumonia. He never regained full consciousness after the operation. He could only breathe with the help of a respirator. He was fed intravenously and given massive doses of antibiotics for both the hepatitis and the pneumonia.

During his brief periods of lucidity, Onassis spoke Greek with Artemis and Christina, making it clear to Jackie that she was very definitely an outsider. Mostly, when he could say a few words, it was to worry about the disposition of his business affairs. Onassis was well aware that he was dying.

Artemis and Christina were openly hostile to Jackie and ignored her presence whenever possible. Christina refused to stay in the Avenue Foch apartment with her and moved into a hotel. A French nurse who helped take care of Onassis reported that Christina sat on one side of the bed, Jackie sat on the other side and "the two women never spoke to each other."

Three weeks after the operation, Onassis's condition had stabilized, although he was still gravely ill. Jackie, concerned about John, Jr., who had only Secret Service men and family servants to supervise his comings and goings, flew back to New York. She also wanted to be in Manhattan for the screening of a film that Caroline had worked on, a documentary about Appalachia.

It's entirely possible that no one informed Jackie, who phoned regularly, that Ari's condition was worsening. Or perhaps Jackie was tired of dealing with the hostility that Christina displayed toward her. Perhaps she could even understand it. Of Christina's immediate family, only Onassis was left. In the last two years, she had lost both her mother and her brother. Whereas Jackie still had her two children, her mother, her sister. If Christina did not want to share her father in his final days, maybe Jackie could sympathize.

In any case, only Christina was at his side when Aristotle Socrates Onassis died on March 15, 1975. The cause of death was listed as "bronchial pneumonia."

Jackie left for Paris immediately. Two days later, along with Christina, Onassis's three sisters, and Teddy Kennedy, she accompanied Onassis's body to Greece. Waiting for them at Skorpios were Jackie's mother, Janet Auchincloss, Caroline, and John, Jr. Onassis had wanted a simple funeral, without a eulogy. The brief service was said in the little chapel on Skorpios where he and Jackie had been married six and one-half years earlier. As on the day of their wedding, a light rain was falling. Ari was buried to the left of the chapel. On the right was the grave of his son.

And it emerged that Onassis was older than he had said. For years, he had given his year of birth as 1906, but the coffin bore a simple brass plaque which read:

ARISTOTLE ONASSIS
1900 − 1975

Jackie's statement to reporters when she had arrived in Paris after his death had been brief, eloquent, and gracious: "Aristotle Onassis rescued me at a moment when my life was engulfed with shadows. He meant a lot to me. He brought me into a world where one could find both happiness and love. We lived through many beautiful experiences together which cannot be forgotten, and for which I will be eternally grateful."

Chapter Six

Alone Again

Chapter Six

Alone Again

Once again, Jackie was a widow.

Press speculation began almost instantly on how much money she would inherit from Onassis's estate. The first stories, based on a rudimentary knowledge of Greek inheritance law, said that Jackie would get between $120 and $200 million, plus the bulk of Onassis's art collection and $15 million trust funds for each of her children.

Several weeks after Onassis's death, the first stories appeared stating that he had planned to divorce Jackie. A week after the New York *Times* gave credence to the reports with a page one account of the imminent divorce which had only been shelved due to Ari's illness, Christina denied that her father had ever intended to divorce Jackie.

Hoping to stop the endless parade of stories about family and her father, Christina prepared a rather lengthy statement about her father's second marriage and released it through the Paris office of Olympic Airways:

"Miss Christina Onassis is very much distressed at the distorted stories and speculations which appeared in the international press about her late father and Mrs. Jacqueline Onassis.

"These stories are totally untrue and she repudiates them. In fact, the marriage of the late Mr. Onassis and Mrs. Jacqueline Onassis was a happy marriage and all rumors of intended divorce are untrue.

"Her own relationship with Mrs. Jacqueline Onassis was always and still is based on mutual friendship and respect and there are no financial or other disputes separating them.

"It is the desire of Miss Christina Onassis and she understands it to be also the desire of Mrs. Jacqueline Onassis that they both be left at peace and all detrimental and harmful speculations cease."

Three days later, both Jackie and Christina attended a special Greek Orthodox memorial service at Ari's grave on Skorpios. Side by side, they were apparently trying to present a more unified appearance than at the funeral: Christina and her aunts had locked hands to keep Jackie from walking immediately behind the coffin in the funeral procession, which is the normal Greek custom. Wire service reports described both Jackie and Christina as "dressed in black and with tears in their eyes."

Then, early in May, Jackie and Christina met secretly in London—or tried to—in order to discuss money. Jackie and Ted Kennedy had, by this time, informed Christina that Jackie would contest the will if she didn't get more than the $150,000 a year the prenuptial contract called for.

Although they couldn't keep the meeting a secret, there was no indication of the specific details they discussed. Nigel Neilson, a spokesman for the Onassis family in London, said that "it is certainly safe to assume that the question of finances was one of the things discussed." Almost as an afterthought, he observed, "There is not a lot of love lost between them."

From London, Jackie flew on to Athens and then left immediately for Skorpios where she supervised the packing and shipping of her clothes, books, and other personal belongings.

No matter what difficulties she and Ari had known in the latter years of their marriage, it must have been painful for her to realize that she would spend no more summers on this idyllic paradise in the Ionian Sea. Even with the occasional presence offshore of the *paparazzi* and their telefoto lenses in their hired fishing boats, Skorpios was an unbelievably beautiful and peaceful place.

Though Onassis had left her a share of the island in his will, Jackie knew that it would be impossible for her to visit in the summer and try to share it with Christina. The Greek servants would be loyal to Christina and not to her. Everyone in Ari's family would make her feel like an outsider, just as they had done at his funeral.

During her last visit to Skorpios, Jackie took many long walks along the shore and along the six miles of roads that Ari had built. The peace and stillness of the place were almost tangible. She would miss Skorpios very much.

* * * * *

On June 5, Caroline was graduated from Concord Academy, a coeducational prep school in Concord, Massachusetts. Caroline chewed bubble gum during the commencement exercises and then lined up for photographers with Jackie, John, Jr., Rose and Ted Kennedy, and Janet Auchincloss.

These were the first news photos of Jackie that had appeared since Onassis's funeral, and the strain she had suffered in the ensuing months was evident. Her famous wraparound smile seemed strained and forced.

Part of the reason for her apparent unease may have been reports that appeared in most newspapers alongside Caroline's graduation story. Christina had announced in Athens that she would spend half of Onassis's fortune on public welfare programs "in accordance with the instructions and wishes of my deceased father." She said the charitable foundation would be set up in Vaduz, Lichtenstein, presumably for tax purposes, but that most of the good works would be done in Greece. (Lichtenstein is a tiny country and tax haven located between Switzerland and Austria.)

Christina's statement was released through a lawyer and made no mention of Jackie. When reporters asked her at Caroline's graduation what she thought of Christina's statement, Jackie cooly ignored them.

Two days later, Onassis's will was published in its entirety. There for the entire world to see were the humiliating financial conditions he had imposed on Jackie.

While it is true that most of us would be able to endure receiving a largely tax-free annual income of a quarter of a million dollars without finding it unduly humiliating, it must be kept in mind that Onassis left a fortune that some estimates put as high as $1 billion. Jackie's minimum legal share of $1 billion under the Greek marriage law in force at the time of their wedding would be $125 million, which, if invested at 8 per cent, would yield an annual income of $10 million, a sum that can support a lifestyle considerably more lavish than a mere $250,000. (In addition to the $150,000, each child got $50,000 yearly until age 21.)

Jackie had a lot at stake, and it was worth fighting for. Christina knew that.

Onassis had wanted to make sure that his pre-nuptial agreement with Jackie would be considered valid and binding should she try to get a minimum widow's share of his estate after his death.

Through his influence with powerful members of the military junta, the Greek Parliament, in the summer of 1974, passed a law which, in effect, recognized the validity of the document in which Jackie gave up her rights under *nomimos mira,* the Greek law which guarantees a widow at least one-eighth of her husband's estate. If the husband makes no written provision, she gets one-fourth.

That is why Onassis said in his will that should Jackie contest the will, win her petition, and the decision not be appealable, she should get one-eighth of Christina's inheritance. Onassis knew that once democratic rule returned to Greece, the special law he had engineered into being to protect his fortune, might be repealed. If it were, he wanted to make sure that Jackie got the minimum allowable under the old *nomimos mira* laws.

In Greece, wills need not be probated and made public as they are in America. In a separate letter that Onassis wrote to Christina, he left it up to her to decide whether its contents should be made public. He ended the letter, which was opened only after his death, with the words, "the last kiss from Daddy."

Judging from the sequence of events in the three months after Onassis's death, Christina probably used the threat of public humiliation to try to force Jackie to accept the will as written.

First, Christina undercut all the "let's you and her fight" scenarios when she said that Jackie and Ari had had a happy marriage, that he had not planned to divorce her, and that she and her stepmother were friends and respected each other. That statement had obviously had no effect on Jackie, who still wanted more money.

Then Christina announced that her father had decided to give half his assets to charity. No mention was made of Jackie—who continued to say she wanted more money. It was, after all, a little late in the day for her to worry about coming across as greedy and grasping. She had the name, she might as well have the game.

Finally, Christina made the will public, an act she need not have taken (and undoubtedly would not have taken) if Jackie had agreed to accept quietly what Onassis had been willing to give her.

Christina was successful in embarrassing Jackie. Friends say she was depressed that summer over its provisions appearing in the papers. But Jackie was definitely not so depressed that she would give up. Her lawyers continued to negotiate with Christina's lawyers, making it clear that a lawsuit was in the offing if Jackie didn't get a better deal.

While the lawyers wrote their letters and made their threats via trans-Atlantic telephone, Jackie quietly moved on to a different sort of life than the one she had been living as Onassis's wife.

Actually, the new life had begun in 1974, during that difficult year of estrangement caused by Ari's deepening guilt and grief over Alexander's death and his own deteriorating health. Jackie's priorities seem to have shifted that year. Maybe she had had enough of the International Super-Rich. Maybe, as an astute politician in her own right, she thought she should do something about the public image that had developed of her as the compulsively extravagant wife of a man who had been characterized once as "a nice gangster." Knowing how ill Ari really was, she also knew that she had best create another way of life, because the one she had known with Onassis would surely vanish with his death.

In October, she and Caroline had driven over to Newark, definitely not one of the garden cities in the Garden State, to see the premiere of *Horace and Fred,* a comedy starring old Kennedy friend and former pro football star Roosevelt Grier whom she greeted when she walked in with a hug and a "Hiya, Rosey." (He had been there the night Bobby Kennedy was killed. They say it took five grown men to keep him off Sirhan Sirhan.)

Grier had wanted the premiere held in Newark because "it is a city that needs help." The premiere was held at a local high school and helped raise money for special inner-city educational programs dear to Rosey's heart. Jackie said she believed in them, too.

In January, just before Ari was stricken with his final illness, Jackie joined the fight to save New York's historic Grand Central Terminal. Penn Central wanted to erect a fifty-nine-story office tower over the site.

Putting in a rare appearance before the television news cameras, Jackie spoke briefly at a luncheon in Grand Central's underground restaurant, the Oyster Bar. "We've all heard that it's too late," she said. "We've been told that it has to happen, but we know that it's not so. Even in the eleventh hour, it's not too late. . . . If we don't care about our past, we cannot hope for our future."

After the luncheon, she went outside the terminal with Bess

Myerson, architect Philip Johnson, who was leading the Grand Central salvation, and then-Congressman Ed Koch. She quite willingly posed for the still photographers who wanted to get her with the station's distinctive facade in the background. They were amazed at the patience of the usually aloof Jackie.

That month she also put down permanent roots in the New Jersey fox-hunting country. She had rented a house there for years and had long planned to buy when the right property came on the market. Now it had—a four-bedroom converted barn in Bernardsville, New Jersey. The rambling, white clapboard house stood on over five acres located at the end of a private, unpaved road. It was further hidden behind high hedges.

Jackie paid $200,000 for the house and land. The deed is in her name only. Immediately, she called—who else?—the decorators and began planning the interiors. The two-story living room would be done in shades of pink and apricot.

Then came the phone call from Athens that told her Ari was seriously ill. With the long ordeal of his death and funeral and the clashes with Christina over money, it was six months before her life got back to normal.

In September, she told Dave Powers, one of JFK's oldest pals, that she planned on "doing things that really matter." As acting curator of the temporarily housed JFK Memorial Library, Powers was guiding her through the storage rooms so she could begin choosing the items from this vast array of memorabilia that would be on permanent display when the library was finally built.

Then she got Caroline outfitted and off to England where the girl spent the 1975-76 school year participating in a special art appreciation course given by Sotheby's, the prestigious London art gallery.

And then Jackie Onassis did something she hadn't done in over twenty-two years. She went to work . . . got herself a job as a "consulting editor" at Viking Press, a distinguished New York publishing house. Its president, Thomas Guinzberg, said that one of Jackie's duties would be to scout for manuscripts among her wide circle of social, political, and international acquaintances.

Nothing she had done since her marriage to Onassis caused such a stir. His death, of course, had generated numerous newspaper and magazine stories on "what will Jackie do now?" No scrap of gossip was too far-fetched to print and it started even before Onassis was in his grave:

—One sleazy tabloid screamed in large black letters on its front page: JACKIE PROMISES ONASSIS: I'LL FREEZE YOUR BODY WHEN YOU ARE DEAD. (This information shared front page space with another revelation of family life: "8-Year-Old Gives Birth to Twin Boys.")

—London columnist William Hickey claimed that Jackie was going to drop Onassis and use the Kennedy name again: "This latest move is motivated by her loyalty to the Kennedy name rather than disloyalty to her memory of Onassis," Hickey declared. "And in practical terms, who can deny that the name Kennedy carries a lot more weight than that of a former Greek tobacco salesman?" One of Jackie's attorneys denied the story and couldn't resist adding that there had been "so much fiction written about Mrs. Onassis in the past month that it is almost impossible to keep up with it."

—According to UPI reports, John C. Carras, about sixty years old and another Greek shipowner, reportedly told friends he planned to begin courting and wanted to marry her.

—Greek film producer Niko Mastorakis offered Jackie $1 million to play herself in a movie about Onassis's last years. When told that Jackie wasn't interested, he offered the part to English actress Julie Christie.

—Germany's biggest newspaper, Hamburg's *Bilt Zeitung,* said that Jackie was in love with Prince Johannes von Thurn und Taxis, a forty-six-year old bachelor worth $211 million who lives in a sixty-four room palace in Regensburg, Bavaria. The principals were appalled. A spokesman for the prince said, "His Highness authorizes his court marshal to deny he is seeking a liaison with Mrs. Onassis. He has known Mrs. Onassis for a long time. The ties are social ties and ties of friendship." The always dependable Nancy Tuckerman sighed wearily and said, "I can assure you there's no truth to the story." (If Nancy Tuckerman had a dollar for every time she's had to repeat those words on Jackie's behalf, she'd be as rich as Jackie . . .)

Obviously, the last thing any of the Jackie-watchers thought she would do was take a job. Her old friend and White House social secretary Letitia Baldridge thought that Jackie needed to work, emotionally if not financially, and suggested Viking, the house that had published her own autobiographical *Diamonds and Diplomats*. "Look, you know Tommy Guinzberg," Tish said to Jackie. "Why don't you talk to him?"

Guinzberg was understandably amazed to find the world's most celebrated woman knocking on his door to ask for a job, but the idea of having Jackie Onassis as a Viking editor had—let's face it—an undeniable *panache*. "One is not unmindful of the range of contacts the lady has," Guinzberg dryly observed.

When she arrived by taxi for her first day's work, the sidewalk in front of the building was covered curb-to-wall with reporters, photographers, and television news crews. Jackie had long since perfected her techniques of making her way through crowds of journalists and simply smiled and continued on to the elevator.

After Guinzberg had shown her around and introduced her to other Viking employees, she sat for a series of here's-our-new-editor portraits by photographer Alfred Eisenstaedt. She even allowed herself to be interviewed. "I expect to be learning the ropes at first," Jackie told a *Newsweek* reporter. "You sit in at editorial conferences, you discuss general things, maybe you're assigned to a special project of your own. Really, I expect to be doing what my employer tells me to do."

The house in New Jersey was ready by this time, and the shelter magazines were besieging her with requests to let them photograph its interior. Harrison Cultra and Georgine Fairholme were the decorators for Jackie's country hideaway. The Cultra-Fairholme team had also done several rooms in her Fifth Avenue apartment—the library and Onassis's bedroom among others—and Onassis had talked Jackie into letting *Vogue* photograph the study, complete with Greek worry beads on the coffee table. But this time, Jackie gave *Newsweek* first photographic crack at her new country digs.

The kitchen was the only room in the house that wasn't refurbished. Why bother? Jackie has never been known to spend much time in the kitchen. On the New Jersey week-ends, she was contented to eat whatever John, Jr.'s governess fixed for her son's meals. John, Jr., was nearly fifteen years old and did not like the idea of having a governess. He wanted to go away to boarding school, but Jackie felt the boy still needed a closer maternal rein. He had stuck his tongue out at bystanders enroute to Skorpios for the Onassis funeral. His behavior had been widely reported, and Jackie had no doubt explained that such antics were not appropriate for the son of a President—or indeed for any well-mannered person. She decided to keep an eye on him herself, and John, Jr., was enrolled in Collegiate, a Manhattan prep school.

The painters had been working on Jackie's New Jersey house so long they began to seem like part of the family. One day, a crew member addressed the boy by the diminutive nickname that President Kennedy had used for his son. John, Jr., didn't like it one bit. "You may call me John," he rather testily told the man, "or you may call me Mr. Kennedy. But you may never call me John-John."

One of the reasons it took over nine months to get the house ready for use was Jackie's usual insistence on getting exactly what she wanted. The foreman of the painting crew claimed he had to repaint one room fifteen times before he achieved the exact shade of blue that Jackie wanted.

Jackie had been able to enjoy the secluded country house for only a few week-ends before she received news of another disaster, one that had brushed her daughter at frighteningly close range.

In London, Caroline was staying with Sir Hugh Fraser, conservative member of Parliament and a longtime friend of the Kennedy family. In recent months, Fraser had been outspoken in his condemnation of Irish Republican Army terrorism.

On the morning of October 23, Sir Hugh and Caroline had finished breakfast and were about to leave Fraser's Campden Hill Square townhouse in Kensington. He would drive her to her classes at Sotheby's and then go on to his own office near Whitehall. Just then the phone rang. It was a fellow member of Parliament calling Sir Hugh. Caroline ran upstairs to her bedroom on a last minute errand.

Seconds later, at 8:53 A.M., came the blast just in front of the house, shattering windows all over the square. When the smoke cleared, they could see that Sir Hugh's car was totally demolished. Unknown terrorists had planted a bomb under a front wheel. Seven persons were injured. Tragically and senselessly killed was Professor Gordon Hamilton Fairley, a cancer specialist and tumor researcher at St. Bartholomew's Hospital. He had been out walking his dog in the square.

Jackie immediately asked British government officials to provide an around-the-clock armed guard for her daughter. They refused, pointing out that Caroline had not been the primary target of the assassination attempt; it was Hugh Fraser they were trying to kill.

A week after the bomb blast, Caroline's London sojourn was causing Jackie distress in other ways. Two London newspapers reported that Jackie, understandably worried that Caroline might be the target of future terrorist plots, had asked the girl to give up her art history studies at Sotheby's and return to New York. Caroline had flatly refused, but it wasn't her passion for Renaissance painting that kept her in London. It was a new boyfriend.

Caroline, nearly eighteen, was dating Mark Shand, the twenty-four-year-old nephew of Lord Ashcombe, a multi-millionaire whose family had developed Belgravia, one of London's most elegant neighborhoods. Caroline had met Mark three years before when they both turned up as house guests of Lee Radziwill's in the West Indies. Then, Caroline had been very much a little girl. Now, Shand was apparently introducing the sheltered Caroline to a free-wheeling way of life she had never known before.

Fashion writers had noticed for years that Jackie had kept Caroline in little-girl puffed-sleeved dresses long after the girl should have been into more grown-up attire. They cattily hinted that the elegant Jackie was trying to retain her own youth by presenting her daughter as more of a child than she really was.

Now Caroline, or so it seemed, was making up for lost time. London's *Daily Mirror* said that Jackie was very upset by the reports she was getting from friends and relatives "that her daughter has been recruited into the swingingest set in London since the 60's." Jackie was said to have "burned up the telephone lines across the Atlantic telling Caroline not to overdo the party going. Her last two calls particularly were lengthy sermons which can be summed up in two words: 'Cool it!' "

Daily Mirror columnist Paul Callan reported that Caroline's sowing of wild oats had resulted in her being late for her classes at Sotheby's three times in the last two weeks.

"An evening has hardly passed without some party—dancing at clubs, late dinners in chic restaurants, not to mention lively country week-ends," Callan wrote. "What worries Mrs. Onassis particularly is that these reports have also reached Caroline's grandmother—the formidable Rose Kennedy—who is pressing her to bring the girl home."

Callan said that Jackie was having a hard time making her case to Caroline because the girl had been reluctant to go to England in the first place. "Her mother's main purpose in sending her away was to separate her from some less-than-desirable friends," Callan claimed.

Well, maybe. But as every woman who has ever gone back to work knows, that is when your children often trot out their most irritating behavior. They want to see if you really *care,* if you're still going to act like a *mother.* Jackie must have passed the test, because Caroline concentrated on her studies and managed to keep herself out of the gossip columns until the following March when Jackie felt obliged to make an impromptu trip to London. It seems that Caroline had announced that she was going to stay there and work as a photographer. Jackie flew over and told Caroline rather forcefully that she was going to Radcliffe as planned and was definitely not going to stay in London. Caroline didn't give in easily— she and Jackie were seen quarrelling in public several times—but finally promised her mother she would abide by her wishes. Caroline's friends, however, said that she was "furious" at her mother's intervention.

But aside from having to deal with Caroline's growing pains, Jackie spent a rather quiet and industrious year. She was deeply involved with her editing chores at Viking. The biggest project was *In the Russian Style,* a lavish art book that Viking was publishing to coincide with an exhibition of the fashions and furniture of Imperial Russia at the Metropolitan Museum of Art.

Late in July, she flew to Moscow and Leningrad to complete research for the book and, with Met director Thomas P. Hoving, to expedite final arrangements for the shipping of over one hundred costumes from the Pushkin and Hermitage museums.

That summer she also put in an hour-long appearance at the Democratic National Convention, which was in the process of nominating Jimmy Carter for the presidency at Manhattan's Madison Square Garden. It had been twenty years since Jackie had attended a Democratic convention. In 1956 she had been in Chicago when Senator John F. Kennedy saw his bid for the vice-presidential nomination derailed by the southern Democrats. In 1960, she had been pregnant with John, Jr., and had stayed in

Hyannis Port while Jack had gone on to glory in Los Angeles.

Accompanying her to the convention which nominated Jimmy Carter was JFK's former press secretary, Pierre Salinger, and Lee Radziwill, who had divorced Stanislaus Radziwill two years earlier.

Shortly after Jackie took her seat in a VIP box overlooking the convention floor, party chairman Robert Strauss introduced her. Wearing a long, black evening gown and smiling radiantly, Jackie stood up and, rather hesitantly, waved to the delegates. They loved it. They gave her an ovation indicating that Camelot was far from forgotten and was, indeed, remembered with much affection.

Another of her book projects at Viking was a Bicentennial-inspired look at American women between 1750 and 1815. *Remember the Ladies* was adorned with two hundred illustrations of colonial women and the lives they led and contained essays by historians Linda Grant DePauw and Conover Hunt. According to the New York *Times Sunday Magazine,* the idea originated with "Muffie" Brandon, the wife of Henry Brandon, Washington bureau chief of London's *Sunday Times.* The Brandons spend their summers in Plymouth, Massachusetts, and Mrs. Brandon had become involved in the restoration of Plymouth's historic houses. One of them had belonged to a woman reputed to be Abigail Adams's best friend.

It occurred to "Muffie" that a good book could be done on the women of Colonial America, and she made an appointment to see Viking president Tom Guinzberg. "When I walked into the meeting I was quite surprised to see Jackie there—she'd only been with Viking for a few days," she recalled. "As I explained the idea, I saw her eyes begin to light up. . . . She caught the idea immediately and for the next two hours she asked the most penetrating questions. She wanted to know what proportion of the text would be devoted to black women—to working women, to Indian women."

Jackie was very much in favor of doing the book and later showed Mrs. Brandon around the Viking offices. "She was so proud, so professional," Muffie said. "It's obvious she's made her peace, that she was born for this. As for what she's been through in the past—well, life is a river and one searches one's way."

Jackie seemed to be making a deliberate effort to change the image that had developed during the years with Onassis—the image of a wildly extravagant compulsive shopper, an ill-tempered petty tyrant. It was alleged that Jackie once demanded that Onassis replace a bottle of perfume a maid had dropped and broken on Skorpios. Onassis had to call an aide in Paris who had to personally buy the perfume and put it on an Olympic Airways flight to Athens. There it was taken to a waiting seaplane and flown to Skorpios. Then Jackie and Ari had a terrible row: she was furious that she had received the medium-size and not the large bottle of Chanel No. 5. "Thank you for the tiny bottle of perfume," she is supposed to have snapped. "What a big trip for such a small present."

Stories like that are hard to shake off, especially when they come wearing the guise of real, honest-to-God backstairs gossip. After all, surely the servants of the rich can tell us what they're really like behind all the glitter. Perhaps. But the servants of the rich, like all employees anywhere, have their own motives. The truth may be incidental to the money to be made in writing a book crammed with juicy details preferably of a sexual or otherwise degrading nature. And if real life proves to be lacking in such events . . . how terribly easy to make them up.

If the subject of the stories-that-never-happened should decide to sue, all the better. When it comes to gossip, a denial almost equals an affirmation.

Jackie wisely never responded to any of the stories about her although, in selected instances that are important to her, she has allowed her friends to speak for her. Jackie, therefore, must have been terribly upset by the way in which she was excluded at Onassis's funeral and by the implication that she was negligent in not having been at his bedside when he died. Her very close friend, Cheray Duchin, has said, "Those lies were started by the Onassis people who always resented the fact that Jackie took over from Callas. Jackie didn't know Ari was going to die suddenly. He had an abscess on his lung that didn't show up on the original X-rays and one night it suddenly broke and he died. What hurt her was that every knife was out to get her afterward. Nobody gave her a chance to grieve because all the nastiness kept pouring out."

By January, 1977—some sixteen months after she began working at Viking—she felt enough in control of the "new Jackie" to attend a small press luncheon in connection with the publication of *In the Russian Style.* (In an unusual departure from regular publishing practices, her name appeared on the book's cover.)

One of the guests was New York *Times* writer Joyce Maynard, who described Jackie's entrance in the Versailles Room of the Carlyle Hotel like this: "Speaking in a soft, almost girlishly hesitant voice about the coldness of the weather, Mrs. Onassis offered a handshake so fragile it seemed almost as if the fingers would melt."

Wearing brown checked slacks and a black cashmere turtleneck sweater, Jackie said that the idea for both the book and the current exhibition of eighteenth- and nineteenth-century Russian fashions at the Metropolitan Museum of Art had originated with former *Vogue* editor Diana Vreeland, now a consultant to the Met's Costume Institute.

Viking president Guinzberg contradicted her. "Jackie wouldn't have allowed her name to go on the book if she hadn't been the prime mover behind it," he said.

When the assembled reporters had polished off their lunch of *fond d'artichaux Carlyle* and were juggling coffee cups, pencils, and notebooks, one of them dared to speculate about whether Jackie had actually performed all the myriad tasks involved in the editing process herself.

Guinzberg was quick to assure the group that Jackie was not "a Hollywood type of star, with a double doing the hard part of the job."

In spite of her own reputation for high living, Jackie said she had no desire to have worn the opulent clothes or lived in the grandiose style of the Russian nobility. "You love to see it, the way you love to see *Gone With the Wind*," she said over dessert. "But wouldn't you rather wear your blue jeans than wander around in a hoop skirt?"

Guinzberg had told all the reporters as they came in that only questions on the book, *In the Russian Style,* would be permitted. In spite of the ban on personal questions, someone asked Jackie if she was planning to attend the Carter inaugural the following week. Her smile froze, her eyes glazed over, and she lit a cigarette. Guinzberg looked unhappy.

How did Caroline and John, Jr., view *In the Russian Style?*

"Rapidly," Jackie said, laughing.

As the luncheon wound down and all the questions that could conceivably have been asked about the book *had* been asked, Jackie grew reflective. "I always wanted to be some kind of writer or newspaper reporter," she said to no one in particular. "But after college—I did other things."

Two months earlier, Hugh D. Auchincloss, Jackie's seventy-nine-year-old stepfather, had died at his home in Georgetown. The funeral service was held at historic Trinity Church in Newport, Rhode Island, where George Washington had once worshiped. Jackie, along with Caroline, John, Jr., and Lee Radziwill attended the service, held only four days after the thirteenth anniversary of John F. Kennedy's assassination.

The following July, Janet Auchincloss reluctantly put Hammersmith Farm, where Jackie had spent so many happy summers, up for sale. The asking price was $985,000. "All my children hate the idea, and I hate it, but it is absolutely necessary," Janet said. "Jacqueline told me, 'I don't want you to sell it.' "

Auchincloss had sporadically made efforts to sell the farm as far back as 1971 because of the sharply increasing maintenance costs. Hammersmith Farm is adjacent to Fort Adams State Park and Rhode Island had made efforts to buy the farm for its appraisal value of $1,297,000 under an arrangement in which the Federal Bureau of Outdoor Recreation would have donated half the money and the family would have donated the other half to the state, in exchange for a substantial federal tax reduction.

When this deal foundered in Washington's bureaucratic maze, Janet had no choice but to make the farm available to any qualified buyer. Her own income had been sharply reduced after her husband's death—there were many heirs—and she simply couldn't afford to keep the farm going. There were fifty-eight acres to tend, plus the thirty-two-room main house with its elegant entrance hall and eighteen bedrooms, as well as eight smaller buildings including a converted windmill with several bedrooms that Jackie was especially fond of.

It was here, at Hammersmith Farm, that the reception was held when Jackie and JFK had been married in 1953. And Jackie had often returned to the lush farm for visits in the hectic years that followed that breezy September day when she and Jack had cut their wedding cake. She and Caroline had been there the week-end before Janet had announced that the farm was for sale.

A few months after her mother's straitened circumstances were made public, Jackie's fortunes improved considerably. She and Christina Onassis had at last come to terms. To get Jackie permanently out of her life, Christina had been willing to pay somewhere between $20 and $34 million.

The final settlement between Jackie and her Greek stepdaughter was probably negotiated as much as a year earlier—at about the time it was widely reported that Jackie had relinquished her shares in Skorpios and the *Christina* to Onassis's daughter for about $8 million.

The New York *Times* said the settlement was for $20 million, Associated Press said it was $21 million and United Press International said the figure was $26 million. Nobody seemed to know whether these figures included the $8 million that Jackie supposedly got for her shares in the Onassis island and yacht.

After eighteen months of haggling following Ari's funeral, Stelios Papadimitrious, Christina's attorney, told her that she would have to fight Jackie in court unless she agreed to honor her stepmother's claims on the Onassis estate. Christina finally agreed to transfer the money—certainly a minimum of $20 million and probably in cash—to Jackie.

People close to Christina say that she was willing to meet Jackie's demands—which Jackie adamantly refused to lessen—because the young heiress did not want to face a court battle that would keep them connected for years. And if Jackie had gone to court and won, she could conceivably have ended up with much more money than the $20 million she was apparently willing to settle for.

Christina was also concerned about the legal consequences if Jackie should marry again. She worried that if the question of Jackie's share of the inheritance wasn't irrevocably settled, a new husband might somehow aid her in getting a bigger chunk of Onassis money. This last fear seems groundless, even a bit paranoid, but Christina had suffered some rough times after her father's death. They had left her shaken and nervous, had perhaps even affected her judgment.

Her second marriage to Alexandros Andreadis, heir to another Greek fortune, had failed, and since her divorce, she had gained weight and tended to spend most of her free time alone, dividing her time among Monaco, Athens, and Skorpios, with an occasional month or two in New York.

Neither Jackie nor Christina would comment on the exact terms or specific amounts of the settlement.

A month later, Jackie was making headlines again, this time over a book Viking had published that dealt with a fictional assassination attempt on her brother-in-law Ted Kennedy. *Shall We Tell the President?* was written by Englishman Jeffry Archer, a former member of Parliament who had resigned after a $1 million bank business deal went awry. The novel is thematically similar to Frederick Forsyth's *Day of the Jackal,* which dealt with a plot to assassinate General de Gaulle. In Archer's futuristic spin-off, the plot to murder Teddy, who has been elected U.S. President in 1980, is hatched by another Senator and his cohorts. The FBI discovers the plot and quashes it. Teddy, like de Gaulle in the Forsyth novel, knows nothing of his would-be killers' plans and is a peripheral character in the story's telling.

Viking president Tom Guinzberg bought the American rights to the Archer book, originally published in England, in the spring of 1977. Viking insiders say that Jackie knew about the manuscript all along and was "the soul of reason" when she first heard about it.

The question of Jackie's role, if any, in the book's publication came up after New York *Times* reviewer John Leonard ended a negative review of *Shall We Tell the President?* with this paragraph: "There is a word for such a book. The word is trash. Anybody associated with its publication should be ashamed of herself."

Jackie was "extremely upset" by Leonard's implication that she had played a part in the book's publication. Through Nancy Tuckerman, she said she "was never consulted on the matter. Her arrangement as a consultant-editor at Viking does not give her veto power over books purchased by other Viking editors."

In the meantime, the enterprising Boston *Globe* reported that Tom Guinzberg said Jackie "didn't indicate any distress or anger when I told her we bought the book in England several months ago." He added that Jackie had "a feeling of resignation that people will go on using this bleak material.

"I know it's going to bring out more crazies," Guinzberg admitted, "but if we hadn't published it, someone else would have." (In fact, Archer's novel had been turned down by several large publishing houses before Guinzberg bought it for Viking.)

Claiming "the Kennedys are good friends of mine," Guinzberg said that Viking would handle the book more tastefully and sensitively than other publishers. (Kennedy brother-in-law, Stephen Smith, however, had told Guinzberg he thought publication of Archer's novel "an act of venal commerce and in basic bad taste.")

However they were intended, Guinzberg's remarks upset Jackie even further. On Thursday, October 13, 1977, she sent a letter of resignation, written in longhand, to Guinzberg. Her public statement, read to reporters by Nancy Tuckerman, was brief: "Last spring, when told of the book, I tried to separate my lives as a Viking employee and a Kennedy relative. But this fall, when it was suggested that I had had something to do with acquiring the book and that I was not distressed by its publication, I felt I had to resign."

Guinzberg, who seemed especially stung by the fact that Jackie had not even phoned him to discuss the matter, issued his own statement the following day:

"After being friends for more than half our lives, I more than ever deeply regret Mrs. Onassis' decision to resign from the Viking Press without a personal discussion of the incident which resulted in her decision.

"My own affection for the Kennedy family and the extremely effective and valued contribution which Mrs. Onassis has made to Viking over the past two years would obviously have been an overriding factor in the final decision to publish any particular book which might cause her further anguish. . .

"Indeed, it is precisely because of the generous and understanding response of Mrs. Onassis at the time we discussed this book and before the contract was signed which gave me confidence to proceed with the novel's publication."

Guinzberg also had harsh words for *Times* reviewer John Leonard, whose curiously snide barb at the end of his review had launched the entire mess. Guinzberg referred to "the grossly unfair imputation in the New York *Times* connecting Mrs. Onassis with the publication of *Shall We Tell the President?* which precipitated this unfortunate affair."

Leonard backed off slightly by saying that he had been "partially" referring to Jackie, whom he felt "should have objected" to Archer's book. "She could have stopped its publication if she wanted to," Leonard declared. Then he rather coyly added that publishing world insiders might well believe that his reference to "her" could have meant Deborah Schabert Owen, an American literary agent who is married to David Owen, British Foreign

Minister. Ms. Owen sold the book to Viking and also negotiated sale of the paperback rights to Fawcett Publications for $500,000 and movie rights to David Niven, Jr., for $250,000.

A spokesman for the subject of this controversial affair, Senator Ted Kennedy, said that the lone surviving Kennedy son and brother had "flipped through the book" but had nothing to say about it.

The "Viking affair" shares a number of obvious similarities to the 1967 Manchester affair, Jackie's first contretemps with the world of publishing. Just as Jackie herself had freely given Manchester the material that she later objected to, she also had known about the Archer book from the time that Viking was considering it. If she had found the book objectionable and was unable to convince Guinzberg not to publish it, then surely she should have resigned then—in the spring of 1977.

Had she quietly departed, she would not have taken the chance that her ill-timed blast could give Archer's book a publicity boost that could turn it into a bestseller. (Actually, even with all the attention resulting from her resignation, *Shall We Tell the President?* was neither exciting enough nor well written enough to attain bestsellerdom. So much for the alleged value of publicity—any publicity—in selling books.)

Nancy Tuckerman said Jackie had been upset when she learned Viking had acquired the book, but did not feel she should interfere with its publication. When they first discussed the matter, Guinzberg advised Jackie not to read *Shall We Tell the President?*, fearing it would be a terribly distressing experience for her. As with the Manchester work on JFK's assassination, Jackie was willing to take drastic personal action over a book she claimed not to have read.

Both Guinzberg and Jackie are presumably intelligent, sophisticated people and should have anticipated at least a few snide cracks from New York columnists and professional Jackie-watchers. And yet they obviously had not worked out a statement for use in the very likely event that one or both of them should be criticized for the subject matter of *Shall We Tell the President?* Such lack of foresight is difficult to explain.

As is so often the case, it probably boils down to personalities. Guinzberg is a man who publishing associates say has considerable trouble in articulating his needs and concerns. From his statement to the press when Jackie resigned, it appears that he is saying he would not have published Archer's book if Jackie had objected. Jackie obviously felt that she had been *told* about Viking's buying the book, not *asked* her opinion about *whether* Viking *should* buy the book.

Her reluctance to make an issue of the matter can best be understood in the light of her efforts to transcend her past as John Kennedy's widow. She had found it difficult to create a solid life for herself after JFK's death. It was one of the reasons she had married Onassis, a move that had not, in the final analysis, proved to be a satisfactory solution.

The horror of that eternal instant when her husband was shot dead beside her in the warm Texas sun is a horror that can never be totally erased no matter how hard she tries. And her decision not to interfere with the Archer book is evidence that she would very much like to put those years behind her. She has carried them around for a long time now. And she must also have wanted to avoid another Manchester affair, knowing how severely she was criticized at the time. Now, after all the years with Onassis, her image was no longer that of the devastated young widow. She was a seasoned in-fighter who could not use her vulnerability as a shield.

But when it began to appear that people might think she actually had something to do with acquiring the wretched book, when Guinzberg himself told reporters that she had not been upset by it, all of her barely suppressed feelings about the assassination exploded. She just wanted out—and there was no point in calling Guinzberg to tell him so because the whole thing at Viking was ruined now, simply could not be put back together and he should have thought of her feelings before he talked to that reporter in Boston.

* * * * *

Speculation began immediately on what Jackie would do next. In the meantime, she continued living her everyday Manhattan life, which is much quieter than the gossip columnists would have us believe. Jackie does not go to cocktail parties, discotheques, or other crowded scenes of Manhattan's so-called high life. She spends most evenings in the Fifth Avenue apartment where she has lived since 1964. Wearing blue jeans and a T-shirt, she sits in the spacious green, gold, and yellow living room watching television with John, Jr., or helping him with his homework.

Occasionally, she invites a few friends—no more than eight—to dinner. Sometimes she herself attends a more ambitious affair. Shortly after her resignation from Viking, she attended a dinner party given by Lally Weymouth, daughter of Washington *Post* publisher Katherine Graham. It was a very glitzy affair, lots of Manhattan-type literary celebrities were on hand, including tiresomely heterosexual author Norman Mailer and tiresomely homosexual writer Gore Vidal. After dinner, Mailer, for reasons not entirely clear, punched Vidal in the face. (Vidal may have called Mailer an "aging socialist;" Mailer may have called Vidal an "aging faggot.")

Jackie appears to have played a part in this bit of madness. Mailer, who is not the most stable of men, sat next to her at dinner. And throughout the meal, Jackie drew him out, encouraging him to talk about a favorite macho subject: boxing. Jackie has long had the ability to virtually magnetize people in the spotlight of her attention.

Louis Auchincloss, a cousin by marriage, says that "when she talks to you she fixes those eyes on you, and you feel as though you're the only person she's interested in or cares about. Then, when she turns to talk to someone else, it's as though you've dropped off the planet."

Either Mailer was jangled from having been dropped off the planet, or else Jackie inadvertently (one hopes) got him all roiled up with boxing fantasies. Because after talking to her, Mailer was unable to control his own well-advertised aggressions. Close at hand was Gore Vidal, who publishes books far more often than Mailer and provides a perfect foil for Mailer.

Jackie's interest in boxing, by the way, was perfectly real and honest. For some months she had been seeing writer and journalist Pete Hamill who had a novel coming out soon about a prizefighter and his incestuous relationship with his still-young and attractive mother.

Hamill's publisher was Doubleday, the company which had published Rose Kennedy's memoirs, *Times to Remember,* in 1974. Doubleday's president, John T. Sergeant, was a long-time friend and occasional escort of Jackie's. Tish Baldridge had also joined

Doubleday as an author, having recently agreed to revise Amy Vanderbilt's etiquette book. And for the last eighteen months, Nancy Tuckerman had been working in the offices of Doubleday as assistant to publisher and vice-president Samuel Vaughn.

So it was not exactly unexpected in publishing circles when Doubleday announced that Jackie was becoming an associate editor there. Her new job appeared to be a better deal than the one she left behind. As a consulting editor at Viking her pay had been about $10,000; as an associate editor at Doubleday, she would make between $15,000 and $20,000.

Happily, she did not really need the money . . . a circumstance that always makes working more enjoyable.

* * * * *

As she approaches her fiftieth birthday, Jacqueline Lee Bouvier Kennedy Onassis seems to be living a female version of the life her father always wanted but never quite achieved. After two successful (if not wildly happy) marriages, she is at last a rich woman. She is famous and celebrated to a degree that few women (or men) in history have achieved. She can pick and choose her escorts (and lovers, if she wants any) from among dozens of men who are eager to be at her side. Her address is one of the best in New York. Located just a few blocks from the East 74th Street apartment where her father lived from his 1940 divorce to his death in 1957, Jackie's apartment, with its windows overlooking Central Park and the afternoon sun, is a far different place from Jack Bouvier's cramped and sunless bachelor digs. There is an easel set up at one of those windows. Jackie still likes to occasionally get out her oils or watercolors and paint what she sees—or thinks about—when she looks out over the park.

On sunny days, she walks in the park or rides her bike with Caroline and John, Jr. Her children seem attached to her in the close, easy way that Jack Bouvier was never quite able to manage with her and Lee. And now she even has a job in one of the "glamour" industries: publishing.

Even though she has been a chain-smoker all her life, she is jogging, along with a great many other New Yorkers, around the Central Park reservoir. If her looks are any indication of her health, she is fairly bursting with vitality and well-being. She hardly seems to have grown older since that much-photographed year of 1960 when Jack Kennedy made his long-anticipated bid for the presidency and won it. The ensuing eighteen years have refined her features, rather than aged them. Even under the harsh lights of photographers, her skin looks like porcelain, translucent and lit from within.

Inside this carapace of celebrity and beauty, Jackie does a great many very ordinary things: the photographers rarely follow her to New Jersey. She can ride her horses, read her books and joke with her children and her nieces and nephews in a setting not dissimilar to Lasata, the Bouvier menage on Long Island where she spent so many of her own girlhood summers.

The many improbable and often ridiculous stories that have appeared about her, along with the harassment of Ron Gallela and others like him, means that her friends take a great deal of care to protect her. And not just her friends look out for Jackie. Recently, she attended the preview of a new musical, "The Best Little Whorehouse in Texas."

When photographers closed in on Jackie and her companion, investment banker Ship Stein, other playgoers quickly came to her defense.

"Throw the photographers out," a dozen people were yelling at once.

"Leave Jackie and her boyfriend alone!" one woman said angrily.

How could Jackie, a woman of such privilege, come across to this crowd of sophisticated New York playgoers as a woman in need of protection? But hasn't Jackie always been a mass of contradictions? It's one of the chief reasons why she's so interesting.

She is very much a private person and yet she enjoys her fame, managing it deftly, skillfully turning it to her own ends. Instinctively, she has followed much of the advice that the Mexican sorcerer, Don Juan, gave to his apprentice, Carlos Castaneda:

—A warrior is never accessible.

—A warrior is never available: do not exhaust yourself or others.

—A warrior lives her life strategically.

—No one can push her.

—No one can make her do anything against her better judgment.

—A warrior does not feel sorry for herself.

—A warrior puts herself in total control and performs all the acts she deems necessary.

And in this regard, she departs rather radically from her father's example. Jack Bouvier doesn't appear to have done many of the things that a warrior must.

Perhaps Jackie's biggest contradiction is this: she is, above everything else, a survivor. She is also fragile. Ironically, it has been the fragility that necessitated the development of her considerable skills as a survivor.

And where does it come from, this ability to survive tragedy, this knowledge that, as Gerald and Sara Murphy put it, "Living well is the best revenge."

Much is made of Jackie's French Provencal heritage. Why has no one noticed that Jackie has more Irish genes than French? Janet Lee Bouvier Auchincloss, Jackie's mother, was descended a few generations back from Irish immigrants on both her father and mother's side.

During their sojourn in America, the Bouviers, on the other hand, often married persons who were not of French descent. So Black Jack did not give his daughters an undiluted Midi heritage. But Janet was Irish through and through, which means that Jackie is half Irish, maybe more. It explains a lot, including her love for Jack Kennedy, her continuing and warm affection for her Kennedy in-laws and even her attraction for Pete Hamill, an Irish kid from Brooklyn, who was once involved for years with another Irish lady named Shirley MacLaine.

Jackie's Irishness also explains her stubborn streak, her temper, her persistence, and her courage.

A Tammany Hall politician of Irish descent was once asked how he had amassed his rather substantial fortune with no other apparent source of income than his modest City Hall job. George Washington Plunkitt's answer remains a model of accuracy and candor:

"I seen my opportunities and I took 'em."

So did Jackie.

Chapter Seven

The Price of the Pedestal

Chapter Seven

The Price of the Pedestal

Detonated by the Watergate explosion, the floodgates of scandal have burst open in Washington, D.C., and other arenas of public life. The public has learned what the FBI and the Washington press corps knew all along: that behind the campaign speeches and the pending legislation, many of our lawmakers have private lives that are unsavory, shabby, and degrading.

Certainty on the topic of bedroom behavior is not easy to attain. Nearly everyone has something to gain by either maximizing or minimizing reality. Who should one believe—the former mistress turned "author" with a book to sell or the faithful retainers who say there's nothing to it, the disgraceful stories are all a pack of lies.

The truth lies somewhere in between, its exact location not yet pinpointed.

Whatever pain Jack's infidelity caused Jackie during their marriage has surely increased an incalculable amount now that at least one of his extra-curricular women claims to have told, with the help of writer Ovid Demaris, her "story." Judith Exner was a professional party girl who was "dating" Frank Sinatra and Chicago mob leader Sam Giancana at the same time that she was visiting Jack Kennedy in the White House. He subsequently broke all ties with her after he learned of her connection with Giancana.

Exner's is an ugly story of rich and powerful men passing silly and stupid young women around as if they were a box of Kleenex. It is also an ugly story of a young woman who obviously hopes to use well-placed beds to advance herself.

Nobody emerges from this tale with any merit. The best that can be said about Jack Kennedy—and it isn't much—is that women like Exner were virtually a commodity to him and not really existing on the same plane as his wife and daughter, mother and

203

sisters. Kennedy was brought up in an era and in a religion in which there were good girls and bad girls. You married the first and used the second.

After Exner, it was only a matter of time before journalists started using all the stories they'd been sitting on for so long, until writers started checking out all the gossip that buzzed around Washington during the late 1950's and early 1960's.

Washington *Post* columnist Maxine Cheshire has written about Jack Kennedy trying, with the help of Senator George Smathers of Florida, to lure actress Sophia Loren to his bedroom. Loren was already secretly married to Carlo Ponti, spoke only a few words of English, and just plain wasn't interested in going off for a midnight tete-a-tete with Kennedy, whose idea of a seduction ploy was to have Smathers tell her that he was going to be the next president of the United States.

Loren appears to have been one of the few women to turn down a JFK proposition. Jack, like his father, was always attracted to Hollywood actresses and showgirl types. He continued collecting them even after he was in the White House.

Cheshire says that members of the White House staff, out of loyalty and kindness, went to great lengths to keep Jackie from finding out the full extent of Jack's behavior. Cheshire's statement calls to mind a strange little episode that appears in Mary Barelli Gallagher's account of her years as Jackie's personal secretary. It is mid-December, 1962, and Jackie is leaving with the children to spend the Christmas holidays at Palm Beach. She puts her arms around Mary Gallagher and wishes her and her family a Merry Christmas. Then Gallagher notices that Jackie has tears in her eyes. "You know," Jackie confides, "you're my only friend in this impersonal White House. What would I ever do without you? Jack has Ted Reardon, Evelyn Lincoln, and the others. . . . But you work so hard upstairs in that office—always messy with my clothes. . . ."

Her loneliness, even across the space of sixteen years, seems almost palpable.

When each First Lady leaves the White House, the chief usher gives her the daily log book which lists every person who has visited the family quarters during her and her husband's tenure there. Cheshire says that when Jackie left, the book was given, instead, to Bobby. The Kennedys claim it has disappeared but Cheshire isn't sure it really has.

"Unless Bobby personally got around to destroying it, I believe someone has it and is holding on to it as their old age insurance," the Kentucky-born columnist declares.

No doubt increasingly explicit bedroom stories about JFK will find their way into print in the years to come. Some of them will be true, some of them won't, and it will be difficult to know the difference.

Washington writer Kitty Kelly has interviewed aging playboy and former Senator George Smathers, who purports to give the lowdown on his one-time fellow swinger, Jack Kennedy: "There's no question about the fact that Jack had the most active libido of any man I've ever known. He was really unbelievable . . . absolutely incredible in that regard, and he got more so the longer he was married. I remember one night he was making it with a famous movie star and, by God, if Jackie almost didn't catch him in the act."

The behavior that Smathers credits to Jack's libido, however, quite possibly has a rather less exciting explanation. In 1947, Jack Kennedy learned he was suffering from Addison's disease, a condition characterized by a failure of the vital adrenal glands. As Joan and Clay Blair, Jr., demonstrate in *The Search for JFK*, there was a massive cover-up of the fact that Kennedy had this illness, but their research leaves no doubt that he was diagnosed as having Addison's disease in 1947 and took drugs—primarily cortisone—to control it for the rest of his life.

One of the symptoms of Addison's disease is fatigue and exhaustion, which is one of the reasons that Jack took a nap every day after lunch while he was in the White House. And one of the side-effects of cortisone treatment is a marked increase of sexual desire along with an "increased sense of well-being approaching a state of euphoria accompanied by a real increase of energy, concentrating power, muscular strength and endurance." There is also a "marked improvement in appetite and an increased feeling of warmth in the skin."

The carefully manicured Kennedy family image of good health and "vigah" based on touch football, sailing, and skiing was grossly inaccurate as far as Jack was concerned. The fact is that he had never in his life enjoyed good health. As the Blairs document in their book on JFK's young manhood, "his health, almost from birth, was disastrously poor. He was born with an unstable back which progressively deteriorated throughout his life, necessitating first a brace or "corset" and later, two spinal operations. . . . Throughout his childhood and especially during the period 1935-1947, he was tormented by an almost continual series of illnesses, most of which we are unable to identify because the medical records are still closed."

The almost constant pain in his back—*not* an aphrodisiac—in opposition with the drug-induced increase in his sex drive along with the conflicted emotional inheritance that Jack received from his philandering and domineering father, Joe Kennedy, gives a sad, even pitiable aura to the stories of his frenetic sexual activity.

Many persons have noticed a sudden surge of sexual desire after an exposure to death and suffering or after a close brush with death or injury—after, for example, narrowly avoiding an auto accident. Jack Kennedy had been frail since birth and close to death on several occasions, *not* including the PT boat experience. More than most of us, perhaps, JFK needed sex to blunt his awareness of death.

If writers and journalists are determined to dig out the truth and nothing but the truth about Jack Kennedy, they seem equally determined to keep Jackie hidden behind a scrim of myth, fantasy, and plain wishful thinking.

Jackie first turned up as a barely disguised fictional character in Jacqueline Susann's novel, *Dolores,* which purports to tell the story of a well-dressed woman, widow of a Catholic President, who marries a shipping magnate.

In the Susann version of Jackie's life, she is Dolores Cortez, daughter of an aristocratic family that has fallen on hard times. She is beautiful, and she also has a beautiful younger sister. Dolores is a whiz with languages and works as a United Nations translator before she lucks out and marries into the rich and powerful Ryan family.

The Ryans may have money, but they can't touch Dolores when it comes to style and class. In case this difference should ever leave their minds for a moment, Dolores continually underscores her true worth by such tactics as bringing her own pate and cucumber sandwiches to the Cape Cod beach picnics where her in-laws are happily munching their hot dogs.

Later, after the assassination of her husband, Dolores marries Baron Erik de Savornee, a man with "vast holdings in the Near and Middle East" who bears an astonishing resemblance to you-know-who.

Jackie and Ari provided material for a virtual sub-genre of the pop novel. French writer Pierre Rey wrote about them in *The Greek* and *The Widow.* Nicholas Gage includes an Onassis character in his *The Bourlotas Fortune* and Sidney Sheldon's *The Other Side of Midnight* has a character and an island which are obviously Onassis and Skorpios. Later, Sheldon's novel became a dazzingly vulgar movie.

Far more vulgar, for example, than *The Greek Tycoon,* which began filming in the early summer, 1977, and opened in New York in May, 1978. Behind *The Greek Tycoon* was Niko Mastorakis, a Greek television producer who once sneaked aboard the *Christina* disguised as a *Bouzouki* musician. Anthony Quinn played Onassis and Jacqueline Bisset played Jackie. The drawings for the newspapers ads fudged a bit, making the two actors, especially Bisset, look more like their real-life counterparts than they actually did. The ads were the most creative part of the whole project:

"SHE WAS THE MOST FAMOUS WOMAN IN THE WORLD.
"HE WAS A PEASANT, A PIRATE, A SHARK.
"WHAT HE COULDN'T BUY WITH MONEY HE STOLE WITH CHARM."

The Greek Tycoon could have been a marvelous piece of jet-set junk—a kind of *Zorba the Greek* with money and servants. Alas, it was merely dull and trite, leaving one with not even bad taste on a grand scale to marvel at and feel superior to, an important function of the very best trash.

The story, surely apocryphal, is told that a young editor at Doubleday ran into his colleague, Mrs. Onassis, in the hall several weeks after the movie opened. He said he'd seen *The Greek Tycoon* over the week-end. The look on Jackie's face hinted that a *faux pas* of staggering proportions had just been committed.

Resourcefully, the young man recouped: "You were very . . . dull in it."

Aristotle Onassis always got the deference the rich always get from most of the people they deal with. He was never idolized in the way that Jack and Jacqueline Kennedy were. During their White House years, the two of them were courted by the media in a way that no American President and his wife had ever before achieved.

After JFK's assassination, Jackie, as the gallant young widow, was embued with a madonna-quality by her public. There was the unstated but clearly felt belief that history itself had put her on a pedestal. And she was left to deal with that uncomfortable and ultimately impossible position as best she could.

Her solution to the untenable role of permanent political widow was to marry Aristotle Onassis. And as we have seen, the marriage turned both their lives into a media circus, focusing public attention on their every move with a laser like intensity.

Now that her second rich and powerful husband is dead, Jackie is quietly going about her life in Manhattan. Publicly, she ignores the continuous stream of speculation, reportage, and gossip about her even though it has taken a rather disconcerting turn. Some of the things now being written and filmed about Jackie have a crude, bludgeoning quality about them—the revelations about JFK's sex life and her reactions to his infidelities and *The Greek Tycoon* being examples of this new, destructive spirit.

It's as if the people who create our media fantasies, having put her on an impossible pedestal of public adulation, interest, and attention now feel compelled to somehow degrade her. This, they perhaps imagine, will prove effective in getting behind that radiant, but impersonal, smile . . . that cool aloofness that rarely makes a public utterance.

So far it hasn't worked. When *The Greek Tycoon* opened, Jackie was on a brief trip to Israel. The first week in June found her at the all-too-familiar Arlington National Cemetery in Washington, D.C. She was there with her Kennedy in-laws to attend a memorial mass on the tenth anniversary of Bobby's death.

Several weeks later, as *The Greek Tycoon* was about to close in Manhattan, Jackie attended a Newport Jazz Festival concert and went to a Sixth Avenue saloon afterwards for a hamburger in the company of *Daily News* columnists Pete Hamill and Jimmy Breslin.

Just trying to live an ordinary life.

Ordinary.

CHAPTER ONE: "Daddy's Girl," pages 13-42

Page

14   "A man with a great sense of style . . .": John H. Davis, *The Bouviers: Portrait of an American Family* (New York: Farrar, Straus and Giroux, 1969) 212.

16   "Have you ever glimpsed . . .": quoted in Mary Van Rensselaer Thayer, *Jacqueline Bouvier Kennedy* (New York: Doubleday, 1961) 10.

19   "Those were terribly silly . . .": Ibid., 27.

     "Little Jackie Bouvier will not . . .": Ibid., 12.

20   "My nurse is lost.": Ibid., 16.

     "How can you say . . .": Ibid., 16.

21   "Living with their mother . . .": Davis, op.cit., 243-44.

23   "Dear Jacqueline: What in one . . .": Thayer, op.cit., 29.

24   "I just know no one . . .": Ibid., 63.

     "Everybody ordered steaks . . .": Ibid., 66.

     "During the winter of 1948 . . .": Davis, op.cit., 301.

26   "We really saw . . .": Thayer, op.cit., 81.

27   "No, thanks . . .": Susan Sheehan, "The Happy Jackie, The Sad Jackie, The Bad Jackie, The Good Jackie." *New York Times Magazine* (May 31, 1970).

28   "I began to feel . . .": Thayer, op.cit., 60.

     "I always love it . . .": Ibid., 60.

29   The Arthur Krock-Frank Waldrop anecdote: Ibid., 83-84.

     Pat Nixon's reply to the Inquiring Camera Girl: Washington *Times-Herald* (November, 1952).

30   "You behave yourself . . .": Thayer, op.cit., 87.

31   Jackie's reaction to Kennedy's presidential ambitions: Davis, op.cit., 307.

41   "They were very much alike . . .": "Jackie," *Time*, January 20, 1961.

42   Story of Jackie's call to her Aunt Maude: Thayer, op.cit., 92.

CHAPTER TWO: "Marriage to Senator Kennedy," pages 45-62

Page
47   "Carrere does not remember . . .": Davis, op.cit., 311.

48   "Since Jack is such a . . .": George Carpozi, Jr., *The Hidden Life of Jacqueline Kennedy* (New York: Pyramid Books, 1967) 17.

"American history is for men.": Thayer, op.cit., 106.

"You ought to write . . .": "Jackie," *Time*, January 20, 1961.

49   *"You can't take it . . ."*: Ibid.

"the only one who really knew . . .": quoted in Carpozi, op.cit., 25.

Description of Jack Kennedy's health drawn from: Joan and Clay Blair, Jr., *The Search for JFK* (New York: Berkley Medallion Books, 1976) 589-608.

52   "She's not feeling too well . . .": Carpozi, op.cit., 34.

53   "In all the years . . .": Richard J. Whalen, *The Founding Father* (New York: New American Library, 1964) 442.

54   "I've been in the news enough.": Carpozi, op.cit., 36.

55   "Joe is said to have . . .": Ibid., 39.

"he had to do something . . .": Ibid., 39.

57   "I want everything to look . . .": Davis, op.cit., 316.

"It's the most exciting life . . .": Carpozi, op.cit., 43.

58   "Not many people know . . .": Ibid., 41.

"She is simply . . .": Ibid., 40.

"I don't think she's . . .": Ibid., 42.

"more interested in what Byron . . .": Ibid., 42.

"My husband likes . . .": Ibid., 46.

"I'm so sick . . .": Marianne Means, "The New White House Hostess," New York *Journal-American* (November 27, 1960).

59   "Every summer, my husband's parents . . .": Carpozi, op.cit., 46.

"It's the only way . . .": Ibid., 44.

"I wouldn't say ...": Ibid., 43.

60   "It's a good thing...": Ibid., 45.

"I feel I should ...": Ibid., 45.

61   "serve as a source ...": Ibid., 50.

"He said a long time ago ...": Ibid., 50.

62   "Now my wife and I ...": quoted by numerous newspapers and magazines and carried live on national television, November 9, 1960.

CHAPTER THREE: "The White House Years," pages 65-110

Page

65   "When somebody cuts Jack ...": "Jackie," *Time*, January 20, 1961.

"As a wife, I'm happy ...": David Wise, "Mrs. Kennedy, Spectacular Woman, Cultured, Beautiful," New York *Herald Tribune* (October 2, 1960).

66   "My major effort...": Ruth Montgomery, "How Jackie Raises White House Children," New York *Journal-American* (June 25, 1961).

"As long as the father ...": Ibid.

"It was so crowded ...": Mary Van Rensselaer Thayer, *Jacqueline Kennedy: The White House Years* (Boston: Little, Brown and Company, 1971) 11.

67   "I think you can understand ...": Ibid., 26.

"The dress is a full-length ...": Ibid., 26.

68   "I am determined ...": "Jackie," *Time*, January 20, 1961.

"When Jacqueline Bouvier Kennedy ...": Martha Weinman, "First Ladies, in Fashion, Too?" *New York Times Magazine*, September 11, 1960.

"Oh, I will ...": Thayer, op.cit., 21.

"What I need are ...": Ibid., 22.

69   "Mrs. Kennedy realizes ...": Ibid., 23.

"What difference could ...": Ibid., 24.

70 "Am I going to . . .": Carpozi, op.cit., 54.

"I had come straight . . .": Thayer, op.cit., 8.

71 Rose Kennedy at Palm Beach anecdote: Mary Barelli Gallagher, *My Life with Jacqueline Kennedy* (New York: David McKay Co., 1969) 76.

72 "I don't know why . . .": Thayer, op.cit., 67.

"if it gets in the newspapers . . .": Gallagher, op.cit., 79.

73 The Harry Truman visit: Gallagher, op.cit., 54, and Thayer, op.cit., 58.

75 "I had heard it in bits . . .": Thayer, op.cit., 75.

"Jack, you were so wonderful.": Ibid., 75.

76 "When it was time . . .": Ibid., 85.

"A Caesarean is major surgery.": Ibid., 44.

"it was probably easier . . .": Davis, op.cit., 327.

77 "I just crumpled . . .": Thayer, op.cit., 94.

78 "I think a wife's happiness . . .": Carpozi, op.cit., 65.

"A man marries a woman . . .": Ibid., 62.

"What husband wants . . .": Ibid., 62.

79 "The only furniture . . .": Thayer, op.cit., 101.

"When we had lived . . .": Ibid., 36.

Jackie having her room repainted: Gallagher, op.cit., 117.

80 "I always loved . . .": Thayer, op.cit., 281.

"Without him on the committee . . .": Ibid., 283.

"Everything in the White House . . .": Ibid., 281.

81 "She's enthralled and engrossed . . .": Carpozi, op.cit., 60.

"I do not think it . . .": Ibid., 73.

82 "Fresh from her triumphs . . .": quoted in Ibid., 74.

83 "It was just an informal affair. . .": Ibid., 77.

85 "Since some discussion . . .": Thayer, op.cit., 207.

86 "she possessed a mysterious authority . . .": Davis, op.cit., 298.

"Nixon says we're having a baby.": Carpozi, op.cit., 88.

Salinger update on India-Pakistan trip: Ibid., 94-95.

88   "Through a wise provision . . .": Gallagher, op.cit., 145.

90   Account of the state dinner for Andre Malraux: Thayer, op.cit., 183-84.

"I think this is the most extraordinary . . .": Ibid., 184.

91   "It is one of the finest male portraits . . .": Ibid., 338.

92   "Mrs. Kennedy's reception . . .": quoted in Carpozi, op.cit., 105.

Other details of Jackie's trip to India and Pakistan: Joan Braden, "An Exclusive Chat with Jackie Kennedy," *Saturday Evening Post* (May 12, 1962).

95   "most Bouviers who saw . . .": Davis, op.cit., 352.

96   "How could you fill his life?": "Jackie," *Time*, January 20, 1961.

97   "Her total expenditures . . .": Gallagher, op.cit., 223.

99   "This baby mustn't be born dead,": Ibid., 285.

101   "The ship will go . . .": Frank Brady, *Onassis: An Extravagant Life* (Englewood Cliffs, New Jersey: Prentice-Hall, Inc., 1977) 163.

102   FDR, Jr., as 1968 presidential candidate: Benjamin C. Bradlee, *Conversations with Kennedy* (New York: W.W. Norton, 1975) 227.

Jack's use of Jackie's guilt feelings: Ibid., 220.

103   Mrs. Connally's comment to JFK: *The Torch Is Passed* (compiled by The Associated Press, 1964) 11.

104   "I want them to see . . .": quoted in Carpozi, op.cit., 192.

"He didn't even have . . .": Ibid., 141.

106   "I want to take . . .": *The Torch Is Passed*, op.cit., 81.

107   "Rose Kennedy dined upstairs . . .": William Manchester, *Death of a President* (New York: Harper & Row, 1967) 555.

108   "There came then the strangest . . .": *The Torch Is Passed*, op.cit., 93.

109   "I had expected her to look . . .": Davis, op.cit., 362.

CHAPTER FOUR: "Building a New Life," pages 113-139

Page

113   "Michel was deeply moved . . .": Ibid., 364.

"to ease her loneliness . . .": Kenneth P. O'Donnell and
David F. Powers with Joe McCarthy, *Johnny, We
Hardly Knew Ye* (Boston: Little, Brown and Company,
1972) 452 (Pocket Book edition).

114   "The sad thing . . .": John G. Mitchell, "The Lonely
Year of Jackie Kennedy," New York *Journal-American*
(November 24, 1964).

115   "We certainly have rotten luck,": Carpozi, op.cit., 168.

"I was looking this way . . .": quoted in Ibid., 191-92.

117   "I know from my talks . . .": quoted in Ibid., 183.

120   "It is nearly a year . . .": Jacqueline Kennedy, "Memoir,"
Look (November 17, 1964).

121   "It's just a teeny, tiny dance . . .": T. F. James, "The
Bouviers," *This Week* (July 11, 1965).

122   "Why don't we make these rumors . . .": Maxine Cheshire
with John Greenya, *Maxine Cheshire, Reporter* (New
York: Houghton Mifflin, 1978) 36.

"shocked and saddened . . .": Carpozi, op.cit., 204.

"All my nieces and nephews . . .": Liz Smith, "Jackie
Comes Off Her Pedestal," New York *World-Journal-
Telegram* (January 10, 1967).

"For five years, . . .": Fred Sparks, *The $20,000,000
Honeymoon: Jackie and Ari's First Year* (New York:
Bernard Geis Associates, 1970) 19.

123   "When Jackie wants to go out . . .": Ibid., 21.

"very married, very old . . .": Ibid., 21.

124   "They're just good friends . . .": Carpozi, op.cit., 216.

"It is a great honor, . . .": Ibid., 218.

"It is a sad . . .": Liz Smith, op.cit.

"Our family has known . . .": Carpozi, op.cit., 219.

125   "On behalf of Mrs. Kennedy, . . .": Ibid., 219.

126 "alive and vital.": Bradlee, op.cit., 219.

"George and Helen were used to . . .": Christian Cafarakis, *The Fabulous Onassis* (New York: William Morrow, 1972) 126 (Pocket Book edition).

128 Account of Jackie's attempt to prevent Jim Bishop from
writing about the assassination: Jim Bishop, *The Day
Kennedy Was Shot* (New York: Funk and Wagnalls,
1968) pp. xi-xviii (Bantam Books edition), and "The
Presidency: Battle of the Book," *Time* (December
23, 1966).

129 Jackie's conversation with Manchester: William Manchester, op.cit., in Foreword, p. ix.

Account of "the Manchester affair" drawn primarily
from: *Time*, December 23, 1966, op.cit.

131 Examples of deletions in Manchester book: Carpozi, op.
cit., 231-34.

134 "Although she found nothing . . .": Ibid., 230.

135 "She's a totally misunderstood woman . . .": quoted in
Brady, op.cit., 165.

136 "I'd go to hell for him, . . .": Ibid., 170.

137 "It's a tragedy for America . . .": Ibid., 172.

138 "She was in a state of panic . . .": Ibid., 173.

"Bobby's death filled her cup . . .": Willi Frischauer,
Jackie (London: Michael Joseph, 1976).

"When Bobby was killed . . .": Lester David and Jhan
Robbins, "To Jackie, Ari was a stout defense against
a hostile world," New York *Daily News* (January 27,
1976).

139 "They're so talkative . . .": David and Robbins, "Why
Jackie Married Ari Onassis," New York *Daily News*
(January 25, 1976).

"And with contemplation . . .": Rose Kennedy, *Times
to Remember* (New York: Doubleday, 1974) 523
(Bantam Books edition).

"As I did not expect . . .": Nicholas Fraser, Philip Jacobson, Mark Ottaway, and Lewis Chester, *Aristotle*

Onassis (Philadelphia and New York: J.B. Lippincott, 1977) 250.

CHAPTER FIVE: "An Island of One's Own: Marriage to Onassis," pages 143-174

Page
143   The "We love Jackie" anecdote: Ibid., 252.

Details of marriage contract: Cafarakis, op.cit., 129-32.

145   "It was a businesslike agreement.": Fraser, et al., op.cit., 252.

"his mistress, mother, . . .": Ibid., 323.

146   "my father's unhappy compulsion . . .": Brady, op.cit., 185.

147   "Mrs. Hugh D. Auchincloss has asked me . . .": quoted in Fraser, et al., op.cit., 255.

"I am going to marry her . . .": Ibid., 259.

148   "We know you understand.": quoted in Brady, op.cit., 180.

Description of the Onassis-Kennedy wedding drawn from: *The London Times* (October 21, 1968).

150   "My father needed a wife . . .": Brady, op.cit., 185.

Public reaction to Onassis-Kennedy wedding: Fraser, et al., op.cit., 256-58.

151   Account of Baldwin's visit to Skorpios: Billy Baldwin, *Billy Baldwin Remembers* (New York: Harcourt Brace Jovanovich, 1974) 113-21.

152   "Jackie is a little bird . . .": Brady, op.cit., 190.

153   "If his 'permanent' address . . .": Ibid., 196.

"He was happy to stay in the background.": Fraser, et al., op.cit., 306.

Jackie's conversation with wife of British diplomat: David and Robbins, op.cit., New York *Daily News* (January 27, 1976).

154   Ari's conversation with fleet operator: Ibid.

       Account of Jackie's fortieth birthday party: Brady, op. cit., 193, and Fraser, et al., op.cit., 309-10.

155   Account of "the Gallela affair": Fraser, et al., op.cit., 311-13.

157   "I always answer the phone.": Fraser, et al., op.cit., 232.

158   "the retailer's best friend.": quoted in Ibid., 307.

       Onassis reaction to Jackie's spending: Ibid., 308.

159   "Since I have a chauffeur-driven limousine . . .": Brady, op.cit., 69.

161   "I go cruising with Mr. Onassis . . .": Brady, op.cit., 138.

162   "All Greek husbands, . . .": Brady, op.cit., 61.

       "I thought Ari was a man of the world . . .": David and Robbins, "She makes all the other nude ladies look like bags of bones," New York *Daily News* (January 28, 1976).

       "Ari would pretend . . .": Ibid.

163   "Dearest Ros": New York *Daily News* (January 10, 1970).

164   "I have great respect for . . .": Fraser, et al., op.cit., 311.

       "Responding like a dalmation": quoted in Ibid., 311.

165   "He was furious, . . .": Fraser, et al., op.cit., 317.

       "He may soon be just . . .": Ibid., 318.

166   "I have to take my pants off . . .": David and Robbins, op.cit., New York *Daily News* (January 28, 1976).

167   Account of Alexander Onassis's death: Fraser, et al., op.cit., 320-336, and Brady, op.cit., 200-203.

170   Description of Onassis's new will: Fraser, et al., op.cit., 348.

171   "Today she appears serene": Liz Smith, "A Serene Jackie Onassis Turns 45 Today," *Long Island Press* (July 28, 1974).

       "he asked Roy Cohn . . .": Fraser, et al., op.cit., 355.

       "the top public relations genius . . .": quoted in Fraser, et al., op.cit., 232.

173   "the two women never spoke . . .": David and Robbins, "What Does the Future Hold for Jackie?" New York *Daily News* (February 1, 1976).

174   "Aristotle Onassis rescued me . . .": Brady, op.cit., 212.

CHAPTER SIX: "Alone Again," pages 177-200

Page
177   "Miss Christina Onassis is . . .": "Ari Never Planned to Divorce Jackie: Christina," New York *Daily News* (April 18, 1975).

178   "dressed in black": "Jackie and Tina Weep at Rite for Onassis," New York *Daily News* (April 21, 1978).

"it is certainly safe": "Tina, Jackie Talk Money in London," New York *Daily News* (May 9, 1975).

179   "in accordance with the wishes . . .": "Tina Will Share Onassis Billion with Charity," New York *Daily News* (June 6, 1975).

180   "the last kiss from Daddy.": "Onassis Will: 250 G a Year for Jackie," New York *Daily News* (June 8, 1975).

181   Account of Roosevelt Grier premiere: "Jackie Bear-Hugs Rosey and Embraces a Cause," Newark *Sunday Star-Ledger* (October 27, 1974).

"We've all heard that": "Jackie Onassis Fights for Cause," New York *Times* (January 31, 1975).

182   "doing things that really matter.": David and Robbins, "What Does the Future Hold for Jackie?" New York *Daily News* (February 1, 1976).

184   "Look, you know Tommy Guinzberg . . .": Stephen Birmingham, "The Public Event Named Jackie," *New York Times Magazine* (June 20, 1976).

"One is not unmindful . . .": "Jackie on Her Own," *Newsweek* (September 29, 1975).

"I expect to be learning . . .": Ibid.

185 "You may call me . . .": Maxine Cheshire, "Jackie Ready to Move In," Newark *Sunday Star-Ledger* (September 14, 1975).

186 Account of Caroline's nightlife in London: "Say Caroline Cuts Up, Miffs Mom," New York *Daily News* (November 14, 1975).

188 "When I walked into . . .": Birmingham, op.cit.

"She was so proud, so professional . . .": Ibid.

189 "Thank you for the tiny bottle . . .": Cafarakis, op.cit., 134.

"Those lies were started . . .": "Jackie on Her Own," *Newsweek* (September 29, 1975).

Account of Jackie's press luncheon: Joyce Maynard, "Jacqueline Onassis Makes a New Debut," New York *Times* (January 14, 1977).

193 Account of Jackie's resignation from Viking Press: Deirdre Carmody, "Mrs. Onassis Resigns Editing Post," New York *Times* (October 15, 1977); Marsha Kranes, "Novel about Ted Upsets Jackie O," New York *Post* (October 13, 1975); and Owen Moritz, "Jackie Quits Job in Protest Over 'Assassin' Novel," New York *Daily News* (October 15, 1977).

197 "when she talks to you . . .": Birmingham, op.cit.

199 The "Best Little Whorehouse" incident: Earl Wilson's column, New York *Post* (April 7, 1978).

200 "I seen my opportunities": William L. Riordon, *Plunkitt of Tammany Hall* (New York: E.P. Dutton, 1963) 3.

CHAPTER SEVEN: "The Price of the Pedestal," pages 203-208

Page
204 The Sophia Loren anecdote: Cheshire, op.cit., 55.

"You know, you're my only friend . . .": Gallagher, op.cit., 243.

205   "Unless Bobby personally . . .": Cheshire, "Intimate Secrets of all the Presidents' Wives," *The Star* (June 13, 1978).

"There's no question": quoted in Liz Smith's column, "Still More on JFK and Jackie," New York *Daily News* (June 1, 1978).

Discussion of JFK's battle with Addison's disease: Joan and Clay Blair, Jr., op.cit., 589-608.

"his health, almost from birth": Ibid., 613.

207   "You were very . . . dull . . .": "New York Intelligencer," *New York Magazine* (July 3, 1978).

BIBLIOGRAPHY

Associated Press. *The Torch Is Passed.* 1964.

Baldwin, Billy. *Billy Baldwin Remembers.* New York: Harcourt Brace Jovanovich, 1974.

Bishop, Jim. *The Day Kennedy Was Shot.* New York: Funk and Wagnalls, 1968.

Blair, Joan and Clay, Jr. *The Search for JFK.* New York: Berkley Medallion Books, 1976.

Bouvier, Jacqueline and Lee. *One Special Summer.* New York: Delacorte Press, 1972.

Bradlee, Benjamin C. *Conversations with Kennedy.* New York: W.W. Norton & Co., 1975.

Brady, Frank. *Onassis: An Extravagant Life.* Englewood Cliffs, New Jersey: Prentice-Hall, 1977.

Cafarakis, Christian. *The Fabulous Onassis: His Life and Loves.* New York: William Morrow & Company, 1972.

Cameron, Gail. *Rose.* New York: G.P. Putnam's Sons, 1971.

Carpozi, George, Jr. *The Hidden Side of Jacqueline Kennedy.* New York: Pyramid Books, 1967.

Clinch, Nancy Gager. *The Kennedy Neurosis: A Psychological Portrait of an American Dynasty.* New York: Grosset & Dunlap, 1973.

Davis, John H. *The Bouviers: Portrait of an American Family.* New York: Farrar, Straus & Giroux, 1969.

Fay, Paul B., Jr. *The Pleasure of His Company.* New York: Harper & Row, 1966.

Fraser, Nicholas; Jacobson, Philip; Ottaway, Mark; and Chester, Lewis. *Aristotle Onassis.* Philadelphia and New York: J.B. Lippincott Co., 1977.

Frischauer, Willi. *Jackie.* London: Michael Joseph, 1976.

Gallela, Ronald. *Jacqueline.* New York: Sheed and Ward, 1974.

Gallagher, Mary Barelli, with Frances Spatz Leighton. *My Life with Jacqueline Kennedy.* New York: David McKay Co., 1969.

Kennedy, Rose Fitzgerald. *Times to Remember.* New York: Doubleday & Co., 1974.

Lester, David, and Robbins, Jhan. *Jackie and Ari: The Inside Story.* New York: Pocket Books, 1975.

Manchester, William. *The Death of a President.* New York: Harper & Row, 1967.

O'Donnell, Kenneth P., and Powers, David F., with Joe McCarthy. *Johnny, We Hardly Knew Ye.* Boston: Little, Brown, 1972.

Riordon, William L. *Plunkitt of Tammany Hall.* New York: E.P. Dutton & Co., 1963.

Schlesinger, Arthur, Jr. *A Thousand Days.* Boston: Houghton Mifflin, 1965.

Sorenson, Theodore C. *Kennedy.* New York: Harper & Row, 1965.

Sparks, Fred. *The $20,000,000 Honeymoon: Jackie and Ari's First Year.* New York: Bernard Geis Associates, 1970.

Shaw, Maude. *White House Nannie: My Years with Caroline and John Kennedy, Jr.* New York: New American Library, 1966.

Shulman, Irving. *Jackie! The Exploitation of a First Lady.* New York: Trident Press, 1970.

Thayer, Mary Van Rensselaer. *Jacqueline Bouvier Kennedy.* New York: Doubleday & Co., 1961.

_____. *Jacqueline Kennedy: The White House Years.* Boston: Little, Brown, 1971.

Vlachose, Helen. *House Arrest.* Boston: Gambit, 1971.

West, J. B. *Upstairs at the White House: My Life with the First Ladies.* New York: Coward, McCann & Geoghegan, 1973.

Whalen, Richard J. *The Founding Father: The Story of Joseph P. Kennedy.* New York: Coward, McCann & Geoghegan, 1973.

INDEX

le noir. Lorsqu'elle se fut rendormie, il lui ôta la main du grand dragon tatoué et la posa sur son visage.

Il ne s'endormit qu'à l'aube. Reba McClane s'éveilla à neuf heures et écouta sa respiration régulière. Elle s'étira paresseusement, mais il ne bougea pas. Elle se remémora la disposition de la maison, l'emplacement des tapis et des escaliers, la direction du tic-tac de la pendule. Quand tout fut en place, elle se leva pour se rendre dans la salle de bains.

Elle se doucha longuement. Il dormait toujours. Ses sous-vêtements déchirés étaient épars sur le sol. Elle les retrouva du bout du pied et les fourra dans son sac. Elle passa sa robe de coton, ramassa sa canne et sortit.

Il lui avait dit que la cour était vaste et plane, bordée de haies démesurées, mais elle ne s'y aventura qu'avec précaution.

La brise matinale était fraîche, le soleil chaud. Elle demeura dans la cour et laissa le vent fouetter ses mains de graines de baies de sureau. Le vent découvrit les contours de son corps. Elle leva les bras et le vent s'engouffra entre ses seins, entre ses jambes. Des abeilles voletaient autour d'elle. Elle n'en avait pas peur, et elles la laissèrent tranquille.

Dolarhyde s'éveilla à son tour, étonné un instant de ne pas se retrouver dans la chambre du premier étage. Il se souvint, et ses yeux jaunes s'écarquillèrent. Un regard furtif vers l'autre oreiller. Vide.

Était-elle en train de se promener dans la maison ? Que pourrait-elle y trouver ? À moins qu'il ne se fût passé quelque chose dans la nuit. Des traces. Il serait soupçonné. Il lui faudrait s'enfuir.

Il regarda dans la salle de bains, dans la cuisine. Dans la cave où était rangé l'autre fauteuil roulant. L'étage supérieur. Il ne voulait pas s'y rendre. Il fallait pourtant qu'il sache. Le tatouage fléchit quand il monta les marches. Le Dragon resplendissait sur la reproduction accrochée au mur de la chambre. Il ne pouvait rester dans cette pièce en compagnie du Dragon.

Par la fenêtre, il l'aperçut qui se promenait dans la cour.

« FRANCIS. » Il savait que la voix venait de sa chambre. Il savait que c'était la voix du Dragon. Cette nouvelle dualité avec le Dragon le désorientait. Il l'avait déjà éprouvée une fois, quand il avait posé la main sur le cœur de Reba.

Le Dragon ne lui avait jamais directement parlé auparavant. C'était effrayant.

« FRANCIS, VIENS ICI. »

Il s'efforça de faire taire la voix qui l'appelait, l'appelait, pendant qu'il se précipitait dans l'escalier.

Qu'aurait-elle donc pu trouver ? Le dentier de grand-mère avait tinté contre le verre, mais il l'avait ôté pour lui apporter de l'eau. Et puis, elle ne pouvait rien voir.

La bande magnétique de Freddy. Elle était dans un magnétophone à cassettes, dans le bureau. Il vérifia. La cassette était entièrement rembobinée. Il ne parvenait pas à se rappeler s'il l'avait rembobinée après l'avoir passée au téléphone au *Tattler*.

Il ne fallait pas qu'elle revienne dans cette maison. Il ne savait pas ce qui pourrait s'y produire. Elle pourrait avoir une surprise. Le Dragon pourrait très bien descendre l'escalier. Il savait avec quelle facilité elle craquerait.

Les femmes l'avaient vue monter dans son van. Warfield se souviendrait parfaitement d'eux. Il s'habilla à la hâte.

Reba McClane sentit l'ombre fraîche d'un tronc d'arbre, puis retrouva le soleil. La chaleur du soleil et le bourdonnement de l'air conditionné lui indiquaient avec précision où elle se trouvait. La navigation, cette discipline vitale, se pratiquait sans problèmes dans cette cour. Elle se promenait en tous sens, faisant courir ses doigts sur les arbrisseaux ou les fleurs trop poussées.

Un nuage passa devant le soleil, et elle s'arrêta de marcher. Elle ne savait plus où elle se trouvait. Elle guetta le moteur de l'air conditionné. Il était coupé. Elle éprouva un malaise passager, puis battit des mains et entendit l'écho que lui renvoyait la maison. Reba palpa sa montre. Elle allait devoir réveiller Dolarhyde. Il fallait qu'elle rentre chez elle.

La contre-porte claqua.

« Bonjour », dit-elle.

Ses clefs tintèrent quand il s'avança vers elle.

Il marchait très lentement, comme si le souffle de son arrivée allait la projeter à terre, et il constata qu'elle n'avait pas peur de lui.

Elle ne paraissait pas gênée de ce qui s'était passé entre eux cette nuit. Elle ne semblait pas non plus lui en vouloir. Elle ne s'était pas enfuie, elle ne l'avait pas menacé. Il se demanda si c'était parce qu'elle n'avait pu voir ses parties intimes.

Reba le prit par le cou et posa la tête sur sa poitrine. Son cœur battait la chamade.

Il parvint à dire : « Bonjour.

— J'ai passé un moment formidable. »

Vraiment ? Qu'est-ce qu'il faut répondre dans ce cas-là ? « Oui, moi aussi. » *Cela semblait correct. Qu'elle s'en aille, à présent.*

« Mais il va falloir que je rentre chez moi. Ma sœur doit venir me chercher pour déjeuner. Vous pouvez nous accompagner si cela vous amuse.

— Il faut que j'aille à la boîte, dit-il subitement.

— Je vais aller chercher mon sac. »

Non ! « Restez là, j'y vais. »

321

Presque sourd à ses sentiments les plus sincères, incapable de les exprimer, Dolarhyde ne comprenait pas ce qui lui était arrivé avec Reba McClane, ni comment cela avait pu se produire. Il se sentait paralysé, terrorisé par sa nouvelle Dualité.

Elle le menaçait, elle ne le menaçait pas.

Tel était le sens de ses gestes d'acceptation dans le lit de grand-mère, de ses gestes de femme vivante.

Bien souvent, Dolarhyde ne savait pas ce qu'il éprouvait avant d'avoir agi. Et il ne savait pas ce qu'il éprouvait pour Reba McClane.

Alors qu'il la raccompagnait, un incident fâcheux lui permit d'y voir un peu plus clair.

Tout de suite après le boulevard Lindbergh, Dolarhyde s'arrêta dans une station-service Servco Supreme afin d'y faire le plein.

Le pompiste était une sorte de lourdaud dont l'haleine empestait l'alcool. Il fit la grimace quand Dolarhyde lui demanda de vérifier le niveau d'huile.

Il en manquait. Le pompiste décapsula un bidon d'huile, y adapta un bec verseur, et retourna le tout sur l'orifice du moteur.

Dolarhyde descendit pour le régler.

Mais le pompiste manifestait un zèle particulier à nettoyer le pare-brise. Du côté du passager. Il frottait inlassablement la vitre.

Reba McClane était installée dans le siège-baquet, les jambes croisées, la jupe relevée sur les genoux. Sa canne blanche était posée entre les deux sièges.

Le pompiste s'attardait devant le pare-brise. Son regard remontait le long des jambes de Reba.

Dolarhyde leva les yeux et le surprit. Il plongea la main en direction du tableau de bord et mit les essuie-glaces à la vitesse maximum, cinglant ainsi les doigts du pompiste.

« Hé, ça va pas, non ? » Le pompiste se hâta d'ôter le bidon d'huile du moteur. Il savait qu'il s'était fait

322

surprendre et ne put réprimer un petit sourire satisfait, jusqu'à ce que Dolarhyde fasse le tour du van pour venir à lui.

« Espèce de salope. » Pas de problèmes avec les *s.*

« Dites donc, qu'est-ce qui vous prend ? » Le pompiste avait à peu près la taille de Dolarhyde, mais il était loin d'en avoir la musculature. Il était jeune pour avoir un râtelier, et en plus il n'en prenait pas soin.

Sa couleur verdâtre dégoûta Dolarhyde. « Qu'est-ce qui est arrivé à tes dents ? lui demanda-t-il doucement.

— Ça vous regarde ?

— C'est pour plaire à ton giton que tu te les fais arracher ? » Dolarhyde était bien trop près de lui.

« Laissez-moi tranquille. »

Très doucement : « Pauvre con. Taré. Ordure. Pourri. »

D'une seule main, Dolarhyde le propulsa contre le van. Le bidon d'huile et son bec verseur tombèrent à terre.

Dolarhyde les ramassa.

« Ne te sauve pas. Je peux te rattraper si je veux. » Il ôta le bec verseur et en observa l'extrémité la plus pointue.

Le pompiste était livide. Il y avait dans le visage de Dolarhyde quelque chose qu'il n'avait jamais vu, jamais.

L'espace d'une seconde, Dolarhyde entrevit le bec verseur enfoncé dans la poitrine de l'homme, le cœur qui se vide comme un bidon d'huile. Il vit le visage de Reba de l'autre côté du pare-brise. Elle secouait la tête, disait quelque chose. Elle cherchait la poignée de la vitre.

« Tu t'es déjà fait péter la gueule, trouduc ? »

Le pompiste secoua la tête, nerveusement. « J'pensais pas à mal, j'vous l'jure. »

Dolarhyde lui brandit devant les yeux le bec verseur métallique. Il le tenait à deux mains et ses pectoraux se gonflèrent quand il le tordit en deux. Il tira le pompiste par la ceinture et lui enfonça le bec verseur dans le pantalon.

« Occupe-toi de tes fesses, pigé ? » Il lui fourra un billet de banque dans la poche de sa chemise. « Tu peux te tirer, maintenant, dit-il, mais je peux te rattraper quand je veux. »

36

LA bande magnétique arriva le samedi sous forme d'un petit paquet adressé à Will Graham c/o Siège du F.B.I., Washington. Elle avait été postée à Chicago le jour même de la mort de Lounds.

Le laboratoire et les « Empreintes » ne trouvèrent rien d'intéressant sur le boîtier ou sur l'emballage.

Une copie de la bande fut expédiée à Chicago par le courrier de l'après-midi. L'agent spécial Chester l'apporta aussitôt à Graham dans la salle des délibérations. Une note de Lloyd Bowman y était jointe.

« Les empreintes vocales sont bien celles de Lounds. Visiblement, il répétait ce qu'on lui dictait », avait écrit Bowman. « C'est une bande neuve, utilisée pour la première fois et fabriquée au cours des trois derniers mois. La section Sciences du comportement en étudie le contenu. Le Dr Bloom pourra l'écouter dès qu'il sera remis — c'est à vous d'en décider. Il est clair que le tueur essaye de vous ébranler. Cela m'étonnerait qu'il y arrive. »

Un témoignage de confiance dont Graham avait bien besoin.

Graham savait qu'il lui fallait écouter cette bande. Il attendit le départ de Chester.

Il ne voulait pas faire cela dans la salle des délibérations. Le prétoire lui paraissait plus agréable — le soleil entrait par les hautes fenêtres. Les femmes de ménage venaient de passer, un peu de poussière flottait dans la lumière.

Le magnétophone était gris, petit. Graham le posa sur la table de l'avocat et appuya sur la touche.

La voix monotone d'un technicien : « Affaire numéro 426238, cote 814, message ci-joint, bande magnétique sur cassette. Copie d'enregistrement. »

Une différence dans la qualité du son.

Graham serra les mains sur la barre des jurés.

Freddy Lounds paraissait épuisé et terrorisé.

« J'ai eu un grand privilège. J'ai vu... j'ai vu avec émerveillement... émerveillement et effroi... effroi... la force du Grand Dragon Rouge. »

L'enregistrement original était fréquemment interrompu. Le magnétophone avait capté le bruit des touches. Graham vit le doigt enfoncer la touche. Le doigt du Dragon.

« J'ai menti à Son propos. Tout ce que j'ai écrit, c'était des mensonges que m'avait racontés Will Graham. Il m'a obligé à les écrire. J'ai... j'ai blasphémé contre le Dragon. Malgré cela... le Dragon est magnanime. Il souhaite que je Le serve. Il... m'a aidé à comprendre... Sa splendeur et je Le louerai à tout jamais. Journalistes, lorsque vous imprimerez ceci, mettez toujours des majuscules quand vous parlerez de Lui.

« Il sait que vous m'avez obligé à mentir, Will Graham. Comme j'ai été forcé à mentir, Il se montrera plus... plus clément envers moi qu'envers vous, Will Graham.

« Posez la main sur vos reins, Will Graham... juste entre les reins... vous sentez votre colonne vertébrale ?... C'est là, très exactement... que le Dragon vous atteindra. »

Graham ne lâcha pas la barre. Oh oui, je la sens. Le Dragon ne connaît pas le nom de l'os iliaque ou a-t-il fait exprès de ne pas l'employer ?

« Vous avez beaucoup... beaucoup à redouter. De mes... de mes propres lèvres, vous allez savoir ce que vous pouvez redouter. »

Une pause, puis un hurlement effrayant. Pis encore, le cri d'une bouche privée de lèvres : « Eshèce de halaud, hous h'ahiez hourtant hromis... »

Graham baissa la tête entre les genoux et attendit que les petites taches lumineuses cessent de danser devant ses yeux. Il ouvrit la bouche et prit une profonde aspiration.

Une heure s'écoula avant qu'il puisse réécouter la bande.

Il emporta le magnétophone dans la salle des délibérations. Trop étouffant. Il laissa tourner la bande et revint au prétoire. Par la porte ouverte, il pouvait entendre :

« J'ai eu un grand privilège... »

Il y avait quelqu'un à la porte du prétoire. Graham reconnut le jeune employé du F.B.I. de Chicago et lui fit signe d'entrer.

« Il y a une lettre pour vous », dit le jeune homme. « M. Chester m'a demandé de vous la porter. Je dois vous dire de sa part que l'inspecteur l'a radiographiée. »

Il tira la lettre de la poche intérieure de son veston. Une enveloppe mauve foncé. Graham espérait qu'elle venait de Molly.

« Elle a été tamponnée, vous voyez ?
— Merci.

« — Il y a aussi la paye. » Le jeune homme lui tendit un chèque.

Sur la bande, Freddy se mit à hurler.

Le jeune homme ferma les yeux.

« Désolé, dit Graham.

— Je me demande comment vous pouvez supporter ça, dit l'autre.

— Allez-vous-en. »

Il prit place dans le box du jury pour lire la lettre. Il avait besoin de se remonter le moral. La lettre avait été envoyée par le Dr Hannibal Lecter.

Mon cher Will,

Quelques mots pour vous féliciter de la façon dont vous avez utilisé Lounds. J'avoue que je suis très admiratif. Vous êtes un type vraiment malin !

M. Lounds m'a souvent offensé par ses bavardages inconsidérés, mais il m'a tout de même éclairé sur un point : votre internement à l'hôpital psychiatrique. L'incapable qui m'a servi de défenseur aurait dû en faire mention devant le tribunal, enfin, tant pis.

Vous savez, Will, vous vous en faites beaucoup trop. Vous vous sentiriez mieux si vous cessiez de vous torturer.

Nous n'inventons pas notre nature, Will ; elle nous est donnée en même temps que nos poumons, notre pancréas, tous nos organes. Pourquoi chercher à la combattre ?

Je veux vous aider, Will, et j'aimerais commencer en vous posant cette question : quand vous avez été si déprimé après avoir abattu M. Garrett Jacob Hobbs, ce n'est pas le *geste* qui vous a fait craquer, n'est-ce pas ? En vérité, n'est-ce pas *parce que cela avait été si bon de le tuer* que vous vous êtes senti si mal par la suite ?

Pensez-y, mais ne vous tourmentez pas. Pourquoi ne serait-ce pas agréable, après tout ? Dieu doit trouver ça agréable — Il n'arrête pas de le faire. Et n'avons-nous pas été créés à Son image ?

Peut-être l'avez-vous lu dans le journal d'hier, mercredi soir, au Texas, Dieu a fait ébouler le toit d'une église sur trente-quatre de Ses fidèles alors qu'ils entonnaient un cantique à Sa gloire. Vous ne croyez pas que cela Lui a procuré du plaisir ? *Trente-quatre*. Il ne peut vous en vouloir d'avoir descendu Hobbs.

La semaine dernière, Il s'est offert cent soixante Philippins dans un accident d'avion. Il ne peut vous en vouloir pour Hobbs. Il ne vous reprochera pas un misérable petit assassinat. Pardon, deux. Ne vous en faites pas.

Lisez le journal. Dieu est imbattable.

Sincèrement,

Docteur Hannibal Lecter.

Graham savait bien que Lecter se trompait pour Hobbs mais, pendant une demi-seconde, il se demanda s'il n'avait pas un peu raison pour Freddy Lounds. L'ennemi intérieur de Graham acceptait tous les chefs d'accusation.

Il avait posé la main sur l'épaule de Freddy pour bien prouver qu'il lui avait vraiment dit toutes ces horreurs sur le Dragon. Mais est-ce qu'il n'avait pas eu un tout petit peu envie de lui faire courir quelques risques ? Il était perplexe.

La certitude de ne pas accorder la moindre chance au Dragon le rassura un peu.

« J'en ai plein les bottes de tous ces enfoirés », dit-il tout haut.

Il avait besoin d'un instant de répit. Il appela Molly mais personne ne répondit chez les grands-parents de Willy. « Ils doivent encore être dans leur foutu mobile-home », grommela-t-il.

Il sortit prendre un café, un peu pour se prouver à lui-même qu'il ne se cachait pas dans la salle des délibérations.

Il vit à la devanture d'une bijouterie un magnifique bracelet d'or ancien. La quasi-totalité de sa paye y passa. Il le fit emballer et timbrer pour le mettre à la poste. Ce n'est qu'une fois arrivé à la boîte à lettres qu'il l'adressa à Molly, dans l'Oregon. À la différence de Molly, Graham ne savait pas qu'il ne faisait des cadeaux que lorsque les choses ne tournaient pas rond.

Il n'avait pas envie de revenir travailler dans la salle des délibérations, mais pourtant, il le fallait. Le souvenir de Valérie Leeds lui donna du courage.

Je suis actuellement absente, avait-elle dit.

Il aurait voulu la connaître. Il aurait voulu — une idée bien inutile, bien enfantine.

Graham était épuisé, égoïste, rancunier. La fatigue l'avait fait régresser vers une mentalité enfantine où les critères de mesure étaient ceux qu'il avait appris en premier ; où « nord » se traduisait par Nationale 61 et où « un mètre quatre-vingts » serait à jamais la taille de son père.

Il s'obligea à établir un profil des victimes extrêmement détaillé à partir d'une kyrielle de rapports et de ses propres observations.

La richesse. C'était un point commun. Les deux familles étaient riches. Bizarre que Valérie Leeds ait économisé sur ses collants.

Graham se demanda si elle avait été une enfant pauvre. Il pensait que oui ; ses enfants étaient un peu trop bien habillés.

Graham avait été un enfant pauvre, qui avait suivi son père des chantiers navals de Biloxi et de Greenville à ceux du lac Érié. À l'école, il avait toujours été le nouveau, l'étranger. Il en voulait plus ou moins consciemment aux riches.

Valérie Leeds avait peut-être été une enfant pauvre. Il fut tenté de revoir le film au prétoire. Non. Les Leeds n'étaient pas prioritaires. Il les connaissait parfaitement. Mais il ne connaissait pas les Jacobi.

Son absence de connaissance intime des Jacobi le paralysait. L'incendie de Detroit avait tout détruit

— les albums de famille et, probablement, les journaux intimes.

Graham tentait de les connaître au travers des objets qu'ils désiraient, achetaient, utilisaient. Il n'avait rien d'autre.

Le dossier envoyé par Metcalf mesurait plus de sept centimètres d'épaisseur et se composait en majeure partie de listes de biens — tout ce qu'il faut pour meubler une nouvelle maison. *Regarde-moi toute cette merde.* Tout était assuré, accompagné des numéros de série à la demande des assurances. Chat échaudé...

Byron Metcalf lui avait envoyé des doubles au carbone au lieu des photocopies des déclarations d'assurance. Les doubles étaient peu nets, difficiles à lire.

Jacobi avait un canot pour le ski nautique. Leeds avait un canot pour le ski nautique. Jacobi avait une moto d'enduro. Leeds avait une moto de cross. Graham s'humecta le pouce et tourna les pages.

Le quatrième objet répertorié sur la deuxième page était un projecteur de cinéma Chinon Pacific.

Graham s'arrêta. Comment avait-il pu passer à côté ? Il avait fouillé toutes les caisses de l'entrepôt de Birmingham afin d'y trouver un indice qui pourrait lui apporter une connaissance plus intime des Jacobi.

Où se trouvait le projecteur ? Il pouvait comparer la déclaration d'assurance à l'inventaire dressé par Byron Metcalf et contresigné par le responsable des entrepôts.

Cela ne lui prit que quinze minutes. Il n'y avait ni projecteur, ni caméra, ni films.

Graham s'appuya au dossier de la chaise et regarda les Jacobi lui sourire sur la photographie posée devant lui.

Qu'est-ce que vous en avez foutu ?
On vous les a volés ?
C'est le tueur qui les a volés ?
S'il les a volés, est-ce qu'il les a revendus à un receleur ?

Mon Dieu, faites qu'il y ait un receleur fiché...

Graham n'était plus fatigué. Il voulait savoir s'il manquait autre chose. Pendant une heure, il compara les déclarations d'assurance à l'inventaire effectué dans l'entrepôt. Tout était enregistré, à l'exception des petits objets précieux. Ils devaient apparaître sur la liste des objets enfermés par Byron Metcalf dans le coffre de la banque de Birmingham.

Ils se trouvaient tous sur la liste. Tous sauf deux.

« Coffret en cristal, 7 x 10, couvercle en argent » — il était sur la déclaration d'assurance mais pas au coffre. « Cadre en argent, 18 x 24, décoré de pampres et de fleurs » — il n'était pas non plus au coffre.

Volés ? Égarés ? C'était de petits objets, facilement dissimulables. D'habitude, l'argent est immédiatement fondu et ne laisse pas de traces. Mais un matériel de projection comporte des numéros de série et laisse par conséquent des traces.

Le voleur était-il l'assassin ?

Le regard fixé sur la photographie des Jacobi, Graham envisageait déjà un nouveau point commun. Mais la réponse qu'il devait obtenir était plutôt décevante.

Il y avait un téléphone dans la salle des délibérations. Graham appela la criminelle de Birmingham. On lui passa le responsable de la tranche horaire trois-onze.

« Dans l'affaire Jacobi, j'ai remarqué que vous aviez tenu un registre des personnes qui s'étaient présentées à la maison après la pose des scellés. Exact ?

— Je vais faire vérifier. »

Graham savait qu'ils avaient un tel registre. C'était une excellente manière de travailler. Il attendit cinq minutes qu'un documentaliste prenne le téléphone.

« J'ai le registre des entrées et sorties. Que désirez-vous savoir ?

— Niles Jacobi, le fils du défunt — il est sur la liste ?

— Euh... oui. 2 juillet, à sept heures du soir. Il avait la permission de prendre des effets personnels.

— Vous savez s'il avait une valise ?

— Non. Désolé. »

Byron Metcalf lui répondit d'une voix rauque, haletante. Graham se demanda ce qu'il pouvait bien être en train de faire.

« J'espère que je ne vous dérange pas.

— Qu'est-ce que je peux pour vous, Will ?

— J'ai un petit problème avec Niles Jacobi.

— Qu'est-ce qu'il a encore fait ?

— Je crois qu'il a sorti quelques objets de la maison après l'assassinat.

— Ah...

— Il manque un cadre en argent que vous aviez répertorié sur l'inventaire des objets déposés au coffre. Quand j'étais à Birmingham, j'ai pris une photo des Jacobi dans le dortoir de Niles. Elle avait été encadrée — je me souviens de la marque sur les bords.

— Le petit salaud... Je lui avais donné la permission de prendre des livres et des vêtements, dit Metcalf.

— Niles a des amis qui lui reviennent cher. Je cherche de ce côté-là. Ah, il manque également une caméra, un projecteur et un film. Je veux savoir s'il les a emportés. Il y a de grandes chances que oui ; sinon, c'est peut-être le tueur qui les a pris. Dans ce cas, il faudra faire parvenir les numéros de séries à tous les revendeurs. C'est une priorité nationale. Pour le cadre, il est certainement déjà fondu à l'heure qu'il est.

— Il ne pensera certainement qu'au cadre quand je l'interrogerai.

— Attention, si Niles a pris le projecteur, il a dû garder le film. Il ne pourrait rien en tirer. Je veux le film. Il faut absolument que je le voie. Si vous annoncez la couleur, il niera tout en bloc et jettera le film dès que vous serez parti.

— Compris, fit Metcalf. La voiture fait partie des biens de la famille, je peux la fouiller sans autorisation. Quant à sa piaule, mon ami le juge d'instruction se fera un plaisir d'y jeter un coup d'œil. Je vous tiens au courant. »

Graham se remit au travail.

La richesse. Il serait utile d'introduire cette notion dans le profil demandé par la police.

Graham se demanda si Mme Leeds et Mme Jacobi étaient du genre à faire leurs courses en tenue de tennis. Cela passait pour très chic dans certains quartiers. Dans d'autres, c'était assez stupide et doublement provocateur, car cela suscitait simultanément des pensées lubriques et une jalousie de classe.

Graham les imagina en train de pousser leur Caddie avec des chaussettes à pompons et une jupette dissimulant à peine leurs cuisses bronzées — passant à côté du costaud aux yeux de requin qui achète de la viande froide pour manger sur le pouce, en voiture.

Combien pouvait-il y avoir de familles avec trois enfants et un animal domestique, et combien étaient-elles à ne pas interposer de portes blindées entre elles et le Dragon ?

Quand Graham imaginait les victimes potentielles, il voyait des gens riches et intelligents se prélasser dans une demeure agréable.

Pourtant, celui qui allait devoir maintenant affronter le Dragon n'avait ni enfants ni animal domestique, et sa maison n'avait rien d'agréable. Celui qui allait devoir affronter le Dragon avait pour nom Francis Dolarhyde.

37

L<small>E</small> bruit des haltères retombant sur le plancher du grenier résonnait dans toute la maison.

Dolarhyde s'entraînait avec effort et les charges qu'il soulevait n'avaient jamais été aussi lourdes. Sa tenue était différente ; un pantalon de survêtement cachait le tatouage. La veste recouvrait *Le Grand Dragon Rouge et la Femme vêtue de soleil.* Le kimono pendait au mur ainsi que la mue d'un serpent et dissimulait le miroir.

Dolarhyde ne portait pas de masque.

Un épaulé-jeté. Deux cent quatre-vingts livres à bout de bras.

« À QUI PENSES-TU ? »

Surpris par la voix, il faillit laisser tomber les haltères. Il les reposa et le sol trembla sous le choc.

Il se tourna, les bras ballants, dans la direction de la voix.

« À QUI PENSES-TU ? »

Elle semblait venir de derrière la veste, mais le volume et l'intonation lui arrachaient la gorge.

« À QUI PENSES-TU ? »

Il savait qui parlait, et il avait peur. Dès le début, le Dragon et lui-même n'avaient fait qu'une seule et même personne. Il connaissait le Devenir, et le Dragon était son moi supérieur. Leur corps, leur voix, leur volonté ne faisaient qu'un.

Plus maintenant. Pas depuis Reba. Ne pense pas à Reba.

« QUI EST ACCEPTABLE ? demanda le Dragon.

— Mme... erhman... Sherman. » Dolarhyde avait du mal à prononcer.

« PARLE PLUS FORT. JE NE COMPRENDS RIEN. À QUI PENSES-TU ? »

Dolarhyde se tourna vers la barre. Un arraché à deux bras. Encore plus difficile.

« Mme... ehrman dans l'eau.

— TU PENSES À TA PETITE AMIE, C'EST ÇA, HEIN ? TU VEUX QU'ELLE SOIT TA PETITE AMIE, DIS ? »

Les haltères retombèrent lourdement.

« He n'ai pas de hetite... amie. » La peur l'empêchait de parler correctement. Il dut boucher ses narines à l'aide de sa lèvre supérieure.

« MENSONGE ! » La voix du Dragon était claire et puissante, les s ne lui posaient aucun problème. « TU OUBLIES LE DEVENIR. PRÉPARE-TOI POUR LES SHERMAN. SOULÈVE CE POIDS. »

Dolarhyde empoigna la barre et rassembla ses forces. Son esprit se tendait en même temps que ses muscles. Il tentait désespérément de penser aux Sherman. Il s'obligea à penser au poids de Mme Sherman dans les bras. C'était le tour de Mme Sherman. C'était Mme Sherman. Il se battait dans le noir contre M. Sherman. Le clouait au sol jusqu'à ce que le sang qui s'écoule fasse frissonner son cœur comme celui d'un oiseau. Le seul cœur qu'il eût jamais entendu. Il n'entendait pas le cœur de Reba. Non, il ne l'entendait pas.

La peur vint à bout de ses forces. Il leva la barre à hauteur des cuisses mais ne réussit pas un épaulé. Il pensa aux Sherman disposés autour de lui, les yeux grands ouverts, pour le service du Dragon. Mais ce n'était pas bon. C'était une pensée vide et creuse. La barre retomba.

« PAS ACCEPTABLE.

— Mme...

— TU N'ES MEME PAS CAPABLE DE DIRE MME SHERMAN. TU N'AS PAS L'INTENTION DE PRENDRE LES SHERMAN. CE QUE TU VEUX, C'EST REBA MCCLANE. TU VEUX QU'ELLE SOIT TA PETITE AMIE, HEIN ? TU VEUX ETRE COPAIN AVEC ELLE ?

— Non.

— MENSONGE !

— Hou ègueu han heuman.

— POUR QUELQUE TEMPS SEULEMENT ? MISÉRABLE DÉBILE PLEURNICHARD, QUI VOUDRAIT ETRE COPAIN AVEC TOI ? VIENS ICI. JE VAIS TE MONTRER CE QUE TU ES. »

Dolarhyde ne bougea pas.

« JE N'AI JAMAIS VU UN ENFANT AUSSI DÉGOUTANT QUE TOI. VIENS ICI.

« OTE CETTE VESTE. »

Il l'enleva.

« REGARDE-MOI. »

Sur le mur, le Dragon resplendissait.

« PRENDS LE KIMONO, REGARDE-TOI DANS LE MIROIR. »

Il regarda. Il ne pouvait détourner son visage des lumières brûlantes. Il se vit en train de baver.

« REGARDE-TOI. JE VAIS TE DONNER UNE SURPRISE POUR TA PETITE AMIE, ENLÈVE CE HAILLON. »

Dolarhyde tira sur la ceinture de son pantalon, qui se déchira. Il en arracha des lambeaux de la main droite, les tendit de la main gauche. Sa main droite les saisit dans sa main gauche tremblante et les jeta dans un coin de la pièce. Dolarhyde retomba sur le tapis, recroquevillé comme un homard coupé vif. Il étreignit ses genoux en gémissant, le souffle court. Le tatouage brillait sous la lumière crue de la salle de gymnastique.

« JE N'AI JAMAIS VU UN ENFANT AUSSI DÉGOUTANT QUE TOI. VA LES CHERCHER.

— Anmé.

— VA LES CHERCHER. »

Il quitta la pièce pour revenir avec les dents du Dragon.

« METS-LES DANS LA PAUME DE TA MAIN. FAIS-LES FONCTIONNER AVEC TES DOIGTS. »

Les pectoraux de Dolarhyde se gonflèrent.

« TU VOIS COMMENT ELLES SE REFERMENT ? METS-LES SOUS TON VENTRE À PRÉSENT. COINCE-LA ENTRE LES DENTS.

— Non.

— OBÉIS. REGARDE, À PRÉSENT. »

Les dents commençaient à lui faire mal. Des larmes et de la salive coulèrent sur sa poitrine.

« Hère ihi.

— TU N'ES QU'UNE CHAROGNE ABANDONNÉE DANS LE DEVENIR. TU ES UNE CHAROGNE ET JE TE DONNERAI UN NOM. TU T'APPELLES TÊTE DE NŒUD. RÉPÈTE.

— Je m'appelle Tête de Nœud. » Il fermait ses narines à l'aide de sa lèvre pour prononcer ces paroles.

« BIENTÔT, JE SERAI DÉBARRASSÉ DE TOI, dit le Dragon sans le moindre effort. EST-CE QUE CE SERA BIEN ?

— Bien.

— QUI VIENDRA ENSUITE, L'HEURE VENUE ?

— Mme... ehrman. »

Une douleur très vite le déchire. La peur et la douleur.

« JE VAIS TE LA COUPER.

— Reba. Reba. Je vous donnerai Reba. » Déjà, son langage s'améliore.

« TU N'AS RIEN À ME DONNER. ELLE EST À MOI. ILS SONT TOUS À MOI. REBA MCCLANE PUIS LES SHERMAN.

— Reba puis les Sherman. La loi le saura.

— J'AI TOUT PRÉVU POUR CE JOUR. EN DOUTERAIS-TU ?

— Non.

— COMMENT T'APPELLES-TU ?

— Tête de Nœud.

— TU PEUX ÔTER MES DENTS. PITOYABLE BEC-DE-LIÈVRE, TU VOUDRAIS ME PRIVER DE TA PETITE AMIE, N'EST-CE PAS ? JE LA DÉCHIRERAI ET TE JETTERAI LES MORCEAUX AU VISAGE. JE TE PENDRAI AVEC SON GROS INTESTIN SI TU T'OPPOSES À MOI. TU SAIS QUE J'EN SUIS CAPABLE. METS 300 LIVRES SUR LA BARRE. »

Dolarhyde ajouta des disques à la barre. Il n'avait jamais dépassé les 280 livres.

« SOULÈVE. »

337

S'il n'était pas aussi fort que le Dragon, Reba mourrait. Il le savait. Il força jusqu'à ce que la pièce se teinte de rouge sous ses yeux exorbités.

« Je ne peux pas.

— TOI, TU NE PEUX PAS, MAIS MOI, JE LE PEUX. »

Dolarhyde saisit la barre. Elle se courba lorsqu'il la hissa à hauteur des épaules. À bout de bras, maintenant. Sans la moindre difficulté. « AU REVOIR, TETE DE NŒUD », dit-il, fier Dragon frissonnant dans la lumière.

38

FRANCIS Dolarhyde ne se rendit pas au travail le lundi matin.

Il quitta la maison à l'heure habituelle. Son allure était impeccable, sa conduite précise. Il mit des lunettes noires pour se protéger du soleil matinal quand il tourna en direction du pont enjambant le Missouri.

La glacière crissait sur le siège du passager. Il tendit le bras et la posa à terre, ce qui lui fit penser qu'il devait se procurer de la glace et aller chercher le film au...

Il franchit ensuite le canal du Missouri, regarda les crêtes d'écume sur la rivière mouvante et éprouva l'impression soudaine de se déplacer au-dessus d'un fleuve immobile. Un sentiment étrange, décousu, l'envahit. Il leva le pied de l'accélérateur.

Le van ralentit puis s'arrêta. Derrière, les voitures

s'entassaient et commençaient à klaxonner, mais il ne les entendit pas.

Il glissait lentement vers le nord, sur une rivière immobile, face au soleil levant. Des larmes coulaient sous ses lunettes noires et tombaient sur ses mains.

Quelqu'un tapa à la vitre. Un conducteur au visage blême et bouffi de sommeil était descendu de voiture. Il lui criait des choses qu'il ne comprenait pas.

Dolarhyde le regarda. Des lumières bleues clignotaient de l'autre côté du pont. Il savait qu'il lui fallait rouler. Il demanda à son corps d'appuyer sur l'accélérateur, et son corps lui obéit. L'homme debout près de la vitre fit un bond en arrière.

Dolarhyde s'engagea sur le parking d'un grand motel proche de l'échangeur routier. Un car scolaire y était garé ; le pavillon d'un tuba reposait contre la vitre arrière.

Dolarhyde se demanda s'il allait devoir prendre le car avec les vieillards.

Non, ce n'était pas cela. Il chercha du regard la Packard de sa mère.

« *Monte en voiture. Ne mets pas tes pieds sur le siège* », lui dit sa mère.

Ce n'était pas cela non plus.

Il se trouvait sur le parking d'un motel, à l'ouest de Saint Louis, il désirait être capable de choisir, et il ne le pouvait pas.

Dans six jours, s'il pouvait attendre jusque-là, il tuerait Reba McClane. Il émit un son suraigu avec le nez.

Peut-être le Dragon aimerait-il commencer par prendre les Sherman et attendre une autre lune...

Non. Il ne le voudrait pas.

Reba McClane ne savait rien du Dragon. Elle se croyait en compagnie de Francis Dolarhyde. Elle voulait coller son corps contre celui de Francis Dolarhyde. Elle attirait Francis Dolarhyde vers elle dans le lit de grand-mère.

« *J'ai passé un moment formidable.* »

Peut-être appréciait-elle Francis Dolarhyde. C'était une chose perverse et méprisable de la part d'une femme. Il avait conscience qu'il lui faudrait la mépriser, mais c'était si agréable...

Reba McClane était coupable d'aimer Francis Dolarhyde. Irrémédiablement coupable.

S'il n'y avait eu le pouvoir de son Devenir, s'il n'y avait eu le Dragon, il n'aurait jamais été capable de l'emmener chez lui. Il n'aurait jamais pu lui faire l'amour. Mais est-ce bien sûr ?

« *Mon Dieu, c'est si bon.* »

Voilà ce qu'elle avait dit. C'est si bon.

Les clients sortaient du motel après avoir pris le petit déjeuner et passaient devant le van. Leurs regards curieux le foulaient ainsi qu'une myriade de pieds.

Il avait besoin de réfléchir. Rentrer chez lui était impossible. Il prit une chambre au motel, appela le bureau et raconta qu'il était souffrant. La chambre était paisible, agréable. Des gravures représentant des vapeurs en constituaient l'unique décoration. Et rien ne resplendissait sur le mur.

Dolarhyde s'allongea tout habillé. Il y avait des traces de peinture au plafond. Il dut se relever plusieurs fois pour uriner. Il frissonna, puis sua à grosses gouttes. Une heure s'écoula.

Il ne voulait pas donner Reba McClane au Dragon, mais il pensa à ce que le Dragon lui ferait s'il refusait de la lui offrir.

La peur intense arrive par vagues, le corps humain ne peut la supporter trop longtemps. Dolarhyde profita des accalmies pour réfléchir.

Comment pouvait-il s'y prendre pour ne pas la livrer au Dragon ? Une idée, toujours la même, l'obsédait. Il se leva.

Le verrou claqua dans la salle de bains. Dolarhyde

observa la tringle du rideau de la douche ; c'était un solide tuyau de plus de deux centimètres de diamètre, fixé aux murs de la salle de bains. Il décrocha le rideau et le jeta sur le miroir.

Il saisit la tringle et s'y balança ; ses pieds effleuraient la paroi de la baignoire. La tringle était solide, de même que sa ceinture. Il pourrait y arriver. *Ça, ça* ne lui faisait pas peur.

Il noua la ceinture autour de la tringle. Elle formait un nœud coulant assez raide.

Il s'assit sur le siège des toilettes et regarda son installation. Il n'y aurait pas de chute, mais cela irait tout de même. Il réussirait à ne pas porter les mains au nœud coulant jusqu'à ce qu'il fût trop faible pour lever les bras.

Mais comment pouvait-il être certain que sa mort affecterait le Dragon, maintenant que le Dragon et lui-même étaient Deux ? Cela ne servirait peut-être à rien. Comment pouvait-il être sûr que le Dragon la laisserait tranquille ?

Des jours pourraient se passer avant qu'on retrouve son corps. Elle se demanderait ce qu'il était devenu. Déciderait-elle de venir chez lui pour voir s'il ne s'y terrait pas ? Monterait-elle au premier ? Une surprise l'y attendrait.

Le Grand Dragon Rouge mettrait bien une heure à la recracher en bas des marches.

Devait-il l'appeler pour la prévenir ? Même prévenue, que pourrait-elle contre Lui ? Rien. Espérer connaître une fin rapide, espérer que, dans Sa fureur, il la mordrait profondément, tout de suite ?

Là-haut, dans la maison de Dolarhyde, le Dragon attendait sur une reproduction qu'il avait encadrée de ses propres mains. Le Dragon attendait, dans d'innombrables magazines, dans des livres d'art, il renaissait toutes les fois qu'un photographe... faisait quoi ?

Dolarhyde entendait dans son esprit la voix puissante du Dragon maudire Reba. Il commencerait par la maudire, puis il la mordrait. Il maudirait également Dolarhyde et le traiterait de moins que rien devant Reba.

« Ne fais pas cela... ne fais pas cela », lança Dolarhyde vers la paroi de céramique. Il écouta sa voix, la voix de Francis Dolarhyde, la voix que Reba McClane comprenait parfaitement, sa propre voix. Il en avait eu honte toute sa vie et s'en était servi pour proférer des paroles de haine.

Mais il n'avait jamais entendu la voix de Francis Dolarhyde le maudire.

« Ne fais pas cela... »

La voix qu'il entendait à présent ne l'avait jamais maudit, jamais. Elle avait répété les insultes du Dragon. Ce souvenir lui faisait honte.

Il n'était probablement pas un homme à part entière, se dit-il. Il se rendit compte qu'il ne s'était jamais vraiment penché sur la question, et voici que cela l'intéressait.

Il avait désormais une once de fierté, et c'était Reba McClane qui la lui avait donnée. Et sa fierté lui disait que mourir dans une salle de bains était une bien triste fin.

Mais quoi d'autre ? Quelle solution lui restait-il ?

Si, il y avait une solution, et elle lui apparut comme un blasphème. Mais c'était tout de même une solution.

Il arpenta la chambre du motel, entre les lits, de la porte à la fenêtre. Et tout en marchant, il fit des exercices d'élocution. Les mots venaient bien s'il respirait à fond entre chaque phrase et s'il prenait tout son temps.

Il pouvait parler correctement entre deux bouffées de peur. Celle qui montait actuellement en lui était assez violente, au point qu'il en vomit. Il attendit le creux de la vague. Et quand elle vint, il se précipita au téléphone et composa un numéro à Brooklyn.

Les membres d'un orchestre de jeunes remontaient dans le car garé sur le parking du motel. Ils virent Dolarhyde arriver, et il dut passer au milieu d'eux pour regagner son van.

Une sorte de bouffi fit la grimace, bomba le torse et gonfla ses biceps derrière Dolarhyde. Deux filles se mirent à glousser. Le tuba tonna par la vitre du car quand il démarra, mais Dolarhyde n'entendit pas les rires qui l'accompagnaient.

Vingt minutes plus tard, il arrêtait le van dans l'allée, à trois cents mètres de la maison de grand-mère.

Il s'épongea le visage, prit son souffle. Sa main gauche se referma sur la clef de la maison ; de la droite, il tenait le volant.

Une sorte de gémissement s'échappa de son nez. Puis un autre, et encore un autre, de plus en plus fort. Vas-y !

Il fonça à toute allure vers la maison, les roues du van projetaient du gravier en tous sens. Le van dérapa dans la cour et Dolarhyde en sortit à toute allure.

À l'intérieur, sans regarder à gauche ni à droite, il dévala l'escalier de la cave et chercha à ouvrir une malle fermée à clef. Mais il n'avait pas la clef sur lui.

Le trousseau était à l'étage. Il ne s'accorda pas le temps de la réflexion. Pour s'interdire de penser, il émit une sorte de bourdonnement sonore avec son nez et se lança dans l'escalier.

Le bureau, le tiroir qu'il retourne pour y trouver les clefs, sans jeter le moindre regard au portrait du Dragon posé au pied du lit.

« QU'EST-CE QUE TU FAIS ? »

Mais où étaient donc les clefs ?

« QU'EST-CE QUE TU FAIS ? ARRETE-TOI. JE N'AI JAMAIS VU UN ENFANT AUSSI DÉGOUTANT QUE TOI. ARRETE-TOI. »

Ses mains ralentirent.

« REGARDE... REGARDE-MOI. »

Il s'agrippa au bord du bureau — surtout, ne pas se retourner vers le mur. Il ferma les yeux quand sa tête commença de tourner malgré lui.

« QU'EST-CE QUE TU FAIS ?

— Rien. »

Et le téléphone sonnait, sonnait, sonnait. Il décrocha le combiné, le dos tourné au mur.

« Salut, D. Alors, comment ça va ? » La voix de Reba McClane.

Il se racla la gorge. « Bien. » Tout juste un murmure.

« Je vous appelle parce qu'on m'a dit au bureau que vous étiez souffrant. Vous n'avez pas l'air en forme.

— Parlez-moi.

— Bien sûr, c'est pour ça que je vous appelle. Qu'est-ce que vous croyiez ? Ça ne va pas ?

— C'est la grippe, dit-il.

— Vous allez voir le docteur ?... Hé ? J'ai dit, vous allez voir le docteur ?

— Parlez plus fort. » Il fouilla dans le tiroir puis chercha à ouvrir le tiroir voisin.

« La ligne est mauvaise, on dirait. D., vous ne devriez pas rester tout seul si vous êtes malade.

— DIS-LUI DE VENIR CE SOIR ET DE S'OCCUPER DE TOI. »

Dolarhyde parvint juste à temps à poser la main sur le microphone.

« Bon sang, qu'est-ce que c'est que ça ? Il y a quelqu'un avec vous ?

— C'est la radio, j'ai tourné le mauvais bouton.

— Dites, vous voulez que je vous envoie quelqu'un ? Ça n'a vraiment pas l'air d'aller. Non, je viendrai plutôt. Je demanderai à Marcia de m'accompagner à l'heure du déjeuner.

344

— Non. » Les clefs étaient dissimulées sous une ceinture roulée dans le tiroir. Il s'en saisit, puis sortit dans le couloir avec le téléphone. « Tout va bien, rassurez-vous. On se rappelle. » Il avait failli trébucher sur les *s*. Il dévala les escaliers. Le cordon du téléphone s'arracha du mur et le combiné roula sur les marches.

Un hurlement de fureur. « REVIENS, TÊTE DE NŒUD. »

La cave. Il y avait dans la malle, juste à côté de la caisse de dynamite, une petite valise bourrée de billets de banque, de cartes de crédit et de permis de conduire établis à divers noms, un revolver, un poignard et un nerf de bœuf.

Il prit la valise et remonta en courant au rez-de-chaussée sans s'arrêter devant le grand escalier, prêt à se battre si le Dragon descendait à sa rencontre. Dans le van, à présent, puis un démarrage sur les chapeaux de roue.

Il ne ralentit qu'une fois sur la nationale et baissa la vitre pour vomir un peu de bile jaunâtre. La peur s'en allait tout doucement. Il roula à la vitesse autorisée, mit ses clignotants bien avant les croisements, et se rendit ainsi à l'aéroport.

39

DOLARHYDE régla le taxi devant un immeuble d'habitation d'Eastern Parkway, à deux pâtés de maisons du Brooklyn Museum. Il fit le reste du chemin à pied. Des joggers se dirigeaient vers Prospect Park.

Il s'arrêta près de la bouche de métro, afin d'admirer la grande bâtisse de style néo-classique. Il n'avait jamais visité le Brooklyn Museum, bien qu'il eût lu le guide — il avait commandé cet ouvrage après avoir vu la mention « Brooklyn Museum » imprimée en caractères minuscules sous les reproductions de *Le Grand Dragon Rouge et la Femme vêtue de soleil.*

Les noms des grands penseurs, de Confucius à Démosthène, avaient été gravés dans la pierre au-dessus de la porte d'entrée. C'était un bâtiment imposant, flanqué d'un jardin botanique — une demeure parfaite pour le Dragon.

Le métro faisait trembler le sol. Des bouffées d'air vicié se mêlaient à l'odeur de teinture de sa moustache.

Le musée allait fermer dans une heure. Il traversa la rue et entra. L'employée du vestiaire prit sa valise.

« Le vestiaire sera ouvert demain ? lui demanda-t-il.

— Le musée est fermé au public demain. » L'employée était une petite femme ridée en costume bleu. Elle tourna la tête.

« Les gens qui viennent demain, ils peuvent utiliser le vestiaire ?

— Non. Le musée est fermé, le vestiaire est fermé. »

Tant mieux. « Merci.

— Je vous en prie. »

Au rez-de-chaussée, Dolarhyde déambula parmi les grandes vitrines des salles consacrées à l'Océanie et aux deux Amériques — poteries des Andes, armes primitives, objets et masques chamaniques des Indiens de la côte du Pacifique.

Il ne restait plus que quarante minutes avant la fermeture du musée. Il n'avait plus le temps de visiter le rez-de-chaussée. Il connaissait l'emplacement des sorties et des ascenseurs publics.

Il monta jusqu'au quatrième étage. Il se sentait bien

plus proche du Dragon, mais tout allait bien — il ne risquait pas de tomber dessus au détour d'une salle.

Le Dragon n'était pas présenté au public ; l'aquarelle avait été enfermée dans l'obscurité depuis son retour de la Tate Gallery.

Dolarhyde avait appris au téléphone que *Le Grand Dragon Rouge et la Femme vêtue de soleil* était rarement exhibé. Cette aquarelle avait près de deux cents ans, et la lumière risquait de l'abîmer.

Dolarhyde s'arrêta devant un tableau d'Albert Bierstadt, *Orage dans les Rocheuses — Mt. Rosalie, 1866.* De là, il pouvait voir les portes fermées des réserves du musée. C'était là que se trouvait le Dragon. Pas une copie ni une photographie : le Dragon. C'était là qu'il viendrait demain, quand il aurait son rendez-vous.

Il fit tout le tour du quatrième étage et passa devant une multitude de portraits qu'il ne remarqua absolument pas. Tout ce qui l'intéressait, c'était les sorties. Il trouva les sorties de secours en cas d'incendie, le grand escalier, et nota l'emplacement des ascenseurs publics.

Les gardiens étaient des hommes d'âge mûr fort polis ; ils portaient des semelles épaisses et leurs jambes étaient déformées par des années de station debout. Aucun n'était armé, remarqua Dolarhyde, à l'exception d'un seul qui se tenait en faction dans le promenoir. Ce devait plutôt être un policier.

Les haut-parleurs annoncèrent la fermeture du musée.

Dolarhyde resta un instant sur le trottoir sous la figure allégorique de Brooklyn et regarda la foule sortir dans la tiédeur estivale.

Les joggers firent du surplace pour permettre aux gens de regagner la station de métro.

Dolarhyde passa quelques minutes au jardin botanique. Puis il héla un taxi et donna au chauffeur l'adresse d'un magasin qu'il avait relevée dans les pages jaunes de l'annuaire.

40

Lundi, neuf heures du soir. Graham posa sa mallette à terre devant la porte de l'appartement de Chicago et fouilla dans ses poches pour y trouver les clefs.

Il avait passé toute une journée à Detroit à interroger le personnel et à consulter les registres de l'hôpital où Mme Jacobi avait travaillé comme bénévole avant que la famille déménage pour Birmingham. Il cherchait quelqu'un qui aurait pu travailler à Detroit puis à Atlanta, ou encore à Birmingham et à Atlanta ; quelqu'un qui pourrait disposer d'une camionnette et d'un fauteuil roulant, et qui aurait vu Mme Jacobi et Mme Leeds avant de faire irruption chez elles.

Crawford pensait que ce voyage éclair était une perte de temps. Crawford avait raison, une fois de plus.

Graham entendit la sonnerie du téléphone dans l'appartement. Le trousseau de clefs s'accrocha au fond de la poche. Quand il tira dessus, il arracha un long fil. De la menue monnaie tomba à l'intérieur de son pantalon et roula sur le palier.

« Merde... »

Le téléphone cessa de sonner juste avant qu'il le décroche. Molly essayait peut-être de le joindre.

Il l'appela dans l'Oregon.

Le grand-père de Willy lui répondit la bouche pleine. C'était l'heure du dîner, dans l'Oregon.

« Dites seulement à Molly de me rappeler quand elle aura terminé », lui dit Graham.

Il se trouvait sous la douche, du shampooing plein les yeux, quand le téléphone sonna à nouveau. Il se rinça la tête et décrocha. « Salut, ma toute belle.

— Espèce de Don Juan. C'est Byron Metcalf, de Birmingham.

— Oh, pardon.

— J'ai de bonnes nouvelles et des mauvaises. Vous aviez raison pour Niles Jacobi. Il a bien sorti les affaires de la maison. Il s'en est débarrassé, mais je l'ai coincé pour une histoire de hasch dans sa chambre et il m'a tout raconté. Ça, c'étaient les mauvaises nouvelles — vous espériez sûrement que La Mâchoire les avait volées et les avait revendues.

« Les bonnes nouvelles, à présent. Il y avait bien un film. Je ne l'ai pas encore. Niles dit qu'il y a deux bobines coincées sous le siège de la voiture. Vous les voulez toujours ?

— Bien entendu.

— C'est son copain Randy qui utilise la voiture pour l'instant et nous ne lui avons pas encore mis la main dessus, mais ça ne devrait pas traîner. Vous voulez que je les mette dans le premier avion pour Chicago et que je vous rappelle ?

— Oui. Merci, Byron.

— Pas de quoi. »

Molly rappela au moment où Graham commençait à s'endormir. Après s'être mutuellement assurés qu'ils allaient parfaitement bien, il sembla qu'ils n'avaient plus grand-chose à se dire.

Willy s'amusait bien, lui dit Molly. Elle laissa Willy lui dire bonsoir.

Willy ne se contenta pas de lui dire bonsoir — il

apprit à Will la grande nouvelle : Grand-père lui avait
acheté un poney.

Molly n'en avait pas soufflé mot.

<h1 style="text-align:center">41</h1>

L E mardi, le Brooklyn Museum est fermé au grand
public, mais les étudiants des Beaux-Arts et les
chercheurs y sont toutefois admis.

Le musée est très pratique pour ceux qui veulent y
faire des études. Le personnel est compétent et
compréhensif ; il permet souvent aux chercheurs de
venir le mardi, sur rendez-vous, voir des œuvres qui
ne sont normalement pas présentées au public.

Francis Dolarhyde sortit du métro peu après deux
heures de l'après-midi ; il tenait sous le bras un carnet
de notes, un catalogue de la Tate Gallery et une bio-
graphie de William Blake.

Il avait également un automatique extra-plat de
calibre 9 mm, une matraque et un couteau dissimulé
sous sa chemise. Un bandage élastique plaquait les
armes contre son ventre plat. Cela ne le gênait pas
pour boutonner sa veste de sport. Dans la poche, il
transportait un sac en plastique renfermant un tampon imbibé de chloroforme.

Il tenait à la main un étui à guitare neuf.

Trois cabines téléphoniques se dressaient non loin
de la bouche de métro, au milieu d'Eastern Parkway.
Un des appareils avait été arraché, mais il y en avait
tout de même un qui fonctionnait.

Il introduisit des pièces jusqu'à ce qu'il entende Reba dire « allô ».

Derrière elle, il percevait les bruits familiers de la chambre noire.

« Bonjour, Reba, dit-il.

— Salut, D. Comment vous sentez-vous ? »

Il avait du mal à entendre à cause des voitures qui passaient de part et d'autre.

« Bien.

— On dirait que vous êtes dans une cabine publique. Je croyais que vous ne vouliez pas sortir de chez vous.

— Il faut que je vous parle, un peu plus tard.

— D'accord, appelez-moi en fin d'après-midi.

— J'ai besoin de... de vous voir.

— J'en serais heureuse, mais ce soir, c'est impossible. J'ai du travail. Vous me rappellerez ?

— Oui. Si rien...

— Comment ?

— Je vous rappellerai.

— J'espère que vous reviendrez très vite, D.

— Oui. Au revoir... Reba. »

Parfait. La peur lui coulait du plexus au nombril. Il l'épongea et traversa la rue.

Le mardi, on pénètre dans le Brooklyn Museum par une petite porte située à l'extrême droite. Dolarhyde entra derrière quatre étudiants en histoire de l'art. Les étudiants déposèrent leurs sacs et leurs cartables contre le mur avant de présenter leurs laissez-passer. Un gardien assis derrière un bureau les contrôla.

Il s'adressa à Dolarhyde.

« Vous avez rendez-vous ? »

Dolarhyde hocha la tête. « Mlle Harper, aux Réserves.

— Veuillez signer le registre, je vous prie. » Le gardien lui tendit un stylo.

Dolarhyde avait déjà le sien. Il signa « Paul Crane ».

Le gardien appela un numéro intérieur. Dolarhyde tourna le dos au bureau et étudia la *Fête des vendanges,* le tableau de Robert Blum accroché au-dessus de l'entrée, pendant que le garde confirmait le rendez-vous. Du coin de l'œil, il vit un responsable de la sécurité en poste dans le promenoir. C'était bien celui qui était armé.

« Au fond du promenoir, vers la boutique, il y a un banc juste à côté des ascenseurs, dit le gardien. Attendez là-bas. Mlle Harper va venir vous chercher. » Il tendit à Dolarhyde un badge en plastique rose et blanc.

« Je peux laisser ma guitare ici ?

— Je ne la quitterai pas des yeux. »

Le musée était différent avec les lumières éteintes. Les grandes vitrines baignaient dans une sorte de crépuscule.

Dolarhyde attendit trois minutes sur le banc, et Mlle Harper sortit de l'ascenseur public.

« Monsieur Crane ? Je suis Paula Harper. »

Elle était plus jeune qu'il ne l'avait imaginé au téléphone quand il l'avait appelée de Saint Louis ; une femme distinguée, d'une beauté sévère. Elle portait sa jupe et son chemisier comme un uniforme.

« Vous avez appelé pour l'aquarelle de Blake, dit-elle. Montons, je vais vous la montrer. Nous allons prendre l'ascenseur du personnel — par ici. »

Ils traversèrent la boutique du musée, puis une petite salle encombrée d'armes primitives. Il jeta un rapide coup d'œil circulaire pour se repérer. Dans un angle de la salle des Amériques, un couloir menait au petit ascenseur.

Paula Harper appuya sur un bouton. Elle croisa les bras et attendit. Ses yeux bleu clair se posèrent sur le badge rose et blanc épinglé à la veste de Dolarhyde.

« Il vous a donné un laissez-passer pour le cinquième étage, dit-elle. Ça ne fait rien, il n'y a pas de gardien au cinquième aujourd'hui. Quel type de recherches effectuez-vous ? »

Jusqu'à maintenant, Dolarhyde ne s'était adressé à elle que par sourires et hochements de tête. « C'est pour un article sur Butts, dit-il.

— Thomas Butts ? »

Il hocha la tête.

« On ne sait pas grand-chose sur son compte. Son nom n'apparaît dans les biographies que comme celui d'un client de Blake. C'est intéressant ?

— Je commence tout juste. Il va falloir que j'aille en Angleterre.

— Je crois que la National Gallery possède deux aquarelles qu'il a exécutées pour Butts. Vous les avez vues ?

— Pas encore.

— Vous feriez mieux de leur écrire avant d'y aller. »

Il hocha la tête. L'ascenseur arriva.

Quatrième étage. Il éprouvait quelques fourmillements, mais le sang continuait de circuler dans ses bras et dans ses jambes. Bientôt, il ne pourrait plus dire que oui ou non. Si les choses tournaient mal, ses jambes ne réussiraient même pas à le porter.

Elle lui fit traverser une galerie consacrée aux portraitistes américains. Il n'était pas passé par là la première fois, pourtant il savait où il se trouvait. Tout allait bien.

Mais quelque chose l'attendait dans la galerie, qui le paralysa littéralement quand il le découvrit.

Paula Harper se rendit compte qu'il ne la suivait plus et elle fit demi-tour.

Il était immobile devant l'un des portraits.

Elle vit ce qu'il contemplait et dit : « C'est un portrait de George Washington par Gilbert Stuart. »

Non, ce n'était pas cela.

« Vous le voyez reproduit sur le billet d'un dollar.

On l'appelle le portrait de Lansdowne parce que Stuart l'a exécuté pour le marquis de Lansdowne afin de le remercier de son soutien à la cause de la révolution américaine. Ça ne va pas, monsieur Crane ? »

Dolarhyde était livide. Cette peinture était pire que tous les billets d'un dollar qu'il avait pu voir jusqu'ici. Avec ses yeux tombants et ses fausses dents, Washington semblait sortir du portrait. Mon Dieu, il ressemblait à grand-mère. Dolarhyde se sentit soudain comme un petit enfant désemparé.

« Monsieur Crane, ça va ? »

Réponds ou laisse tomber. Vite. *Mon Dieu, c'est si bon.* TU ES L'ENFANT LE PLUS DÉGOUTANT... Non.

Dis quelque chose.

« Je prends du cobalt, fit-il.

— Vous voulez vous asseoir un instant ? » Il dégageait *effectivement* une odeur de médicament.

« Non, allez-y, je vous suis. »

Tu ne vas pas m'avoir, grand-mère. Je te tuerais si tu n'étais déjà morte. Déjà morte. Déjà morte. Grand-mère était morte ! Depuis des années, et à jamais. Mon Dieu c'est si bon...

Mais l'autre n'était pas mort, et Dolarhyde le savait.

Assailli par la peur, il suivit pourtant Mlle Harper.

Ils franchirent une double porte et pénétrèrent dans les réserves du musée. Dolarhyde observa les lieux. C'était une longue pièce paisible, bien éclairée, pleine de présentoirs chargés de tableaux recouverts de draps. De petits bureaux étaient alignés tout le long du mur. La dernière porte était entrouverte, quelqu'un tapait à la machine.

Il ne vit personne en dehors de Paula Harper.

Elle le conduisit à une table de travail et lui apporta un tabouret.

« Attendez-moi là, je vais vous apporter ce tableau. »

Elle disparut derrière les présentoirs.

Dolarhyde défit un bouton de sa veste.

Mlle Harper revint vers lui. Elle portait un coffret noir et plat pas plus grand qu'un carton à dessin. Il était là-dedans. Comment avait-elle la force de le porter ? Il n'aurait jamais imaginé qu'il fût si plat. Il avait relevé les dimensions dans le catalogue — 42 x 34,3 cm — mais n'y avait prêté aucune attention. Il s'attendait à ce que le tableau soit immense, mais il était assez petit. Petit et *ici*, dans cette pièce paisible. Il n'avait jamais vraiment évalué la force que le Dragon pouvait tirer de la vieille maison perdue au milieu des vergers.

Mlle Harper lui parlait. « ... le conserver dans ce coffret parce que la lumière risque de l'affecter. C'est pour cela qu'il n'est que rarement exposé. »

Elle posa le coffret sur la table et commença de le déballer. Un bruit en provenance de la double porte. « Excusez-moi, il faut que j'ouvre à Julio. » Elle referma le coffret et l'emporta avec elle. Un homme attendait à l'extérieur avec un chariot. Elle ouvrit les portes vitrées et l'homme entra.

« Tout va bien ici ?

— Oui, merci Julio. »

Il repartit.

Et Mlle Harper revint avec le coffret.

« Je suis désolée, monsieur Crane. C'est le jour où Julio vient épousseter les cadres. » Elle ouvrit le coffret et en tira une chemise de carton blanc. « Vous comprendrez que vous n'avez pas le droit d'y toucher. Je vous le montre, c'est tout. D'accord ? »

Dolarhyde hocha la tête. Il ne pouvait plus parler.

Elle ouvrit la chemise et ôta le feuillet de protection.

Il était là, sous ses yeux. *Le Grand Dragon Rouge et la Femme vêtue de soleil* — l'Homme-Dragon rampant sur la femme prostrée et suppliante, prisonnière des replis de sa queue.

Le tableau était petit, mais d'une telle puissance.

Fascinant. Les meilleures reproductions ne pouvaient rendre justice aux détails, aux coloris.

En un instant, Dolarhyde le découvrit dans son intégralité — l'écriture de Blake sur le bord de l'œuvre, deux taches brunes en bas, à droite. Il était saisi. C'était trop... Les couleurs étaient si puissantes...

Regarde la femme prisonnière de la queue du Dragon. Regarde-la.

Il vit que ses cheveux avaient exactement la même couleur que ceux de Reba McClane. Il vit qu'il était à un peu plus de six mètres de la porte. Il réprima certaines voix.

J'espère que je ne vous ai pas choqué, dit Reba McClane.

« Il semble qu'il ait utilisé de la craie en plus de l'aquarelle », lui disait Paula Harper. Elle se tenait de telle sorte qu'elle pouvait toujours voir ce qu'il faisait. Ses yeux ne quittaient jamais le tableau.

Dolarhyde glissa sa main sous sa chemise.

Un téléphone se mit à sonner. Le bruit de machine à écrire cessa. Une femme passa la tête hors du bureau du fond.

« Paula, c'est pour toi. C'est ta mère. »

Mlle Harper ne tourna pas la tête. Ses yeux ne quittaient jamais Dolarhyde et le tableau. « Tu peux prendre un message ? dit-elle. Non, dis-lui que je rappellerai. »

La femme disparut dans le bureau. À nouveau, le crépitement de la machine à écrire.

Dolarhyde n'y tenait plus. Il fallait attaquer, tout de suite.

Mais le Dragon fut plus rapide que lui. « je n'ai jamais vu...

— Quoi ? s'écria Mlle Harper, affolée.

— Un rat aussi gros ! dit Dolarhyde, le doigt tendu. Là, sur ce tableau !

— Où cela ? » fit-elle en se retournant.

La matraque glissa de sa chemise. D'un mouvement

du poignet il lui en assena un coup à l'arrière de la tête. Elle commença à s'affaisser, mais Dolarhyde la rattrapa par le pan de son chemisier et lui plaqua sur le visage le tampon de chloroforme. Elle poussa un petit cri puis s'affaissa.

Il l'allongea à terre, entre la table et les présentoirs, tira à lui la chemise contenant l'aquarelle et s'accroupit au-dessus d'elle. Un bruissement de papier, un bruit de déchirure, une respiration haletante, et à nouveau la sonnerie du téléphone.

La femme sortit du bureau du fond.

« Paula ? » Elle chercha du regard dans la pièce. « C'est ta mère, dit-elle. Il faut absolument qu'elle te parle *tout de suite.* »

Elle s'approcha de la table. « Je m'occuperai de ton visiteur si tu... » C'est alors qu'elle les vit. Paula Harper allongée à terre, les cheveux dans la figure, et accroupi au-dessus d'elle, un revolver à la main, Dolarhyde, qui enfonçait dans sa bouche le tout dernier morceau de l'aquarelle. Sans cesser de mâcher, il se leva et fonça vers elle.

Elle courut vers le bureau, referma la porte, s'empara du téléphone qu'elle fit tomber à terre, rampa vers lui et chercha à composer un numéro sur la ligne occupée, quand la porte fut enfoncée. Le voyant rouge explosa devant ses yeux quand la matraque s'abattit sur son crâne. Le combiné retomba à terre avec un bruit sec.

Dans l'ascenseur du personnel, Dolarhyde regardait défiler les chiffres des étages ; le revolver était plaqué sur son ventre et dissimulé par les livres.

Rez-de-chaussée.

Ses chaussures semblaient voler sur le dallage des galeries désertes. Une erreur de parcours, et il se retrouva devant les masques de baleines, les grands masques des Sisuits ; il perdit plusieurs secondes, se retrouva devant les mâts totémiques des Haidas, aperçut à gauche les armes primitives et sut où il se trouvait.

Il jeta un coup d'œil discret dans le promenoir.

Le gardien se tenait près du panneau d'affichage, à une dizaine de mètres de son bureau.

Celui qui portait une arme se trouvait plus près de la porte. Son étui craqua quand il se baissa pour frotter une tache sur la pointe de sa chaussure.

Si ça barde, descends-le en premier. Dolarhyde coinça le revolver sous sa ceinture et boutonna sa veste. Il traversa le promenoir et défit le badge.

Le gardien se retourna en entendant des pas.

« Merci », fit Dolarhyde. Il déposa le laissez-passer sur le bureau.

Le garde hocha la tête. « Voudriez-vous le mettre dans cette fente, s'il vous plaît ? »

Le téléphone du bureau sonna.

Il eut du mal à ramasser le badge.

Le téléphone sonna à nouveau. Vite.

Dolarhyde récupéra le laissez-passer et le glissa dans la fente. Il prit son étui à guitare au milieu des cartables.

Le gardien se dirigeait vers le téléphone.

Il franchit la porte et tourna en direction du jardin botanique, prêt à faire feu si quelqu'un le poursuivait.

Il pénétra dans le jardin, tourna à gauche et se dissimula entre un abri et une haie. Il ouvrit l'étui à guitare et en sortit une raquette de tennis, une balle, une serviette-éponge, un sac en papier et une grande branche de céleri.

Les boutons volèrent sous ses doigts et il se débarrassa prestement de sa veste et de sa chemise, avant d'ôter son pantalon. Dessous, il portait un tee-shirt du Brooklyn College et un pantalon de survêtement. Il enfourna les livres et les vêtements dans le sac en papier, puis il y rangea les armes avant de disposer la branche de céleri. Il essuya la poignée et la fermeture de l'étui à guitare, puis le dissimula sous la haie.

La serviette autour du cou, il coupa par les jardins en direction de Prospect Park, et déboucha sur Empire Boulevard. Des joggers couraient devant lui. Il les suivit à l'intérieur du parc quand les premières sirènes de police retentirent. Les joggers n'y prêtèrent aucune attention, et Dolarhyde ne leur en prêta pas plus qu'eux.

Il faisait alterner la marche et le petit trot ; avec son sac à provisions et sa raquette de tennis, il paraissait s'être arrêté pour faire des courses en revenant de l'entraînement.

Il s'obligea à ralentir ; il valait mieux ne pas courir l'estomac plein. Il pouvait choisir son rythme, à présent.

Il pouvait tout choisir.

42

Assis au dernier rang du box des jurés, Crawford mangeait des cacahuètes pendant que Graham tirait les stores du prétoire.

« Il faut absolument que tu me communiques le profil en fin d'après-midi, dit Crawford. Tu avais dit mardi, et on est mardi.

— J'ai presque terminé, mais je veux d'abord voir ça. »

Graham ouvrit l'enveloppe que Byron Metcalf lui

avait adressée par exprès et en vida le contenu
— deux bobines poussiéreuses de film super-8, enve-
loppées chacune dans un sac en plastique.

« Est-ce que Metcalf va chercher à faire inculper
Niles Jacobi ?

— Pas pour vol, en tout cas. Il va probablement
hériter, lui et le frère de Jacobi, dit Graham. Quant
au hasch, je n'en sais rien. Je crois que le juge de
Birmingham a envie de le faire plonger.

— Tant mieux », dit Crawford.

L'écran descendit du plafond du prétoire et fit face
au box des jurés ; ce dispositif avait été installé pour
permettre la projection de pièces à conviction au jury.

Graham brancha le projecteur.

« À propos des kiosques où La Mâchoire aurait pu
se procurer le *Tattler* si rapidement, j'ai déjà des rapports en provenance de Cincinnati, Detroit et
quelques quartiers de Chicago, dit Crawford. Il y a des
pistes à suivre. »

Graham lança le film. Une partie de pêche.

Les enfants Jacobi étaient installés au bord d'un
étang avec des gaules et des épuisettes.

Graham s'efforça de ne pas les imaginer dans leurs
petites boîtes, dans la terre. Il voulait les voir pêcher,
c'est tout.

Le bouchon de la fille s'agita puis disparut. Un pois-
son avait mordu.

Crawford froissa le sac de cacahuètes. « C'est fou ce
qu'ils mettent comme mauvaise volonté à Indianapo-
lis pour interroger les marchands de journaux et les
employés des stations Servco Supreme, dit-il.

— Tu veux voir ça ou quoi ? » lui lança Graham.

Crawford réussit à ne pas dire un mot pendant les
deux minutes que durait le film. « Formidable, elle a
attrapé une perche, dit-il. Bon, pour le profil...

— Jack, tu t'es rendu à Birmingham juste après la
tuerie, et moi, j'y suis allé un mois plus tard. Tu as vu

la maison comme elle était du temps de leur vivant. Pas moi. Elle avait été complètement transformée entre-temps. Maintenant, pour l'amour de Dieu, laisse-moi regarder et je le ferai ensuite, ton profil. »

Il lança la seconde bobine.

Une réception d'anniversaire apparut sur l'écran du prétoire. Les Jacobi étaient assis autour d'une table. Ils chantaient.

Graham put lire sur leurs lèvres : « Happy birthday to you. »

Donald Jacobi, onze ans, était face à la caméra. Il avait pris place au bout de la table, et le gâteau était posé devant lui. Les bougies se reflétaient dans ses lunettes.

À côté de lui, son frère et sa sœur le regardèrent souffler les bougies.

Graham remua sur sa chaise.

Mme Jacobi se pencha en avant — ses longs cheveux noirs lui caressèrent les épaules — et chassa le chat qui avait sauté sur la table.

À présent, Mme Jacobi tendait à son fils une grande enveloppe d'où pendait un long morceau de ruban. Donald Jacobi ouvrit l'enveloppe et en tira une carte de vœux. Il se tourna vers la caméra et montra la carte. « Bon anniversaire — suis le ruban. »

Une image tressautante tandis que la caméra suit la procession en direction de la cuisine. Une porte fermée au crochet. L'escalier de la cave, Donald en tête, puis les autres, et le ruban qui court toujours le long des marches. L'extrémité du ruban était attachée au guidon d'une bicyclette à dix vitesses.

Graham se demanda pourquoi on ne lui avait pas offert la bicyclette dans la cour.

La séquence suivante apporta une réponse à sa question. Elle avait été tournée en extérieur. Visiblement, il avait beaucoup plu. De l'eau stagnait dans la cour. La maison paraissait différente. Geehan, l'agent immobilier, l'avait fait repeindre d'une autre couleur après la tuerie.

La porte du sous-sol s'ouvrit et M. Jacobi apparut avec la bicyclette. C'était la première fois qu'on le voyait dans le film. Un coup de vent lui ébouriffa les cheveux. Il déposa la bicyclette avec force cérémonie.

Le film s'acheva sur les débuts de coureur cycliste de Donald Jacobi.

« C'est bien triste, tout ça, dit Crawford, mais on le savait déjà. »

Graham rembobina le film de l'anniversaire.

Crawford secoua la tête et lut des papiers à l'aide d'une lampe de poche.

Sur l'écran, M. Jacobi sortit la bicyclette du sous-sol. La porte se referma derrière lui. Un cadenas y était accroché.

Graham arrêta sur l'image.

« Là. C'est pour cela qu'il avait besoin d'un coupe-boulons. Pour couper le cadenas et entrer par le sous-sol. Pourquoi a-t-il changé d'avis ? »

Crawford éteignit la lampe de poche et jeta un coup d'œil à l'écran. « À propos de quoi ?

— On sait qu'il possédait un coupe-boulons : il s'en est servi pour tailler la branche qui le gênait pour observer la maison. Mais pourquoi ne s'en est-il pas servi pour pénétrer par la porte du sous-sol ?

— Il n'aurait pas pu. » Crawford attendit, un sourire énigmatique aux lèvres. Il adorait donner la pichenette qui fait s'écrouler le château de cartes.

« Est-ce qu'il a essayé et a été contraint d'abandonner ? Je n'ai même pas pu voir cette porte — Geehan l'a fait remplacer par une porte blindée avec une serrure à pompe. »

Crawford ouvrit enfin la bouche. « *Tu supposes* que Geehan a fait poser cette porte. Eh bien, non. Geehan ne l'a pas fait poser. La porte blindée était déjà là quand ils ont été tués. C'est certainement Jacobi qui l'a installée — les gens de Detroit raffolent des serrures à pompe.

— *Quand* Jacobi l'a-t-il fait poser ?

— Je n'en sais rien. Certainement après l'anniversaire du gosse. Quelle date était-ce, au juste ? Ce doit être marqué dans le rapport d'autopsie, il faudra qu'on vérifie.

— C'était le 14 avril, un lundi », dit Graham. Il contemplait fixement l'écran, le menton dans la main. « Je veux savoir quand Jacobi a changé cette porte. »

Le front de Crawford se plissa, puis redevint lisse lorsqu'il vit où Graham voulait en venir. « Tu crois que La Mâchoire a repéré la maison des Jacobi quand il y avait encore la vieille porte, dit-il.

— Il avait bien un coupe-boulons, n'est-ce pas ? Comment fais-tu pour entrer quelque part avec un coupe-boulons ? demanda Graham. Tu coupes les cadenas, les barres ou les chaînes. Il n'y avait ni barre ni chaîne à la porte, exact ?

— Exact.

— Il pensait trouver un cadenas. Un coupe-boulons est un objet assez lourd et assez encombrant. Il s'est déplacé en plein jour, et il avait pas mal de chemin à parcourir entre sa voiture et sa maison. Il aurait été obligé de revenir en courant au cas où les choses auraient mal tourné. S'il a emporté un coupe-boulons, c'est qu'il pensait en avoir besoin. Il croyait trouver un cadenas.

— Tu crois qu'il a repéré la maison avant que Jacobi ne change la porte ? Ensuite, il est revenu pour les tuer, il a attendu dans les bois.

— On ne peut voir cette façade de la maison depuis la forêt. »

Crawford hocha la tête. « Il attend dans les bois. Ils vont se coucher et lui arrive avec son coupe-boulons, c'est alors qu'il trouve la nouvelle porte avec la serrure à pompe.

— D'accord, il trouve la nouvelle porte. Tout avait bien marché jusque-là, dit Graham. Il est terriblement déçu, mais il faut absolument qu'il rentre dans la place. Il s'excite contre la porte du patio et fait tellement de bruit qu'il réveille Jacobi — c'est pour cela qu'il l'a tué dans l'escalier. C'est trop brouillon, cela ne ressemble pas au Dragon. Il prend beaucoup de précautions et ne laisse pas de traces derrière lui. Il a fait du beau boulot quand il est entré chez les Leeds.

— D'accord, dit Crawford. Si nous pouvons savoir quand Jacobi a fait changer la porte, nous connaîtrons le laps de temps qui s'est écoulé entre le jour où il a repéré les lieux et celui où il a tué, à quelque chose près. Cela peut être assez utile. Peut-être que l'intervalle correspondra avec l'intervalle entre deux conventions ou deux manifestations à Birmingham. Il faudra revoir les loueurs de voitures. Nous demanderons aussi pour les camionnettes. Je vais en toucher un mot au bureau de Birmingham. »

Crawford dut faire plus que « toucher un mot » : au bout de quarante minutes très exactement, un agent du F.B.I. de Birmingham, accompagné de l'agent immobilier Geehan, parlait à un charpentier travaillant dans le chevronnage d'une maison en construction. L'information donnée par le charpentier fut aussitôt transmise à Chicago.

« Pendant la dernière semaine d'avril, dit Crawford en reposant le combiné. C'est à ce moment-là qu'ils ont fait installer la nouvelle porte. Bon sang, c'est deux mois avant la mort des Jacobi. Pourquoi a-t-il repéré la maison deux mois plus tôt ?

— Je n'en sais rien, mais il y a une chose dont je suis sûr : il a vu Mme Jacobi ou toute la famille avant de repérer leur maison. À moins qu'il ne les ait suivis depuis Detroit, il a vu Mme Jacobi entre le 10 avril, date de leur déménagement à Birmingham, et la fin avril, époque où la porte a été changée. Il se trouvait à Birmingham. Le bureau va s'en occuper ?

— Oui, les flics aussi, dit Crawford. Mais il y a autre chose : comment pouvait-il savoir qu'une porte permettait d'accéder directement du sous-sol dans la maison proprement dite ? Ce n'est pas du tout évident — dans cette région, je veux dire.

— Il n'y a pas de doute possible, il a vu l'intérieur de la maison.

— Ton copain Metcalf, il a les relevés de banque de Jacobi ?

— Certainement.

— Je voudrais voir s'ils ont eu des travaux ou des livraisons à domicile entre le 10 avril et la fin du même mois. Je sais bien qu'on a déjà vérifié pour les semaines précédant la tuerie, mais nous ne sommes peut-être pas remontés assez loin. Idem pour les Leeds.

— Nous avons toujours pensé qu'il avait vu l'intérieur de la maison des Leeds, dit Graham. De l'extérieur, on ne peut pas voir la porte vitrée de la cuisine. Il y a une véranda en bois. Pourtant, il avait un diamant. Et personne n'est venu chez eux au cours du trimestre précédant leur mort.

— Dans ce cas, c'est peut-être nous qui ne sommes pas remontés assez loin. Enfin, on verra bien. Mais attends... quand il relevait les compteurs derrière la maison des Leeds deux jours avant de les tuer, il les a peut-être vus entrer dans la maison. Il a peut-être aperçu l'intérieur quand la porte de la véranda était ouverte.

— Ce n'est pas possible, les portes ne sont pas en enfilade. Tu te souviens ? Tiens, regarde. »

Graham chargea la bobine des Leeds sur le projecteur.

Le scottish des Leeds pointa les oreilles et courut

vers la porte de la cuisine. Valérie Leeds et les enfants arrivèrent, les bras chargés de commissions. On n'apercevait que la paroi de la véranda par la porte de la cuisine.

« Bon, tu veux que Byron Metcalf reprenne les relevés de banque d'avril, pour voir s'ils n'ont pas eu la visite d'un réparateur ou d'un démarcheur à domicile ? Non, je vais m'en occuper pendant que tu travailles au profil. Tu as le numéro de Metcalf ? »

Graham était absorbé par le film des Leeds. D'un air distrait, il dicta à Crawford trois numéros de téléphone où il pourrait joindre Byron Metcalf.

Il se repassa les films pendant que Crawford téléphonait de la salle des délibérations.

Il commença par le film des Leeds.

Le chien des Leeds. Il ne portait pas de collier et les chiens étaient nombreux dans les environs ; malgré tout, le Dragon savait exactement lequel était leur chien.

Valérie Leeds. Graham se sentit troublé en la voyant. Derrière elle, il y avait cette porte, si fragile avec sa vitre. Les enfants jouaient sur l'écran du prétoire.

Graham ne s'était jamais senti aussi proche des Jacobi que des Leeds. Pourtant, leur film le préoccupait. Et il se rendit compte qu'il n'avait jamais pensé aux Jacobi que sous forme de tracés à la craie effectués sur un sol ensanglanté.

Les enfants des Jacobi étaient assis à table, les bougies d'anniversaire éclairaient leurs visages.

Pendant une fraction de seconde, Graham entrevit la marque de cire sur la table de nuit des Jacobi, les taches de sang sur le mur de la chambre des Leeds. Quelque chose...

Crawford revint dans le prétoire. « Metcalf m'a dit de te demander...

— *Ne dis rien !* »

366

Crawford ne s'en offusqua pas. Il se figea et posa sur Graham un regard devenu intense, brûlant.

Le film se poursuivit, les lumières et les ombres dansaient sur le visage de Graham.

Le chat des Jacobi. Le Dragon savait pertinemment que c'était *leur* chat.

La porte intérieure.

Puis la porte du sous-sol avec son cadenas. Le Dragon avait apporté un coupe-boulons.

Le film était terminé. La bande claqua contre la bobine.

Tout ce que le Dragon avait besoin de connaître se trouvait sur ces films.

Ils n'avaient pas été montrés en public ni présentés dans un club ou dans un festi...

Graham regarda à nouveau la boîte dans laquelle était rangé le film des Leeds. Il y lut leur nom et leur adresse. Et aussi : Laboratoires Gateway, Saint Louis, Missouri, 63102.

Son esprit s'arrêta sur « Saint Louis » comme sur un numéro de téléphone qu'il aurait déjà rencontré. Qu'y avait-il donc à Saint Louis ? C'était l'une des villes où le *Tattler* était disponible dès le lundi soir, jour où il était imprimé — la veille du jour où Lounds avait été enlevé.

« Bon sang, murmura Graham. Oh ! nom de Dieu ! »

Il se boucha les oreilles comme pour empêcher les idées de s'enfuir.

« Tu as toujours Metcalf au téléphone ? »

Crawford lui tendit le combiné.

« Byron, c'est Graham. Écoutez, les bobines que vous m'avez envoyées, est-ce qu'elles étaient dans des boîtes ? Oui, je sais bien que vous me les auriez expédiées en même temps. J'ai besoin d'un renseignement très précis. Vous avez les relevés de banque des Jacobi sous les yeux ? Bon, je veux savoir où ils ont fait déve-lopper ce film. Une boutique a dû s'en charger à leur place. S'il y a un chèque rédigé à l'ordre d'un drugs-tore ou d'un magasin de photos, nous saurons où ils se sont adressées. Byron, c'est vraiment urgent, je vous assure. Le F.B.I. de Birmingham va contrôler toutes ces boutiques. Dès que vous avez quelque chose, vous le leur communiquez et ensuite, vous m'appelez. Ça ira ? D'accord. Quoi ? Non, il n'est *pas question* que je vous présente à "ma toute belle" ! »

Les agents du F.B.I. de Birmingham rendirent visite à quatre magasins de photos avant de trouver celui où étaient venus les Jacobi. Le vendeur dit que tous les films des clients étaient envoyés dans un seul et même laboratoire de développement.

Crawford avait eu le temps de visionner douze fois les films avant que Birmingham rappelle. C'est lui qui prit le message.

Avec beaucoup de solennité, il tendit la main à Gra-ham. « C'est Gateway », lui dit-il.

43

CRAWFORD faisait fondre un Alka-Seltzer dans un gobelet en plastique quand la voix de l'hôtesse retentit dans les haut-parleurs.

« M. Crawford est prié de se faire connaître des membres de l'équipage. Je répète, M. Crawford... »

Il leva la main, et l'hôtesse s'approcha de lui.

« Monsieur Crawford, voudriez-vous vous rendre dans la cabine de pilotage ? »

Crawford ne s'absenta que quatre minutes. Puis il se rassit à côté de Graham.

« La Mâchoire était à New York aujourd'hui même. »

Graham fit la grimace et fit claquer ses dents.

« Pas du tout. Il s'est contenté d'assommer deux femmes au Brooklyn Museum et aussi, tiens-toi bien, il *a mangé* un tableau.

— Il l'a mangé ?

— Oui. La brigade chargée de la protection des œuvres d'art a foncé sur place en apprenant ce qu'il avait mangé. Ils ont relevé deux empreintes partielles sur un laissez-passer en plastique et ils les ont aussitôt communiquées à Price. Il a ameuté tout le monde dès qu'il les a projetées : elles ne correspondent pas à une carte d'identité, mais c'est le même pouce que sur l'œil du gosse des Leeds.

— New York..., dit Graham l'air pensif.

— Cela ne prouve rien, il était à New York aujourd'hui, c'est tout. Ce qui ne l'empêche pas de travailler à Gateway. Il a dû prendre sa journée. Ça nous facilitera la tâche.

— Et qu'est-ce qu'il a mangé ?

— Une peinture intitulée *Le Grand Dragon Rouge et la Femme vêtue de soleil*. Ils disent que c'est de William Blake.

— Et les femmes ?

— Un petit coup de matraque, c'est tout. La plus jeune est en observation à l'hôpital. L'autre a eu quatre points de suture. Elle est un peu secouée.

— Elles ont pu fournir une description ?

— La plus jeune, oui. Calme, baraqué, une moustache et des cheveux noirs — certainement une perruque. Le gardien a confirmé sa déclaration. Quant à l'autre, elle ne sait même pas ce qui s'est passé.

— Et il n'a tué personne.

— Non, fit Crawford. C'est étrange. Il aurait mieux valu qu'il les supprime toutes les deux — cela lui aurait donné le temps de prendre la fuite et surtout évité d'être repéré. Le département des Sciences du comportement a appelé Bloom à l'hôpital. Tu sais ce qu'il a dit ? Selon Bloom, il essaye peut-être de s'arrêter. »

44

DOLARHYDE entendit le gémissement des volets qui se baissent. Les lumières de Saint Louis tournoyèrent lentement sous l'aile noire. Sous ses pieds, le train d'atterrissage sortit et se bloqua avec un bruit sec.

Il fit rouler sa tête sur ses épaules pour dégourdir les muscles puissants de sa nuque.

Retour au bercail.

Il avait pris de grands risques, mais la récompense en était le pouvoir de choisir. Il pouvait choisir de laisser en vie Reba McClane. Il pouvait l'avoir auprès de lui pour lui parler, il pouvait l'avoir dans son propre lit, avec son étonnante et pourtant inoffensive mobilité.

Il n'avait plus à redouter sa maison. Le Dragon était dans son ventre, à présent. Il pouvait rentrer chez lui, s'approcher d'une reproduction du Dragon épinglée au mur et la déchiqueter si bon lui semblait.

Il n'avait pas à s'inquiéter de ressentir de l'Amour pour Reba. S'il éprouvait de l'Amour pour elle, il pourrait livrer les Sherman au Dragon afin de l'apaiser, revenir auprès de Reba, calme et serein, et bien s'occuper d'elle.

Dolarhyde l'appela à son appartement dès qu'il fut dans l'aérogare. Elle n'était pas encore rentrée. Il composa le numéro de la Baeder Chemical. La ligne de nuit était occupée. Il pensa à Reba et la vit se diriger vers l'arrêt d'autobus, son travail terminé ; l'imperméable sur les épaules, elle heurtait le trottoir du bout de sa canne.

La circulation était assez fluide et il ne lui fallut que quinze minutes pour se rendre au laboratoire.

Elle n'était pas à l'arrêt du bus. Il se gara derrière la Baeder Chemical, près de l'entrée la plus proche des chambres noires. Il lui dirait qu'il était venu la chercher, attendrait qu'elle ait fini de travailler et la raccompagnerait. Il était fier de son nouveau pouvoir. Il voulait en faire usage.

Il y avait un certain nombre de choses qu'il pourrait prendre dans son bureau pendant ce temps-là.

Seules quelques pièces de la Baeder Chemical étaient encore éclairées.

La chambre noire de Reba était fermée à clef. Au-dessus de la porte, la lumière n'était ni rouge ni verte, mais éteinte, tout simplement. Il sonna. Pas de réponse.

Peut-être lui avait-elle laissé un message dans son bureau.

Il entendit des pas dans le couloir.

Dandridge, le responsable de Baeder, passa devant les chambres noires sans daigner tourner la tête. Il marchait à vive allure et tenait sous le bras une pile de dossiers provenant du service du personnel.

Une ride imperceptible se creusa sur le front de Dolarhyde.

Dandridge avait franchi la moitié du parking et prenait la direction des bâtiments de Gateway quand Dolarhyde quitta à son tour la Baeder.

Deux camionnettes de livraison et une douzaine de voitures se trouvaient sur le parking. La Buick appartenait à Fisk, le chef du personnel de Gateway. Que pouvaient-ils bien faire à cette heure ?

Il n'y avait pas d'équipe de nuit chez Gateway. La majeure partie du bâtiment était plongée dans l'obscurité. Dans les couloirs, les panneaux lumineux rouges indiquant les sorties étaient allumés. Il y avait également de la lumière de l'autre côté de la porte vitrée du service du personnel. Dolarhyde perçut le bruit de plusieurs voix, celle de Dandridge, celle de Fisk.

Des pas de femme. La secrétaire de Fisk déboucha dans le couloir devant Dolarhyde. Elle avait dissimulé ses bigoudis sous un foulard et transportait des registres comptables. Elle paraissait pressée. Les registres étaient lourds et encombrants. Elle frappa du bout du pied à la porte du bureau de Fisk.

Will Graham lui ouvrit.

Dolarhyde se figea dans l'obscurité. Il avait laissé son automatique dans le van.

La porte du bureau se referma.

Les chaussures de Dolarhyde ne faisaient pas de bruit. Il courut jusqu'à la porte vitrée de la sortie et jeta un coup d'œil au-dehors. Il régnait une certaine agitation sur le parking. Un homme s'approcha d'une des camionnettes de livraison, une lampe-torche à la main. Il épousseta le rétroviseur extérieur afin d'y trouver des empreintes.

Des pas retentirent dans le couloir, derrière Dolarhyde. Quitter cette porte, vite. Il s'engouffra dans l'escalier menant au sous-sol et aux chaudières installées de l'autre côté du bâtiment.

En grimpant sur un établi, il put atteindre les vasistas qui ouvraient au niveau du sol, derrière des broussailles. Il fit un rétablissement et s'avança à quatre pattes devant les buissons, prêt à se battre ou à courir.

Tout était calme de ce côté-ci du bâtiment. Il se releva, mit sa main dans sa poche et traversa la rue. D'un pas rapide quand il faisait très sombre, plus lent lorsque des voitures passaient, il fit un large crochet pour contourner le laboratoire de Gateway et la Baeder Chemical.

Son van était garé derrière la Baeder. Il lui était désormais impossible de se cacher. Tant pis. Il fonça vers le véhicule, ouvrit la portière, sauta sur le siège et agrippa sa valise.

Il mit un chargeur plein dans l'automatique et engagea une balle dans le canon avant de le poser sur le tableau de bord et de le dissimuler sous un tee-shirt.

Il démarra et roula lentement, pour ne pas devoir s'arrêter au feu rouge, puis tourna au coin de la rue et se mêla à la circulation clairsemée.

Il fallait qu'il réfléchisse, tout de suite, mais ce n'était pas aussi facile que ça.

Ce devait être les films. D'une manière ou d'une autre, Graham avait compris pour les films. Il savait *où* aller, mais il ne savait pas encore *qui* arrêter. S'il le savait, il n'aurait pas eu besoin des archives du personnel. Mais qu'allait-il faire des registres comptables ? Pour les absences, bien entendu. Comparer les absences aux dates où le Dragon avait frappé. C'était le samedi, sauf dans le cas de Lounds. Les absences des jours précédents, voilà ce qu'il voulait vérifier. Mais il se casserait le nez : la direction ne conservait pas les fiches de pointage des employés.

Dolarhyde remonta lentement le boulevard Lindbergh tout en comptant sur les doigts de sa main droite les points à analyser.

Ils cherchaient des empreintes. Il ne leur avait jamais donné l'occasion d'en trouver — sauf, peut-être, sur le laissez-passer en plastique du Brooklyn Museum. Dans sa hâte, il l'avait attrapé par les bords.

Ils possédaient déjà une empreinte de lui. Sinon, à quoi compareraient-ils celles qu'ils relevaient sur les véhicules ? Ils contrôlaient les fourgonnettes ; il n'avait pas eu le temps de voir s'ils s'intéressaient aussi aux voitures.

Le van. Il y avait transporté Lounds et le fauteuil roulant. C'était cela. À moins qu'un habitant de Chicago ne l'ait aperçu. Il y avait beaucoup de fourgonnettes de toutes sortes à Gateway, des camionnettes de livraison, des vans privés.

Non, Graham savait qu'il possédait un van, tout simplement. Graham le savait parce qu'il le savait. Graham savait. Graham savait. Ce fils de pute était un monstre.

Ils allaient relever les empreintes de tous les employés de Baeder et de Gateway. S'ils ne tombaient pas sur lui ce soir, ce serait pour demain. Il lui faudrait s'enfuir à tout jamais et voir *son visage* reproduit sur tous les avis de recherche affichés dans les bureaux de poste ou les commissariats. Tout se désagrégeait. Il était totalement impuissant contre eux.

« Reba », dit-il à haute voix. Reba ne pouvait plus le sauver. Le piège se refermait sur lui, et il n'était rien de plus qu'un chétif bec-de-li...

« REGRETTES-TU ENFIN DE M'AVOIR TRAHI ? »

La voix du Dragon résonnait en lui, elle s'élevait des fragments du tableau épars dans ses entrailles.

« Je ne vous ai pas... Je voulais choisir, c'est tout. Vous m'aviez appelé...

— DONNE-MOI CE QUE JE DÉSIRE ET JE TE SAUVERAI.

— Non, je vais m'enfuir.

— DONNE-MOI CE QUE JE DÉSIRE ET TU ENTENDRAS SE BRISER LES REINS DE GRAHAM.

— Non.

— J'AI ADMIRÉ TON GESTE. NOUS SOMMES TRÈS PROCHES À PRÉSENT. NOUS POURRIONS NE PLUS FAIRE QU'UN. SENS-TU MA PRÉSENCE EN TOI ? TU LA SENS, N'EST-CE PAS ?

— Oui.

— ET TU SAIS QUE JE PEUX TE SAUVER. TU SAIS QU'ILS T'ENVERRONT DANS UN ENDROIT PIRE QUE LE PENSIONNAT DU FRÈRE BUDDY. DONNE-MOI CE QUE JE DÉSIRE ET TU SERAS LIBRE.

— Non.

— ILS TE TUERONT. TU TE TORDRAS À TERRE.

— Non.

— QUAND TU NE SERAS PLUS LÀ, ELLE SE TAPERA TOUS LES AUTRES TYPES, ELLES...

— Non ! Taisez-vous !

— ELLE SE TAPERA TOUS LES AUTRES, TOUS CEUX QUI SONT BEAUX, ELLE SE METTRA LEUR...

— Assez ! Silence !

— RALENTIS ET JE NE TE DIRAI PAS CE QU'ELLE FERA. »

Dolarhyde souleva le pied de l'accélérateur.

« C'EST BIEN. DONNE-MOI CE QUE JE DÉSIRE ET CELA NE SE PRODUIRA PAS. DONNE-LE-MOI ET JE TE LAISSERAI TOUJOURS CHOISIR. TU POURRAS TOUJOURS CHOISIR ET TU PARLERAS CORRECTEMENT. JE VEUX QUE TU PARLES CORRECTEMENT. RALENTIS. C'EST BIEN. TU VOIS CETTE STATION-SERVICE ? ARRÊTE-TOI LÀ, IL VA FALLOIR QUE JE TE PARLE... »

45

GRAHAM sortit des bureaux et se reposa un instant la vue dans le couloir plongé dans la pénombre. Il se sentait mal à l'aise, tout cela prenait trop de temps.

Crawford passait en revue les 380 employés de Gateway et de la Baeder Chemical, il effectuait son travail avec le maximum d'efficacité — et Dieu sait s'il était spécialisé de ce genre de boulot — mais les heures s'écoulaient et le secret ne pourrait plus être gardé très longtemps.

Crawford avait réduit au minimum le groupe de travail. (« Nous ne voulons pas le surveiller mais le trouver, leur avait-il expliqué. Si nous le découvrons ce soir, nous pourrons l'arrêter hors de l'usine, chez lui ou sur le parking. »)

La police de Saint Louis coopérait avec eux. Le Lt Fogel, de la criminelle de Saint Louis, et un sergent arrivèrent dans une voiture banalisée avec un Datafax.

Branché sur un téléphone de Gateway, le Datafax ne mit que quelques minutes pour transmettre la liste du personnel au service d'identification du F.B.I. à Washington, et au service des immatriculations du Missouri.

À Washington, les noms seraient confrontés aux listes d'empreintes civiles ou criminelles. Les noms des employés affectés aux postes de sécurité furent écartés pour accélérer la procédure.

Le service des immatriculations étudierait la liste des propriétaires de van.

Quatre employés seulement furent convoqués au laboratoire : Fisk, le chef du personnel ; la secrétaire de Fisk ; Dandridge, de la Baeder Chemical ; et le chef comptable de Gateway.

Ils n'utilisèrent pas le téléphone pour les faire venir ; des agents allèrent les chercher à domicile et leur expliquèrent ce qu'on attendait d'eux. (« Embarquez-les avant de leur dire ce que vous leur voulez, avait dit Crawford. Et ne les laissez pas se servir du téléphone. Ce genre de nouvelles circule très vite. »)

Ils avaient espéré que les dents permettraient une identification rapide, mais aucun des employés ne les reconnut.

Graham regarda les longs couloirs et les lumières rouges des panneaux de sortie. Attendre... Que pouvaient-ils faire d'autre ?

Crawford avait demandé que la femme du Brooklyn Museum — Mlle Harper — les rejoigne dès qu'elle serait en état de voyager. Elle arriverait certainement dans la matinée. La police de Saint Louis disposait d'une camionnette de surveillance très pratique d'où elle pourrait voir passer tous les employés.

S'ils n'aboutissaient pas à un résultat dès ce soir, toutes les traces de l'opération seraient effacées avant que le travail reprenne à Gateway. Mais Graham ne se faisait pas d'illusions — ils disposeraient à peine d'une journée avant que tout le monde ne soit au courant à Gateway. Et le Dragon s'enfuirait à la moindre alerte.

46

Un souper avec Ralph Mandy lui convenait parfaitement. Reba McClane savait qu'elle devait le mettre au courant, et elle n'aimait pas laisser traîner les choses en longueur.

En fait, Mandy devait déjà se douter de quelque chose.

Elle lui parla en voiture, quand il la raccompagna ; elle lui dit qu'il ne devait pas s'en faire, qu'elle s'était bien amusée avec lui et qu'elle désirait rester son amie, mais qu'elle avait fait la connaissance d'un autre homme.

Peut-être cela lui fit-il un peu mal, mais elle savait aussi qu'il se sentait soulagé.

Devant sa porte, il ne chercha pas à entrer. Mais il lui demanda la permission de l'embrasser, et elle accepta. Il ouvrit la porte et lui tendit les clefs. Puis il attendit qu'elle se fût enfermée dans son appartement.

Au moment où il se retourna, Dolarhyde lui tira une balle dans la gorge et deux autres dans la poitrine. Trois détonations étouffées par le silencieux du revolver. Un scooter fait plus de bruit.

Dolarhyde souleva sans peine le cadavre de Mandy pour le déposer entre la maison et le massif d'arbustes, où il l'abandonna.

Dolarhyde avait reçu un coup de poignard en plein cœur en voyant Reba embrasser Mandy, mais sa douleur avait vite disparu.

Il avait toujours l'allure et les intonations de Francis Dolarhyde — le Dragon était vraiment un acteur de tout premier plan, il jouait à merveille le rôle de Dolarhyde.

Reba était dans la salle de bains quand elle entendit le carillon de la porte. Il sonna à quatre reprises avant qu'elle touche la chaîne, sans l'enlever toutefois.

« Qui est là ?

— Francis Dolarhyde. »

Elle entrouvrit la porte, toujours avec la chaîne. « Vous voulez répéter ?

— Dolarhyde. C'est moi. »

Elle savait que c'était bien lui. Elle ôta la chaîne.

Reba n'aimait pas les surprises. « Il me semblait que vous deviez m'appeler avant.

— Oui, mais c'est vraiment urgent », dit-il, en lui pressant sur le visage le tampon de chloroforme et en la repoussant à l'intérieur de l'appartement.

La rue était vide, la lumière éteinte dans la plupart des appartements. Il la porta jusqu'au van. Les pieds de Ralph Mandy dépassaient du massif, mais Dolarhyde n'y prêta pas attention.

Elle revint à elle pendant le trajet. Elle était couchée sur le flanc, la joue posée sur le tapis poussiéreux ; la transmission résonnait dans ses oreilles.

Elle tenta de porter la main à son visage, et cela lui fit mal à la poitrine. Ses avant-bras étaient attachés l'un à l'autre.

Elle parvint à les palper du bout du nez. Ils étaient entourés du coude au poignet par ce qui semblait être des bandes de tissus. Les jambes étaient attachées de la même manière, du genou à la cheville. Quelque chose lui barrait la bouche.

Que... que... D. à la porte et ensuite... Elle se souvint d'avoir détourné la tête, de la force terrible qui l'avait assaillie. Mon Dieu... Qu'est-ce que... D. était à la porte et puis, elle avait respiré quelque chose de froid, elle avait voulu se tourner et il y avait eu cette poigne formidable sur sa tête.

Elle se trouvait dans le van de Dolarhyde, elle en reconnaissait les résonances. Le van roulait. La peur montait en elle. Son instinct lui disait de rester calme, mais sa gorge était pleine de vapeurs d'essence et de chloroforme. Elle voulut se débarrasser du bâillon.

La voix de Dolarhyde. « Il n'y en a plus pour très longtemps. »

Il y eut un virage, puis du gravier, de petits cailloux qui heurtent la caisse et les pare-chocs.

Il est fou. C'est tout simple : il est fou.

Et la folie est une chose effrayante.

Pourquoi tout cela ? Ralph Mandy. Il avait dû les voir ensemble. Et cela avait suffi.

Seigneur Jésus, il fallait être prête. Un homme avait essayé de la frapper, à l'institut Reiker. Elle n'avait pas bougé, et il n'avait pas réussi à la trouver — lui non plus ne pouvait pas voir. Mais celui-ci voyait parfaitement. Etre prête. Prête à parler. Mon Dieu, il pourrait me tuer sans même m'ôter mon bâillon. Sans comprendre ce que j'ai à lui dire.

Prête, oui. Réagir tout de suite sans faire « hein ? ». Lui dire qu'il peut faire marche arrière sans problème. Je ne dirai rien à personne. Reste passive le plus longtemps possible. Et si tu ne peux pas l'être, tâche de trouver ses yeux.

Le van s'arrêta. Une oscillation quand il en descendit. Les portes qui coulissent. Une odeur d'herbe et de pneus chauds. Des criquets. Il monta dans le van.

Malgré elle, elle poussa des cris étouffés et tourna la figure quand il essaya de la toucher.

Une caresse sur l'épaule ne parvint pas à la calmer. Une paire de gifles y réussit bien mieux.

Elle essaya de parler malgré le bâillon. On la soulevait, on la portait. Les pas qui résonnent sur le plan incliné. Elle savait parfaitement où elle se trouvait. Sa maison. Mais où, dans sa maison ? Le tic-tac de l'horloge sur la droite. Du tapis puis du parquet. La chambre où ils avaient dormi. Elle sentit le lit sous elle.

À nouveau, elle voulut parler. Il s'en allait. Du bruit à l'extérieur. La porte du van qui claque. Il revient. Il pose quelque chose à terre — des bidons en métal.

Elle sentit l'odeur de l'essence.

« Reba. » C'est bien la voix de D., mais elle est si calme. Si terriblement et étrangement calme. « Reba, je ne sais pas quoi... quoi vous dire. Vous aviez l'air si bonne, et vous ne saviez pas ce que j'avais fait pour vous. Mais j'ai eu tort, Reba. Vous m'avez diminué et vous m'avez fait souffrir. »

Elle tenta de parler malgré le bâillon.

« Si je vous détache et vous permets de vous asseoir, vous vous montrerez gentille ? N'essayez pas de vous enfuir. Je peux vous rattraper. Vous serez gentille ? »

Elle tourna la tête et fit signe que oui.

Un contact métallique, glacial, contre sa peau ; le souffle d'un couteau qui tranche l'étoffe, et ses bras furent libérés. Puis ce fut le tour des jambes. Ses joues étaient humides quand il ôta le bâillon.

Lentement, sans mouvement brusque, elle s'assit sur le lit. Montre-toi convaincante.

« D., dit-elle, je ne savais pas que vous vous intéressiez tant à moi. J'en suis heureuse mais vous savez, vous m'avez fait peur avec tout ça. »

Pas de réponse. Elle savait qu'il était là.

« C'est parce que j'étais avec ce vieil idiot de Ralph Mandy que vous êtes en colère ? Vous l'avez vu devant chez moi, c'est ça ? J'étais en train de lui dire que je ne voulais plus le revoir. C'est vous que je veux voir. Je ne reverrai plus jamais Ralph.

— Ralph est mort, dit Dolarhyde. Je ne crois pas qu'il ait beaucoup apprécié. »

Il plaisante. C'est cela, il plaisante. « Je n'ai jamais voulu vous faire de mal, D. Soyons amis, envoyons-nous en l'air et oublions toute cette histoire.

— La ferme, dit-il calmement. Je vais vous raconter quelque chose. Ce sera la chose la plus importante que vous ayez jamais entendue. Aussi importante que le Sermon sur la montagne ou les Dix Commandements. C'est compris ?

— Oui, D. Mais je...

— La ferme. Reba, des événements tout à fait remarquables se sont déroulés à Birmingham et à Atlanta. Vous voyez de quoi je parle ? »

Elle secoua la tête.

« Les actualités en ont beaucoup parlé. Deux groupes de gens ont été transformés. Les Leeds. Et les Jacobi. La police croit qu'ils ont été assassinés. Vous voyez de quoi je parle, maintenant ? »

Elle commença de secouer la tête, puis la mémoire lui revint et elle fit signe que oui.

« Savez-vous comment ils appellent l'Etre qui a rendu visite à ces gens ? Vous pouvez le dire.

— La Mâch... »

Une main se plaqua sur sa bouche.

« Réfléchissez et donnez-moi une réponse correcte.

— C'est le Dragon... Attendez, le Dragon Rouge. »

Il était tout près d'elle. Elle pouvait sentir son souffle sur son visage.

« JE SUIS LE DRAGON. »

Le volume et le timbre de sa voix la firent sursauter, au point qu'elle se heurta au chevet du lit.

« Le Dragon te désire, Reba. Il t'a toujours désirée. Je ne voulais pas t'offrir à Lui. Aujourd'hui, j'ai fait en sorte qu'Il ne puisse t'avoir. Et j'ai mal agi. »

C'était bien Dolarhyde, elle pouvait lui parler. « Je vous en prie. Je vous en prie, ne le laissez pas me prendre. Vous ne le laisserez pas, dites, vous ne le... Je suis à *vous*. Gardez-moi avec vous. Vous m'aimez, je le sais.

— Je n'ai pas encore pris de décision. Je ne pourrai peut-être pas m'empêcher de te livrer à Lui. Je n'en sais rien. Je vais voir si tu fais bien ce que je te dis. Tu m'obéiras ? Je peux compter sur toi ?

« — Je vais essayer. Oui, je vais essayer. Mais arrêtez de me faire peur, sinon je ne pourrai plus rien faire.

— Lève-toi, Reba. Tiens-toi au lit. Tu sais où tu te trouves dans la pièce ? »

Elle hocha la tête.

« Tu sais où tu te trouves dans la maison, n'est-ce pas ? Tu t'es promenée dans la maison pendant que je dormais ?

— Pendant que vous dormiez ?

— Ne fais pas l'idiote. Quand nous avons passé la nuit ici. Tu as visité la maison, hein ? Est-ce que tu as trouvé quelque chose d'étrange ? Est-ce que tu l'as emporté pour le montrer à quelqu'un ? Dis, Reba, tu as fait cela ?

— Je suis sortie, c'est tout. Vous dormiez et je suis allée faire un tour dehors, je vous le jure.

— Dans ce cas, tu sais où se trouve la porte d'entrée. »

Elle hocha la tête.

« Reba, pose tes mains sur ma poitrine. Remonte-les, lentement. »

Les yeux !

Les doigts de Dolarhyde effleuraient sa gorge. « Ne fais pas ce à quoi tu penses ou je t'étrangle. Mets tes mains sur ma poitrine. Sur ma gorge, maintenant. Tu sens la clef au bout de la chaîne ? Fais-la passer au-dessus de ma tête. Doucement... là, c'est bien. Maintenant, je vais voir si je peux te faire confiance. Tu vas aller jusqu'à la porte d'entrée, tu vas la fermer à clef et tu me rapporteras la clef. Vas-y. Je t'attendrai ici. N'essaye pas de t'enfuir. Je peux te rattraper sans problèmes. »

Elle tenait la clef à la main, la chaîne se balançait sur sa cuisse. Il était bien plus difficile de se diriger avec des chaussures, mais elle les garda. Le tic-tac de l'horloge était là pour l'aider.

Le tapis, le parquet, du tapis à nouveau. Le bord d'un canapé. À droite.

Qu'est-ce que j'ai de mieux à faire ? Faire semblant d'entrer dans son jeu et foncer à la première occasion ? Est-ce que les autres avaient fait semblant ? La tête lui tournait, elle avait respiré trop profondément pour se calmer. Ne t'évanouis pas. Ne meurs pas.

Cela dépendra de la porte. Si elle est ouverte ou non. D'abord, savoir où il se trouve.

« Je suis dans la bonne direction ? » Elle savait fort bien que oui.

« Encore cinq pas. » La voix venait de la chambre. Elle sentait de l'air frais. La porte était entrouverte. Elle demeura un instant entre la porte et la voix. Elle introduisit la clef dans la serrure. À l'extérieur.

Maintenant. Elle passe la porte, la tire vers elle et tourne la clef. Le plan incliné, pas de canne pour s'aider. Il faut se rappeler où le van est garé, courir. Courir. Elle rentre dans... dans un buisson. Elle crie. « Au secours ! au secours ! au secours ! au secours ! » Elle court sur le gravier. Un klaxon dans le lointain. La nationale est de ce côté-ci, elle court de son mieux, fait des zigzags, change de direction quand elle sent l'herbe sous ses pieds, retrouve le gravier.

Derrière elle, des pas qui se font plus rapides, plus sonores sur le gravier. Elle se baisse et ramasse une poignée de cailloux, elle attend qu'il soit tout près et les lui jette au visage, entend le bruit net qu'ils font au contact de son corps.

Une main sur son épaule la fait tourner sur elle-même, un bras se place sous son menton, il la serre, le sang bourdonne à ses tempes. Elle se débat, donne des coups de pied, le frappe au tibia, et puis... progressivement... elle se calme...

47

IL ne fallut que deux heures pour dresser la liste des employés de sexe masculin âgés de vingt à cinquante ans et possédant des vans. Elle se composait de vingt-six noms.

Le service des véhicules à moteur indiqua la couleur des cheveux à partir des renseignements portés sur les permis de conduire, mais cet élément ne fut pas retenu en priorité. Le Dragon avait très bien pu porter une perruque.

Mlle Trillman, la secrétaire de Fisk, tapa plusieurs exemplaires de la liste et la fit distribuer.

Le Lt Fogel était en train d'examiner la liste quand son beeper se mit à sonner.

Il appela le quartier général de la police, puis posa la main sur le combiné. « Monsieur Crawford — Jack, un certain Ralph Mandy, trente-huit ans, de race blanche, a été retrouvé assassiné il y a quelques minutes aux environs de la cité universitaire — oui, c'est juste au centre-ville —, il se trouvait devant la maison d'une certaine Reba McClane. Les voisins ont dit qu'elle travaillait chez Baeder. Sa porte est ouverte et elle n'est pas chez elle.

— Dandridge ! appela Crawford. Reba McClane, vous la connaissez ?

— Elle travaille à la chambre noire. Elle est aveugle. Elle vient du Colorado et...

— Et Ralph Mandy, ça vous dit quelque chose ?

— Mandy ? fit Dandridge. Randy Mandy ?

— *Ralph* Mandy, il travaille ici ? »

Un coup d'œil jeté à la liste du personnel lui apprit que non.

« C'est peut-être une coïncidence, dit Fogel.

— Peut-être, fit Crawford.

— J'espère qu'il n'est rien arrivé à Reba, dit Mlle Trillman.

— Vous la connaissez ? demanda Graham.

— J'ai déjà bavardé avec elle.

— Et Mandy ?

— Je ne le connais pas. Je ne l'ai vue qu'avec un seul homme, elle était montée dans le van de M. Dolarhyde.

— Le van de M. Dolarhyde ? Mlle Trillman, quelle est la couleur de ce van ?

— Attendez... Marron foncé. Peut-être noir.

— Où travaille M. Dolarhyde ? demanda Crawford.

— Il est chef de fabrication, dit Fisk.

— Où se trouve son bureau ?

— Tout de suite à droite, dans le couloir. »

Crawford se tourna pour s'adresser à Graham, mais celui-ci était déjà parti.

Le bureau de Dolarhyde était fermé à clef. Un passe-partout du service de l'entretien fit l'affaire.

Graham alluma la lumière. Il resta un instant sur le pas de la porte pour s'habituer à l'éclairage. Tout était en ordre. Il n'y avait visiblement aucun objet personnel, et la bibliothèque n'abritait que des ouvrages techniques.

La lampe de bureau était sur la gauche du fauteuil, donc il était droitier. Comment trouver l'empreinte d'un pouce gauche avec un droitier ?

« Voyons s'il a un carnet, dit-il à Crawford qui attendait dans le couloir. Il y aura certainement l'empreinte de son pouce gauche dessus. »

Ils commençaient de fouiller dans les tiroirs quand le calendrier de bureau attira l'attention de Graham. Il tourna les pages pour remonter au 28 juin, date de la mort des Jacobi.

Il n'y avait rien de marqué pour le jeudi et le vendredi précédant ce week-end.

Il tourna à nouveau les pages. La dernière semaine de juillet. Les pages du jeudi et du vendredi étaient encore vierges. Il y avait une note au mercredi : « Am 552.3.45 — 6.15. »

Graham recopia l'inscription. « Je veux savoir de quel vol il s'agit.

— Je vais m'en occuper. Continue à chercher », dit Crawford. Il décrocha un téléphone de l'autre côté du couloir.

Graham venait de trouver dans le tiroir du bas un tube de pâte adhésive pour dentier quand Crawford lui cria :

« C'est l'avion d'Atlanta, Will. Coinçons-le. »

48

DE l'eau froide sur le visage de Reba, de l'eau qui coule dans ses cheveux. Elle se sent mal. Sous son dos, quelque chose de dur. Elle tourne la tête. Du bois. Une serviette humide essuie son visage.

« Ça va, Reba ? » La voix de Dolarhyde.

Elle sursauta. « Oui.

— Respirez à fond. »

Une minute s'écoula.

« Vous croyez que vous pourrez vous relever ? Essayez de vous relever. »

Elle parvint à se relever quand il lui passa le bras autour de la taille. Son cœur se souleva. Il attendit que le spasme fût passé.

« Montez le plan incliné. Vous savez où vous êtes ? »
Elle hocha la tête.

« Tirez la clef, Reba. Entrez. Maintenant, refermez la porte et mettez la clef autour de mon cou. Autour de mon cou, là. Je vais m'assurer que la porte est bien fermée à clef. »

Elle l'entendit tourner le bouton.

« Bien. Allez dans la salle de bains, à présent. Vous connaissez le chemin. »

Elle tituba et tomba sur les genoux, la tête pendante. Il la souleva sous les bras et l'aida à regagner la chambre.

« Prenez place dans ce fauteuil. »

Elle s'assit.

« DONNE-LA-MOI. »

Elle voulut se lever, mais des mains puissantes la plaquèrent aux épaules.

« Restez tranquille, sinon je ne pourrai L'empêcher de vous avoir », dit Dolarhyde.

Elle reprenait ses esprits, malgré elle.

« Essayez, je vous en prie, dit-elle.

— Reba, tout est fini pour moi. »

Il était debout, il s'affairait. L'odeur d'essence était plus forte que tout à l'heure.

« Tendez la main. Touchez cela. Ne le serrez pas, touchez-le simplement. »

Elle sentit quelque chose qui ressemblait à des narines de métal ; l'intérieur était lisse. Le canon d'une arme.

« C'est un fusil de chasse, Reba. Un magnum calibre 12. Vous savez à quoi il va servir ? »

Elle hocha la tête.

« Baissez la main. » Le canon froid se nicha dans le creux de sa gorge.

« Reba, j'aurais voulu pouvoir vous faire confiance. Je voulais vous faire confiance. »

On aurait dit qu'il pleurait.

« Vous aviez l'air si bonne. »

Oui, *il pleurait.*

« Vous aussi, D. J'étais bien avec vous. Ne me faites pas de mal.

— Tout est fini pour moi. Je ne peux vous laisser à Lui. Vous savez ce qu'Il fera ? »

Il se mit à hurler.

« Vous savez ce qu'Il fera ? Il vous mordra jusqu'à ce que vous en mouriez. Il vaut mieux que vous veniez avec moi. »

Elle entendit le craquement d'une allumette, sentit une odeur de soufre. Un souffle soudain. De la chaleur. De la fumée. Le feu. La chose qu'elle redoutait le plus au monde. Le feu. Tout valait mieux que cela. Elle espérait que la première balle serait pour elle. Elle se prépara à s'enfuir.

Des mots presque incompréhensibles.

« Oh, Reba, je ne supporterai jamais de vous voir brûler. »

Le canon abandonna sa gorge.

Les deux gueules du fusil crachèrent en même temps, à l'instant précis où elle se relevait.

Assourdie, elle crut un instant qu'il lui avait tiré dessus et qu'elle était morte ; elle sentit plus qu'elle n'entendit le bruit d'un corps qui tombe à terre.

La fumée, le crépitement des flammes. Le feu. Le feu la ramena à elle. Elle sentit la chaleur sur son visage, sur ses bras. Dehors. Elle se cogna au pied du lit.

Accroupis-toi pour passer sous la fumée, c'est ce qu'on lui avait toujours appris. Ne cours pas, si tu t'assommes dans quelque chose, tu es morte.

Mais elle était enfermée dans la pièce. Enfermée. Elle marcha lentement, se baissa, laissa traîner ses doigts à terre. Elle trouva des jambes. De l'autre côté. Elle trouva des cheveux, posa la main sur quelque chose de mou. Rien que de la chair déchiquetée, des éclats d'os et un œil arraché.

La clef autour du cou, vite. Les deux mains sur la chaîne. Elle tira de toutes ses forces et tomba en arrière quand la chaîne se brisa. Elle se releva, tourna sur elle-même. Il faut sentir, percevoir les bruits malgré le craquement des flammes. Le bas-côté du lit, mais lequel ? Elle buta sur le corps, chercha à percevoir des bruits.

BONG, BONG, l'horloge sonne, BONG, BONG, dans la salle de séjour, BONG, BONG, prends à droite.

La gorge pleine de fumée. BONG, BONG. La porte. La serrure, là, sous le bouton. Ne fais pas tomber la clef. Un déclic. Elle est ouverte. De l'air. Le plan incliné. De l'air. Elle s'effondra dans l'herbe, se mit à quatre pattes.

Elle frappa dans ses mains et perçut l'écho que renvoyait la maison, puis elle s'éloigna à quatre pattes, respirant bien à fond, jusqu'à ce qu'elle puisse se relever, marcher, courir, rentrer dans quelque chose, courir à nouveau.

49

Il ne fut pas facile de retrouver la maison de Francis Dolarhyde. L'adresse qu'il avait laissée à Gateway était celle d'une boîte postale de Saint Charles.

Même le bureau du shérif de Saint Charles dut consulter une carte des branchements électriques pour en être sûr.

L'équipe du shérif attendit l'arrivée de la brigade d'intervention de Saint Louis et les voitures s'engagèrent en silence sur la Nationale 94. Graham se trouvait dans la voiture de tête ; à ses côtés, un shérif adjoint lui indiquait la route. Assis sur la banquette arrière, Crawford se penchait entre eux sans cesser de se curer les dents. Ils ne rencontrèrent que fort peu de véhicules au nord de Saint Charles : un camion bâché plein d'enfants, un car Greyhound, une dépanneuse.

Ils virent les lueurs de l'incendie à l'instant même où ils franchirent les limites nord de la ville.

« C'est *là* ! s'écria l'adjoint. C'est là ! »

Graham écrasa l'accélérateur. Les lueurs se faisaient plus vives au fur et à mesure qu'ils approchaient.

Crawford claqua des doigts pour qu'on lui passe le micro.

« Appel à toutes les unités, c'est sa maison qui est en train de brûler. Attention, il va peut-être sortir. Shérif, il faudra établir un barrage routier ici même. »

Une épaisse colonne d'étincelles et de fumée s'étirait vers le sud-est, au-dessus des champs, puis au-dessus des voitures de police.

« Là, dit l'adjoint, prenez l'allée de gravier. »

C'est alors qu'ils virent la femme, silhouette noire sur fond d'incendie, ils la virent à l'instant où elle les entendit, et elle leva les bras.

Le feu prit alors des proportions extraordinaires, il se propagea vers le haut et vers l'extérieur quand les poutres et les fenêtres s'embrasèrent. Les flammes décrivaient de grands arcs dans le ciel. Renversé sur le côté, le van brûlait également. Soudain, les contours orange des arbres en feu devinrent tout noirs. Le sol trembla et le souffle de l'explosion secoua les voitures de police.

La femme était allongée sur la route, le visage dans

le gravier. Crawford, Graham et les adjoints descendirent de voiture et coururent vers elle. Une pluie de feu s'abattait sur le chemin. Des hommes les dépassèrent, courant vers la maison, revolver au poing.

Crawford enleva Reba à un adjoint qui ôtait les flammèches de ses cheveux.

Il la tint dans ses bras, le visage tout près du sien.

« Francis Dolarhyde », dit-il. Il la secoua doucement. « Francis Dolarhyde, où est-il ?

— Là-dedans. » Elle tendit une main salie vers le brasier, puis la laissa retomber.

« Il est mort.

— Vous en êtes *sûre* ? » Crawford chercha à scruter ses yeux d'aveugle.

« J'étais avec lui.

— Dites-moi tout, je vous en prie.

— Il s'est tiré une décharge en plein visage. J'ai posé ma main dessus. Il a mis le feu à la maison. Il s'est tué. J'ai posé ma main sur son visage. Il était allongé par terre. J'ai posé ma main... Est-ce que je peux m'asseoir quelque part ?

— Oui », dit Crawford. Il monta avec elle à l'arrière d'une voiture de police. Il la prit par les épaules et la laissa pleurer sur lui.

Debout au milieu de la route, Graham contempla les flammes jusqu'à ce qu'il ne puisse plus supporter la chaleur.

La fumée chassée par le vent obscurcissait la lune.

50

Le vent matinal était chaud et humide. Des nuages s'amoncelaient au-dessus des cheminées noircies qui se dressaient à l'endroit où s'était élevée la maison de Dolarhyde. Une fine couche de fumée planait sur les champs alentour.

Quelques gouttes de pluie tombaient sur les vestiges encore fumants et se changeaient en minuscules jets de vapeur et de cendres.

Une voiture de pompiers stationnait non loin de là, le gyrophare allumé.

S.F. Aynesworth, chef de la brigade des explosifs au F.B.I., se tenait près des ruines en compagnie de Graham et versait du café d'une Thermos.

Aynesworth fit la grimace en voyant le capitaine des pompiers fouiller les cendres à l'aide d'un râteau.

« Dieu merci, c'est encore trop chaud pour qu'il s'y risque », dit-il du coin de la bouche. Il avait bien pris soin de se montrer aimable envers les autorités locales, mais il n'avait rien à cacher à Graham : « Il va falloir que je m'y mette. Cet endroit va ressembler à une basse-cour dès que les flics du coin et leurs hommes y auront jeté leurs emballages et coulé leurs bronzes. »

Le véhicule spécial d'Aynesworth n'était pas encore arrivé de Washington, et il dut se débrouiller avec ce qu'il avait pu emporter dans l'avion. Il tira un vieux sac de l'armée du coffre d'une voiture de police et en sortit des sous-vêtements Nomex ainsi qu'une combinaison et des bottes en amiante.

« À quoi cela ressemblait quand ça a pété ?

— Il y a eu un éclair très intense qui n'a pas duré. Puis la base a paru plus sombre. Tout un tas de trucs ont été projetés en l'air, des fenêtres, des morceaux de toiture, des éclats de bois ont volé dans les champs. Il y a eu une onde de choc puis un grand souffle, ça a presque failli éteindre l'incendie.

— Le feu était violent quand il y a eu l'explosion ?

— Oui, les flammes sortaient par le toit et par les fenêtres, au premier comme au rez-de-chaussée. Les arbres avaient pris feu. »

Aynesworth demanda à deux pompiers de l'assister avec leur lance ; un troisième homme portant un costume en amiante devait rester près de lui avec une hache au cas où quelque chose lui tomberait dessus.

Il dégagea l'escalier de la cave, maintenant à ciel ouvert, et descendit dans un amas de poutres noircies. Il ne pouvait rester que quelques minutes à chaque fois, et il dut faire huit voyages.

Il ne rapporta de ses expéditions qu'un morceau de métal déchiqueté mais cela parut le satisfaire.

Le visage rouge et couvert de transpiration, il se débarrassa de ses vêtements en amiante et s'assit sur le marchepied de la voiture de pompiers, un imperméable sur les épaules.

Il posa à terre le morceau de métal et souffla dessus pour en ôter une fine couche de cendres.

« C'est de la dynamite, dit-il à Graham. Tenez, là, vous voyez les dessins sur le métal ? C'est une serrure de malle ou de coffre. Oui, c'est cela. La dynamite était dans un petit coffre. Mais elle n'a pas dû exploser au sous-sol. Je pencherais plutôt pour le rez-de-chaussée. Regardez l'arbre qui a été coupé par le dessus de table en marbre — elle a été projetée horizontalement. La dynamite était rangée dans quelque chose qui l'a protégée momentanément du feu.

— Vous croyez qu'il y aura des restes ?

— Pas beaucoup, mais on trouve toujours quelque chose. Il va falloir tout déblayer. Mais nous le trouverons. Je vous le rapporterai dans une pochette en plastique. »

Reba McClane s'était endormie un peu avant l'aube grâce au somnifère qu'on lui avait administré à l'hôpital DePaul. Elle avait insisté pour qu'une femme de la police reste auprès d'elle. Elle s'éveilla plusieurs fois dans la matinée et tendit la main pour serrer celle de l'inspecteur.

Quand elle demanda le petit déjeuner, ce fut Graham qui le lui apporta.

Comment faire ? Bien souvent, les témoins préfèrent que leur interlocuteur demeure anonyme. Mais il ne pensait pas que Reba McClane aimerait cela.

Il lui dit qui il était.

« Vous le connaissez ? » demanda-t-elle à la femme de la police.

Graham lui tendit ses papiers, mais elle n'y jeta pas le moindre coup d'œil.

« Je sais que c'est un enquêteur fédéral, mademoiselle McClane. »

Finalement, elle lui raconta tout. Tout ce qu'elle avait fait avec Francis Dolarhyde. Elle avait mal à la gorge et devait s'arrêter fréquemment pour sucer un peu de glace.

Il lui posa les inévitables questions indiscrètes et elle répondit à toutes ; mais elle dut lui faire signe de sortir quand la femme lui tendit la cuvette pour vomir son petit déjeuner.

Elle était pâle et son visage brillait quand il revint dans la chambre.

Il lui posa encore quelques questions et referma son carnet.

« Je ne vous importunerai plus avec cette histoire, lui dit-il, mais j'aimerais bien revenir un de ces jours. Pour dire bonjour, pour voir comment vous allez.

— Ne vous en privez pas... Je suis tellement irrésistible. »

Pour la première fois, il la vit pleurer, et il comprit ce qu'elle pouvait endurer.

« Vous pouvez nous laisser un instant ? » dit-il à l'inspecteur de police. Puis il prit la main de Reba.

« Écoutez, il y avait beaucoup de choses à reprocher à Dolarhyde mais pas à vous, vous comprenez ? Vous m'avez dit qu'il se montrait prévenant et aimable avec vous. Je veux bien le croire. C'est vous qui avez suscité ces sentiments en lui. Et en fin de compte, il n'a pas pu vous tuer, il n'a pas pu vous voir mourir. Les gens qui étudient son comportement disent qu'il essayait de s'arrêter. Pourquoi ? Parce que vous l'avez aidé. Vous avez probablement sauvé la vie de plusieurs personnes. Vous n'avez pas aidé un monstre, Reba, mais un homme doublé d'un monstre. Vous n'avez rien à vous reprocher, mais si vous vous persuadez du contraire, vous n'arriverez plus jamais à rien. Je reviendrai dans un jour ou deux. J'ai encore pas mal de choses à faire avec les flics et j'ai besoin de repos. Et puis, essayez de faire quelque chose pour vos cheveux. »

Elle hocha la tête et tendit la main vers la porte. Peut-être souriait-elle — mais il n'en était pas certain.

Graham appela Molly depuis le bureau du F.B.I. de Saint Louis. Le grand-père de Willy décrocha le téléphone.

« Maman, c'est Will Graham, dit-il.

— Bonjour, monsieur Graham. »

Les grands-parents de Willy l'appelaient toujours « monsieur Graham ».

« Maman dit qu'il s'est suicidé. Ils ont interrompu le programme pour l'annoncer. C'est une drôle d'histoire. Ça vous a évité la peine de lui courir après, et ça a évité pas mal de frais aux contribuables. Dites, est-ce qu'il était vraiment blanc ?

— Oui, il était blond, avec un air scandinave. »

Les grands-parents de Willy étaient scandinaves.

« Est-ce que je pourrais parler à Molly ?

— Vous allez retourner en Floride ?

— Bientôt, oui. Est-ce que Molly est là ?

— Maman, il veut parler à Molly. Elle est dans la salle de bains, monsieur Graham. Mon petit-fils est en train de prendre son deuxième petit déjeuner. Il est allé faire du cheval, ça lui a donné faim. Vous devriez le voir à table. Il a bien pris cinq kilos depuis qu'il est ici. Tenez, la voilà.

— Bonjour.

— Salut, toi.

— Alors, les nouvelles sont bonnes ?

— Plutôt, oui.

— J'étais au jardin. Mamaman est venue me raconter ce qu'elle avait vu à la télé. Quand as-tu trouvé qui c'était ?

— Hier soir, assez tard.

— Tu aurais pu m'appeler.

— Je n'aurais pas voulu réveiller Mamaman.

— Elle regardait l'émission de Johnny Carson. Tu sais, je suis heureuse que tu n'aies pas eu à l'arrêter.

— Il va falloir que je reste encore quelque temps.

— Combien ? Quatre ou cinq jours ?

— Je ne sais pas au juste. Peut-être moins. Tu sais, je voudrais bien te voir.

— Moi aussi, je voudrais bien te voir quand tu auras réglé tous tes problèmes.

— On est mercredi aujourd'hui. Vendredi, je devrais avoir...

— Will, Mamaman a invité les oncles et les tantes de Willy. Ils arriveront de Seattle la semaine prochaine et...

— Elle nous barbe, Mamaman. Et puis, qu'est-ce que c'est que cette expression idiote, "Mamaman" ?

— C'est Willy quand il était petit, il n'arrivait pas à dire...

— Reviens à la maison avec moi.

— Will, c'est *moi* qui t'ai attendu. Ils ne voient jamais Willy et quelques jours de plus...

397

— Tu n'as qu'à venir toute seule. Laisse Willy, ton ex-belle-mère pourra le mettre dans l'avion la semaine prochaine. Voilà ce qu'on va faire, on va aller à New Orleans. Je connais un petit endroit qui...

— Ce n'est pas possible. Je travaille — à mi-temps, bien sûr — dans une boutique et je ne peux pas partir comme ça.

— Molly, qu'est-ce qui ne va pas ?

— Rien. Ça va... Will, j'étais si triste. Tu sais que je suis venue ici après la mort du père de Willy. » Elle disait toujours « le père de Willy », comme s'il s'agissait d'une personne morale. Elle ne l'appelait jamais par son nom. « Nous étions tous réunis... J'ai réussi à me ressaisir, à me calmer. Cette fois-ci aussi, je me suis ressaisie et...

— Il y a une petite nuance, tout de même : je ne suis pas mort.

— Ne sois pas comme ça.

— Comme ça quoi ?

— Tu m'en veux. »

Graham ferma les yeux un instant.

« Allô ?

— Je ne t'en veux pas, Molly. Tu fais ce que tu veux. Je te rappellerai quand les choses seront arrangées ici.

— Tu pourrais venir nous retrouver.

— Je ne le pense pas.

— Pourquoi ? Il y a de la place, tu sais. Et Mamaman voudrait...

— Molly, ils ne m'aiment pas, et tu sais très bien pourquoi. Quand ils me voient, je leur fais penser à leur fils.

— Ce n'est pas juste de dire ça, Will. »

Graham était épuisé.

« Bon. Tu préfères que je te dise que ce sont des vieux cons et qu'ils m'emmerdent ?

— Ne dis pas cela.

398

— Ce qu'ils veulent, c'est le gosse. Probablement qu'ils t'aiment bien aussi s'ils y réfléchissent. Mais c'est le gosse qu'ils veulent, et ils te prendront dans le lot. Ils ne veulent pas de moi et je m'en fous complètement. Mais moi, *je te veux*. En Floride. Et Willy aussi, quand il en aura marre de son poney.

— Tu te sentiras mieux quand tu auras dormi un peu.

— Cela m'étonnerait. Écoute, je te rappellerai quand je saurai ce qui se passe ici.

— D'accord. » Elle raccrocha.

« Fait chier, dit Graham. Fait chier. »

Crawford passa la tête à la porte. « Je ne t'aurais pas entendu dire "fait chier" ?

— Exact.

— Eh bien, j'ai de bonnes nouvelles. Aynesworth a appelé. Il a quelque chose pour toi. Il dit que nous devrions venir, les flics locaux ont trouvé quelque chose. »

51

AYNESWORTH était occupé à déposer des cendres dans une boîte en métal quand Crawford et Graham arrivèrent près des ruines carbonisées de la maison de Dolarhyde.

Il était couvert de suie et une grosse cloque s'était formée sous son oreille. L'agent spécial Janowitz, de la brigade des explosifs, travaillait à la cave.

Une sorte de grand flandrin traînait autour d'une Oldsmobile poussiéreuse garée dans l'allée. Il interpella Crawford et Graham au moment où ils traversèrent la cour.

« C'est vous, Crawford ?

— Oui, c'est moi.

— Je m'appelle Robert L. Dulaney. Je suis le coroner[1] de cette juridiction. » Il leur montra une carte marquée : « Votez pour Robert L. Dulaney. »

Crawford attendit.

« Votre collègue détient des preuves qu'il aurait dû me transmettre. Cela fait une heure que j'attends.

— Je suis désolé, monsieur Dulaney, mais il n'a fait que suivre mes instructions. Asseyez-vous dans votre voiture, nous allons régler cela. »

Dulaney les suivit.

Crawford se retourna. « Excusez-moi, monsieur Dulaney, mais j'aimerais mieux que vous restiez dans votre voiture. »

Aynesworth leur adressa un large sourire ; ses dents blanches tranchaient avec la noirceur de son visage. Il avait remué des cendres pendant toute la matinée.

« En tant que chef de brigade, j'ai le plaisir...

— De tirer au cul, on le sait », dit Janowitz. Il venait de ressortir de la cave.

« Silence dans les rangs, soldat Janowitz. Allez plutôt chercher les preuves. » Il lui jeta un trousseau de clefs.

Janowitz sortit une grande boîte en carton du coffre d'une des voitures du F.B.I. Un fusil était attaché au fond de la boîte ; la crosse était carbonisée et les canons tordus par la chaleur. Une boîte de plus petite taille renfermait un automatique noirci.

« Le revolver est en meilleur état, dit Aynesworth.

---

1. Officier civil chargé d'enquêter en cas de mort suspecte ou violente. (*N.d.T.*)

La balistique pourra peut-être en tirer quelque chose. Allez, Janowitz, la suite. »

Janowitz lui tendit trois sacs en plastique.

« Les oreilles et la queue, Graham. » Un instant, Aynesworth perdit sa bonne humeur. Cela faisait partie du rituel des chasseurs, comme marquer de sang le front de Graham.

« On ne peut pas dire qu'il en reste grand-chose. » Aynesworth déposa les sacs dans les mains de Graham.

Le premier contenait une douzaine de centimètres de fémur calciné. Le deuxième, une montre-bracelet. Le troisième, le dentier.

Le palais était brisé, carbonisé, et il n'en restait plus que la moitié, mais sur cette moitié apparaissait l'incisive latérale entaillée reconnaissable entre mille.

Graham pensa qu'il devrait dire quelque chose. « Merci. Merci beaucoup. »

Soudain, la tête lui tourna, mais cela ne dura qu'un instant.

« ... mettre au musée, disait Aynesworth. Il faudra le rendre aux poulets, pas vrai, Jack ?

— Oui, mais il y a quelques types sérieux chez le coroner de Saint Louis. Ils en prendront des empreintes de qualité. Nous pourrons en avoir une. »

Crawford et les autres allèrent rejoindre le coroner.

Graham resta seul près de la maison. Il écouta le vent souffler dans les cheminées. Il espérait que Bloom pourrait venir, une fois rétabli. Oui, il viendrait certainement.

Graham désirait connaître la vérité sur Dolarhyde. Il voulait savoir ce qui s'était déroulé en ces lieux, ce qui avait donné naissance au Dragon. Mais il en savait assez pour aujourd'hui.

Un merle se percha sur le faîte de la cheminée et se mit à siffler.

Graham lui répondit.

Il allait pouvoir rentrer chez lui.

401

52

G RAHAM sourit en sentant le jet le propulser loin de
Saint Louis et prendre la direction du sud-est
pour le ramener chez lui.

Molly et Willy seraient là.

« Écoute, on ne va pas s'occuper de savoir qui a eu
tort ou raison. Je te prendrai à Marathon, c'est tout »,
lui avait-elle dit au téléphone.

Il espérait qu'il ne se souviendrait que des bons
moments de cette affaire — le plaisir de voir à l'œuvre
des gens qui croient vraiment à ce qu'ils font. Même
si cela peut se trouver partout, il suffit de se donner
la peine de chercher.

Il aurait été assez présomptueux de remercier Lloyd
Bowman et Beverly Katz ; il se contenta de leur dire
au téléphone qu'il avait été heureux de retravailler
avec eux.

Il y avait toutefois un détail qui le préoccupait : ce
qu'il avait éprouvé quand Crawford avait posé la main
sur le combiné du téléphone et lui avait dit : « C'est
Gateway. »

La joie qu'il avait éprouvée à cet instant était certainement la plus sauvage, la plus intense qu'il eût
jamais connue. C'était assez troublant de savoir qu'il
avait vécu là, dans une salle de délibérations de Chicago, le moment le plus heureux de toute son existence. *Parce que, avant même de savoir, il savait.*

Il n'avait pas dit à Lloyd Bowman ce qu'il ressen-
tait ; c'était inutile.

« Vous savez, quand Pythagore a vu que son théo-
rème avait fait tilt, il a offert cent bœufs à la muse qui
l'avait inspiré, avait dit Bowman. Il n'y a pas mieux
comme sensation, hein ? Ne dites rien, ça vous gâche-
rait une partie du plaisir. »

Graham faisait preuve de plus d'impatience au fur et à mesure qu'il se rapprochait de Molly. À Miami, il dut descendre sur la piste avant de monter à bord de « Tante Lula », le vieux DC-3 qui assurait le service de Marathon.

Il aimait les DC-3. D'ailleurs, aujourd'hui, il aimait tout.

Tante Lula avait été construite quand Graham avait cinq ans ; ses ailes étaient toujours recouvertes d'une pellicule d'huile noirâtre recrachée par les moteurs.

Il avait entièrement confiance en elle, et il courut pour monter à son bord comme si elle s'était posée en pleine jungle pour venir à sa rescousse.

Les lumières d'Islamorada furent visibles quand l'île passa sous l'aile de l'avion. Graham pouvait déjà apercevoir des moutons sur l'océan. Puis ce fut la descente sur Marathon.

C'était exactement comme la première fois où il était venu à Marathon. Il avait voyagé sur Tante Lula ; et bien souvent, par la suite, il s'était rendu à l'aérodrome à la tombée du jour pour la voir arriver, avec ses ailerons baissés, ses pots d'échappement qui crachaient des flammes et ses passagers derrière les hublots éclairés.

Le décollage constituait également un merveilleux spectacle, mais le vieil avion qui décrivait un vaste arc de cercle pour prendre la direction du nord le laissait toujours triste, frustré, et dans l'air flottaient des au revoir amers. Très vite, il avait appris à ne regarder que les atterrissages, à n'entendre que des bonjours.

Mais c'était avant Molly.

L'avion s'arrêta avec un ultime hoquet. Graham vit Molly et Willy debout derrière la barrière, sous les projecteurs.

Willy se tenait bien droit devant elle, èt il n'en bougerait pas tant que Graham ne les aurait pas rejoints. Alors seulement, il se promènerait en bord de piste et examinerait tout ce qui l'intéressait. Graham l'aimait bien pour cette façon d'être.

Molly était aussi grande que Graham. Quand deux personnes ont la même taille, le baiser qu'ils échangent en public fait immanquablement penser à ces autres baisers qu'on échange au lit...

Willy lui proposa de porter sa valise. Graham ne lui confia que le sac de voyage.

La route de Sugarloaf Key, Molly au volant ; Graham se souvint des détails du paysage révélés par les phares, et il se contenta d'imaginer les autres.

Quand il ouvrit la portière de la voiture dans la cour, il put entendre le bruit de la mer.

Willy rentra dans la maison, le sac de voyage posé sur la tête.

Graham demeura dans la cour, l'air absent ; il chassait d'un geste les moustiques qui lui tournaient autour du visage.

Molly posa la main sur sa joue. « Tu ne crois pas que tu ferais mieux de rentrer avant de te faire dévorer ? »

Il hocha la tête. Ses yeux étaient humides.

Elle attendit encore un peu, pencha la tête de côté et le regarda en battant des paupières. « Martini Tanqueray, steack et gros câlin. Ça te va ? Sans oublier la note d'électricité, la note du gaz et les interminables conversations avec mon fils », ajouta-t-elle du bout des lèvres.

53

GRAHAM et Molly désiraient sincèrement que tout redevienne comme avant, qu'il n'y ait rien de changé dans leur existence.

Quand ils découvrirent que ce n'était plus possible, cette révélation s'installa entre eux comme une présence importune. Les assurances mutuelles qu'ils tentaient d'échanger dans le noir ou en plein soleil passaient au travers d'un prisme qui les déviait de leur cible.

Molly ne lui avait jamais semblé plus belle. Et, de loin, il admirait sa grâce inconsciente.

Elle faisait tout pour lui être agréable, mais elle était allée en Oregon et les souvenirs enfouis étaient remontés à la surface.

Willy le sentait bien, et il faisait preuve envers Graham d'une politesse glaciale.

Une lettre de Crawford arriva un jour. Molly l'apporta avec le reste du courrier et n'y fit pas allusion.

Elle contenait une photographie de la famille Sherman tirée d'un film super-8. Tout n'avait pas brûlé, lui écrivait Crawford. Une fouille effectuée dans les champs alentour avait permis de retrouver cette photo ainsi que d'autres objets projetés loin du brasier par l'explosion.

« Ces gens étaient probablement sur son itinéraire, écrivait Crawford. Ils sont en sécurité à présent. Je me suis dit que tu aimerais le savoir. »

Graham montra la photo à Molly.

« Tu vois ? C'est pour cela, dit-il, c'est pour cela que ça valait la peine.

— Je sais, fit-elle, je te comprends. Parfaitement. »

Les poissons volants bondissaient sous la lune.

Molly prépara le dîner, ils allèrent à la pêche et firent du feu sur la plage ; mais rien de tout cela ne fut agréable.

Grand-père et Mamaman envoyèrent à Willy une photo de son poney, et il l'épingla au mur de sa chambre.

Le cinquième jour était la veille du jour où Graham et Molly iraient retravailler à Marathon. Ils pêchèrent dans les vagues à quelque cinq cents mètres de la maison, sur un emplacement qui leur avait porté bonheur auparavant.

Graham avait décidé qu'il leur parlerait à tous les deux, ensemble.

La partie de pêche ne commença pas très bien. Willy repoussa ostensiblement la gaule que Graham lui avait montée et préféra emporter la canne pour la pêche au lancer que son grand-père lui avait offerte.

Ils pêchèrent en silence pendant trois heures. À plusieurs reprises, Graham ouvrit la bouche pour dire quelque chose mais il n'en fit rien.

Il en avait assez de ne pas être aimé.

Graham attrapa quatre poissons ; il avait appâté à la crevettine. Willy ne prit rien. Il pêchait avec la grosse Rapala équipée de trois triples hameçons que son grand-père lui avait donnée. Il pêchait bien trop vite, lançait ou tournait le moulinet sans réfléchir, au point d'être en nage et d'avoir le visage tout rouge.

Graham s'avança dans la vague et gratta le sable d'où il tira deux crevettines toutes frétillantes.

« Tu en veux une, camarade ? » Il tendit une crevettine à Willy.

« Je préfère la Rapala. C'était celle de mon père — tu le savais ?

— Non », dit Graham. Il se tourna vers Molly.

Elle se tenait les genoux et regardait une frégate prendre son essor.

Elle se leva et épousseta le sable. « Je vais faire des sandwiches », dit-elle.

Quand Molly fut partie, Graham eut la tentation de parler au garçon seul à seul. Non. Willy éprouverait les mêmes choses que sa mère. Il attendrait son retour pour leur parler à tous les deux en même temps. Cette fois-ci, il n'hésiterait pas.

Elle ne fut pas longtemps absente, et elle revint sans les sandwiches. Elle marchait d'un pas rapide sur le sable humide.

« Il y a Jack Crawford au téléphone. Je lui ai dit que tu le rappellerais mais il paraît que c'est urgent », fit-elle. Elle examina l'un de ses ongles. « Tu ferais mieux de te dépêcher. »

Graham rougit. Il enfonça dans le sable l'extrémité de la gaule et coupa par les dunes. C'était bien plus court que par la plage si l'on ne craignait pas de se piquer aux broussailles.

Il entendit une sorte de sifflement prolongé et, craignant un serpent à sonnettes, regarda où il mettait les pieds.

Il vit des bottes dissimulées sous les broussailles, le reflet d'une lentille, une veste kaki. Son regard rencontra les yeux jaunes de Francis Dolarhyde et la peur explosa dans sa poitrine.

Il y eut le déclic d'un pistolet automatique, mais Graham lança son pied en avant ; il heurta le canon au moment où celui-ci tirait une langue jaune pâle dans le soleil couchant et le pistolet vola dans les broussailles. Graham sur le dos, une brûlure terrible dans la poitrine — puis il dévala la dune la tête la première vers la plage.

Dolarhyde prit son élan et arriva sur Graham les deux pieds en avant, le couteau à la main, sans s'occuper des cris qui montaient du bord de l'eau. Il lui enfonça les genoux dans la poitrine, brandit son arme et poussa un grognement sauvage au moment de frapper. La lame manqua de peu l'œil de Graham et s'enfonça profondément dans sa joue.

Dolarhyde bascula en avant et pesa de tout son poids sur le manche du poignard pour qu'il traverse complètement la tête de Graham.

La gaule siffla dans l'air quand Molly l'abattit sur Dolarhyde. Les triples hameçons de la Rapala pénétrèrent dans sa joue, puis le moulinet vrombit quand elle tira un coup brusque avant de frapper à nouveau.

Il poussa un cri et porta la main à sa joue, de sorte que les hameçons s'y enfoncèrent également. De sa main libre, il arracha le couteau et se lança à la poursuite de Molly, une main fixée à sa joue par les hameçons.

Graham roula sur le sol, il parvint à se mettre à genoux puis debout, et il s'enfuit en courant loin de Dolarhyde, les yeux fous, la bouche pleine de sang, avant de s'effondrer.

Molly courut vers les dunes, Willy la devançait. Dolarhyde s'approchait, la gaule à la main. Il trébucha dans les broussailles et arracha un hurlement, le forçant à s'arrêter avant qu'il ne pense à trancher la ligne.

« Cours, je t'en prie ! Ne te retourne surtout pas ! » cria-t-elle. Elle avait de longues jambes et le garçon courait aussi vite qu'elle mais, derrière eux, Dolarhyde gagnait du terrain.

Ils avaient cent mètres d'avance dans les dunes, plus que soixante-dix en arrivant à la maison. Elle se précipita dans l'escalier, ouvrit le placard de Will.

À Willy : « Reste là. »

Dans l'escalier, à nouveau, pour l'affronter. La cuisine. Elle se débattait avec la barrette de chargement rapide.

Elle oublia la position correcte et pratiquement tout ce qu'elle avait appris à l'entraînement, mais elle tint tout de même le pistolet à deux mains et, quand la porte éclata littéralement, elle tira et lui fit un trou énorme dans la cuisse — « Manmon ! » — puis elle tira en pleine figure quand il glissa le long de la porte et encore en pleine figure quand il tomba assis par terre, puis elle courut vers lui et tira de nouveau en pleine figure à deux reprises, et il s'effondra enfin, la calotte crânienne sur le menton, les cheveux en feu.

Willy déchira un drap et se rendit auprès de Will. Ses jambes tremblaient et il tomba à plusieurs reprises en traversant la cour.

Les adjoints du shérif et les ambulances arrivèrent avant même que Molly les appelle. Elle prenait une douche quand ils arrivèrent, l'arme au poing. Elle tentait de se débarrasser des fragments de chair et d'os qui collaient à ses cheveux, et ne put pas répondre quand un adjoint lui adressa la parole au travers du rideau de la douche.

Un des adjoints finit par prendre le combiné du téléphone et parla à Crawford qui, à Washington, avait entendu les coups de feu et avait alerté les hommes du shérif.

« Je ne sais pas, ils sont en train de l'emmener », dit l'adjoint. Il regarda par la fenêtre et vit passer la civière. « Mais il ne m'a pas l'air en très bon état », ajouta-t-il.

54

Sᴜʀ le mur, en face du lit, les chiffres de la pendule étaient si gros qu'on pouvait les lire malgré les médicaments et la douleur.

Quand Will Graham parvint à ouvrir l'œil droit, il vit la pendule et comprit où il était — une unité de soins intensifs. Cette pendule avait quelque chose de rassurant, elle lui prouvait que le temps passait.

C'était d'ailleurs à cela qu'elle servait.

La pendule indiquait quatre heures. Quelles quatre heures ? Il n'en savait rien, et il s'en moquait éperdument, du moment que les aiguilles continuaient de tourner. Il perdit conscience.

Il était huit heures quand il rouvrit l'œil.

Il y avait quelqu'un près de lui. Méfiant, il tourna l'œil. C'était Molly, elle regardait par la fenêtre. Elle était si mince. Il voulut parler, mais une grande douleur lui déchira le côté gauche de la tête quand il remua la mâchoire. Sa tête et sa poitrine ne palpitaient pas au même rythme. Il émit un bruit au moment où elle quitta la chambre.

Il faisait grand jour quand on le manipula en tous sens et le traita de telle sorte que les muscles de son cou se raidirent.

Puis il vit le visage de Crawford penché au-dessus du sien.

Graham réussit à cligner de l'œil. Quand Crawford lui sourit, Graham aperçut un fragment d'épinard coincé entre ses dents.

Étrange. Crawford détestait pratiquement tous les légumes.

Graham fit semblant d'écrire sur le drap où reposait sa main.

Crawford glissa un bloc sous sa main et lui coinça un stylo entre les doigts.

« Willy ? » écrivit-il.

« Il va bien, dit Crawford. Molly aussi. Elle est restée tout le temps avec toi. Dolarhyde est mort, Will. Je te le jure. J'ai relevé moi-même les empreintes et Price les a comparées. Il n'y a plus de doute possible. Il est mort. »

Graham dessina un point d'interrogation.

« Ne t'en fais pas, je te raconterai tous les détails quand tu te sentiras mieux. Ils ne nous donnent que cinq minutes, tu sais. »

« Maintenant », écrivit Graham.

« Le docteur t'a parlé ? Non ? À propos de... Tout ira bien, tu verras. Tu as l'œil enflé à cause du coup de couteau que tu as reçu en pleine figure. Ils t'ont rafistolé mais ça prendra du temps. Tiens, on t'a aussi enlevé la rate. Pour ce que ça sert. Price a bien laissé la sienne en Birmanie en 41. »

Une infirmière tapa au carreau.

« Il faut que j'y aille. Ils ne respectent rien ni personne, pas même les laissez-passer officiels. Tu verras, ils te flanqueront à la porte dès que tu seras sur pied. À bientôt. »

Molly se trouvait dans la salle d'attente de l'U.S.I. À ses côtés, beaucoup de gens fatigués.

Crawford alla la trouver. « Molly...

— Bonjour, Jack, lui dit-elle. Vous avez vraiment bonne mine. Vous ne voulez pas faire l'échange avec lui ?

— Ne dites pas cela, Molly.

— Vous l'avez regardé ?

— Oui.

— Je ne pensais pas y arriver, mais j'ai tout de même réussi.

— Ils vont le remettre en état, c'est le docteur qui me l'a dit. Ils sont très capables, vous savez. Molly, vous voulez que quelqu'un reste avec vous ? Phyllis est descendue avec moi, elle...

— Non. Ne vous occupez plus de moi. »

Elle se détourna et chercha un kleenex dans son sac. C'est alors qu'il vit la lettre : une enveloppe mauve, luxueuse.

Crawford n'aimait pas cela, mais il dut se résoudre à parler.

« Molly ?

— Qu'est-ce qu'il y a ?

— Will a du courrier ?

— Oui.

— C'est l'infirmière qui vous l'a donné ?

— Oui, elle me l'a *donné*. Et ils ont reçu des fleurs de tous ses *amis* de Washington.

— Je peux voir cette lettre ?

— Je la lui donnerai quand il en aura envie.

— Je vous en prie, montrez-la-moi.

— Pourquoi ?

— Parce qu'elle vient d'une certaine personne dont il ne souhaite peut-être pas entendre parler. »

Son visage avait l'air grave, et elle sortit la lettre du sac, mais celui-ci tomba à terre, son contenu se vida, un tube de rouge à lèvres roula sur le sol.

Crawford se pencha pour ramasser les affaires de Molly, mais elle quitta la salle d'attente sans prendre la peine d'emporter son sac.

Il le confia à l'infirmière de service.

Crawford savait que Lecter n'avait pratiquement aucune possibilité d'obtenir ce dont il avait besoin, mais il ne pouvait pas prendre le moindre risque.

Il demanda à un interne de passer la lettre aux rayons X.

Crawford ouvrit l'enveloppe sur les quatre côtés et en examina l'intérieur pour voir s'il n'y avait pas de taches ou de poussière suspectes.

Rassuré, il put lire le texte de la lettre.

Mon cher Will,

Nous voici, vous et moi, languissant dans nos hôpitaux respectifs. Vous souffrez et moi, je suis privé de mes livres — le bon Dr Chilton y a veillé.

Nous vivons dans une époque primitive — vous n'êtes pas d'accord, Will ? — ni sage ni sauvage. Il n'y a rien de pire que les demi-mesures. Toute société raisonnable me mettrait à mort ou me rendrait mes livres.

Je vous souhaite une convalescence rapide et espère que vous ne serez pas trop défiguré.

Je pense souvent à vous.

Hannibal Lecter

L'interne consulta sa montre. « Vous avez encore besoin de moi ?

— Non, dit Crawford. Où se trouve l'incinérateur ? »

Crawford revint quatre heures plus tard pour la visite ; Molly ne se trouvait ni dans la salle d'attente ni dans la chambre de l'U.S.I.

Graham était réveillé. Il dessina un point d'interrogation sur le bloc et ajouta : « D. mort comment ? »

Crawford le lui dit. Graham resta immobile pendant une bonne minute. Puis il écrivit : « Échappé comment ? »

« Bon, fit Crawford. À Saint Louis, Dolarhyde a dû chercher Reba McClane. Il est venu au labo pendant que nous y étions et il nous a vus. On a retrouvé ses empreintes sur une des fenêtres de la chaufferie — on ne l'a su qu'hier. »

Graham écrivit sur le bloc : « Corps ? »

« Nous croyons que c'est celui d'un dénommé Arnold Lang — il est porté disparu. On a retrouvé sa voiture à Memphis. Bon, on va me jeter dans une minute, il vaut mieux que je te raconte tout dans l'ordre.

« Dolarhyde savait que nous étions là. Il nous a filé

entre les doigts à Gateway et s'est rendu dans une station-service Servco Supreme proche du boulevard Lindbergh. C'est là que travaillait Arnold Lang.

« Reba McClane a déclaré que Dolarhyde s'était accroché avec un pompiste de cette station. Nous pensons qu'il s'agissait de ce Lang.

« Il a descendu Lang et a emporté le corps chez lui. Il s'est ensuite rendu chez Reba McClane. Elle embrassait Ralph Mandy sur le pas de la porte. Il a tué Mandy et a caché le corps dans un massif. »

L'infirmière entra.

« Je vous en prie, c'est une affaire officielle », dit Crawford. Il se hâta de parler pendant qu'elle le tirait par la manche. « Il a chloroformé Reba McClane et il l'a emmenée dans la maison. Le cadavre de Lang s'y trouvait déjà », dit Crawford depuis le couloir.

Graham dut attendre quatre heures pour connaître la suite.

« Il lui a fait tout un numéro, tu sais, dans le genre "je ne sais pas encore si je vais vous tuer", dit Crawford dès qu'il eut franchi la porte de la chambre. Tu connais l'histoire de la clef autour du cou — il voulait être sûr qu'elle toucherait bien un corps et, surtout, qu'elle nous le raconterait. Bon, il la fait marcher, il lui dit : "Je ne supporterai jamais de vous brûler", et là-dessus, il fait sauter la tête de Lang avec le calibre 12.

« Lang était parfait, il n'avait plus de dents. Dolarhyde savait peut-être que l'arcade maxillaire résiste souvent au feu — nous ne saurons jamais quelle était la portée de ses connaissances. Quoi qu'il en soit, Lang n'avait plus d'arcade maxillaire après que Dolarhyde lui eut fait sauter la tête. Ensuite, il a dû faire tomber une chaise pour que Reba croie à la chute d'un corps, et il a mis la clef autour du cou de Lang.

« Reba cherche la clef à tâtons. Dolarhyde la

414

regarde faire mais elle ne l'entend pas, elle a été assourdie par la détonation.

« Il y a bien eu un début d'incendie, mais il n'a pas encore mis le feu à l'essence. Bien. Elle est sortie de la maison sans problèmes. Je crois bien qu'il l'aurait assommée et qu'il l'aurait traînée dehors si elle s'était perdue. De toute façon, elle n'aurait pas su ce qui lui était arrivé. Merde, revoilà l'infirmière. »

Graham se hâta d'écrire : « Véhicule comment ? »

« Tu vas admirer la manœuvre, dit Crawford. Il savait qu'il lui faudrait laisser le van devant la maison. D'un autre côté, il ne pouvait pas conduire deux véhicules à la fois, et il lui fallait bien un moyen de transport pour s'enfuir.

« Voilà ce qu'il a fait : il a obligé *Lang* à accrocher le van à la dépanneuse de la station-service, puis il l'a descendu, il a fermé la station et il a conduit la dépanneuse jusqu'à chez lui. Il a alors abandonné la dépanneuse dans les champs, non loin de la maison, et repris le van pour aller chez Reba McClane. Quand elle est sortie saine et sauve de la maison, il est allé chercher la dynamite à la cave et a mis le feu à l'essence avant de sortir par-derrière. Il a *ramené* la dépanneuse à la station-service et pris la voiture de Lang. Tout était prévu.

« Cette histoire m'a rendu dingue tant que je n'ai pas trouvé la solution. Et j'ai su que j'avais raison quand on a retrouvé ses empreintes sur le cabestan de la dépanneuse.

« Nous l'avons probablement croisé sur la route en nous rendant chez lui... Oui, madame, j'arrive. Oui, oui. »

Graham voulut lui poser une question, mais il était trop tard.

Molly entra dans la chambre.

Graham lui écrivit : « Je t'aime » sur le bloc de Crawford.

Elle hocha la tête et lui prit la main.

Une minute plus tard, il écrivit à nouveau.

« Willy en forme ? »

Elle hocha la tête.

« Ici ? »

Elle détourna la tête un peu trop rapidement. Elle lui envoya un baiser et lui désigna l'infirmière qui venait la chercher.

Il la retint par le pouce.

« Où ? » insista-t-il, en soulignant deux fois ce mot.

« Dans l'Oregon », dit-elle.

Crawford lui rendit une ultime visite.

Graham avait déjà préparé sa question. « Dentier ? »

« C'était celui de sa grand-mère, dit Crawford. La police de Saint Louis a retrouvé un certain Ned Vogt — la mère de Dolarhyde était la belle-mère de Vogt. Vogt avait vu Mme Dolarhyde quand il était gosse et il n'avait jamais oublié ses dents.

« C'est pour cela que je t'appelais quand tu es tombé sur Dolarhyde. Le Smithsonian venait de m'appeler. Les autorités du Missouri leur avaient enfin transmis les dents. Ils ont remarqué que la partie supérieure était faite de vulcanite au lieu d'acrylique. On ne fait plus de dentiers en vulcanite depuis trente-cinq ans.

« Dolarhyde avait un dentier neuf en acrylique, c'était la copie exacte de l'autre mais il pouvait le porter. On l'a retrouvé sur son cadavre. Le Smithsonian l'a étudié de près, ils disent qu'il est de fabrication chinoise. L'autre dentier était suisse.

« Il avait également sur lui la clef d'un coffre-fort de Miami. On y a découvert une sorte de gros registre — un drôle de truc. Il est à ta disposition.

« Écoute, mon vieux, il faut que je rentre à Washington. Je redescendrai te voir pendant le week-end si je peux. Ça va aller ? »

Graham dessina un point d'interrogation, puis le raya et écrivit : « Parfait. »

L'infirmière arriva après le départ de Crawford. Elle lui fit une intraveineuse de Demerol et la pendule se brouilla.

Il se demanda si le Demerol agissait sur les sentiments. Il pourrait retenir Molly quelque temps, jusqu'à ce qu'on lui refasse le visage. Mais la retenir pour quoi ? Il se sentait partir à la dérive et espérait qu'il ne rêverait pas.

Il flotta tout de même, entre le rêve et le souvenir. Mais ce n'était pas si désagréable que ça. Il ne rêva ni au départ de Molly ni à Dolarhyde. Ce fut une sorte de souvenir onirique de Shiloh interrompu par des lumières braquées sur son visage ou le sifflement du tensiomètre...

C'était au printemps, peu de temps après la mort de Garett Jacob Hoobs, qu'il avait visité le site de Shiloh.

Par un beau matin d'avril, il avait traversé la route bitumée qui mène au Bloody Pond — l'Étang Sanglant. Les jeunes pousses d'herbe d'un beau vert clair formaient un tapis qui descendait jusqu'à la pièce d'eau. Il y avait eu une crue et la pelouse était encore visible sous l'eau, elle semblait tapisser le fond de l'étang.

Graham savait ce qui s'était passé ici en avril 1862[1].

Il s'assit sur l'herbe en dépit de l'humidité.

Une voiture de touristes passa ; quand elle eut disparu, Graham aperçut quelque chose qui bougeait sur la route. La voiture avait brisé la colonne vertébrale

---

1. La bataille de Shiloh fut l'une des plus meurtrières de la guerre de Sécession. La soudaineté de l'attaque sudiste faillit submerger les troupes nordistes acculées au fleuve en crue. L'armée de l'Union perdit treize mille hommes sur soixante-trois mille. (N.d.T.)

d'une petite couleuvre. Elle se tordait en tous sens au milieu de la route, dévoilant parfois son dos sombre et parfois son ventre pâle.

La terrible présence de Shiloh lui glaçait les sangs, alors même que le soleil printanier le faisait transpirer.

Graham se leva, le pantalon mouillé. Il avait la tête vide.

La couleuvre continuait de se tordre. Graham la saisit par l'extrémité de la queue et la fit claquer comme un fouet.

La cervelle éclata pour retomber dans l'étang. Une brème la happa.

Il avait cru Shiloh hanté, avec sa beauté sinistre comme un étendard.

Et maintenant, à mi-chemin entre le rêve et le sommeil dû aux narcotiques, il découvrait que Shiloh n'avait rien de sinistre ; il était indifférent, c'est tout. Shiloh l'admirable pouvait tout voir. Son inoubliable beauté soulignait tout simplement l'indifférence de la nature, ce Vert Engrenage. Le charme de Shiloh se moque bien de notre désarroi.

Il s'éveilla et découvrit la pendule insouciante, mais il ne put s'empêcher de penser.

Le Vert Engrenage ne connaît pas la pitié ; c'est *nous* qui créons la pitié et l'élaborons dans les excroissances de notre cerveau reptilien.

Le meurtre n'existe pas. C'est nous qui l'inventons, et c'est à nous seuls qu'il importe.

Graham ne savait que trop bien qu'il réunissait en lui tous les éléments pouvant donner naissance au meurtre ; et aussi, peut-être, à la pitié.

Et sa compréhension du meurtre avait quelque chose de dérangeant.

Il se demanda si, dans ce corps immense qu'est l'humanité, dans l'esprit des hommes civilisés, les forces malignes que nous retenons en nous et la redoutable connaissance instinctive de ces mêmes forces n'ont pas la fonction de ces virus affaiblis contre lesquels s'arme le corps humain.

Il se demanda si ces forces anciennes, terribles, ne sont pas les virus d'où naissent les vaccins.

Oui, il s'était trompé à propos de Shiloh. Shiloh n'est pas un lieu hanté — ce sont les hommes qui sont hantés.

Shiloh s'en moque bien.

J'ai pris à cœur d'acquérir la connaissance de la sagesse, de discerner la sottise et la folie ; mais j'ai reconnu que cela aussi, c'est vaine poursuite du vent.

Ecclésiaste 1 : 17

Achevé d'imprimer par GGP Media, Pößneck
en août 2002
pour le compte de France Loisirs,
Paris

N° d'éditeur: 37325
Dépôt légal: juillet 2002